HAVE YOU HEARD THE ONE ABOUT...

HAVE YOU HEARD THE ONE ABOUT...

More Than **500** Side-Splitting Jokes!

JUSTIN SEDGWICK

Skyhorse Publishing

Skyhorse Publishing Publishing books may be purchased in bulk at special discounts for sales promotion, corporate gifts, fund-raising, or educational purposes. Special editions can also be created to specifications. For details, contact the Special Sales Department, Skyhorse Publishing, 307 West 36th Street, 11th Floor, New York, NY 10018 or info@skyhorsepublishing.com.

Skyhorse® and Skyhorse Publishing® are registered trademarks of Skyhorse Publishing, Inc.®, a Delaware corporation.

Visit our website at www.skyhorsepublishing.com.

10 9 8 7 6 5 4 3 2

Library of Congress Cataloging-in-Publication Data is available on file.

Cover art used with permission from iStock.com.
Special thanks to joke contributor, Tyler Ross.

ISBN: 978-1-5107-2922-3

eISBN: 978-1-5107-2926-1

Printed in the United States

TABLE OF CONTENTS

INTRODUCTION

An overweight, middle-aged shirtless man walks into a convenience store, which has a very clear "No Pants, No Shoes, No Service" sign displayed in its front window. It is impossible for the man not to see this sign when walking up to the store, but he still goes in anyway, breaking the store's firm policy, with the sight of his flabby, hairy, sun-burnt torso causing some shoppers to reconsider if they're still hungry for those Cool Ranch Doritos and extra-sized Slim Jims.

Now consider this situation. The same overweight, middle-aged, shirtless man walks into a convenience store, with that same "No Pants, No Shoes, No Service" sign displayed clear as day in its front window. All the same shoppers are there and all the same Doritos and Slim Jims are on the shelves, but this time, the man actually has a tuxedo painted on his chest, with even a little red rose delicately created above his left nipple. This situation is much more humorous, while the former seems a bit more gross.

What makes a joke funny? It's a question that has plagued ancient philosophers and the great thinkers of our time. Countless hours and tireless research has been poured into the humor sciences, hoping to find the true answer of what actually makes a joke funny, if the answer even exists.

Sadly, we are no closer to understanding the true, intangible truth behind a joke. But what has always remained true is that humor is subjective and that it is a certain "unexpectedness" of a punch line that really gets us laughing. Bar jokes, blonde jokes, anti-jokes, pick-up lines, regional and international jokes, Dad jokes, all share a unique sense of unexpectedness. A clever play on words or an outcome that diverted from what you were originally anticipating is enough to get our funny bones dancing. That's why people try to guess the answers to one-liners and are so pleased when they're proven wrong.

Certain types of jokes may be funny to some but are not funny to all. Some jokes may be too "inside baseball" for others to understand: A joke that focuses on a very niche part of Judaic culture may not be appreciated or even understood by non-Jewish persons. Other jokes may be too offensive or tame for audiences: A more rebellious teenager may not laugh at a well-behaved kid's joke, and a person from a conservative background might be appalled by a more risqué, sex-driven joke than someone from a more liberal-leaning background.

Regardless of your age, gender, hair color, religious upbringing, political affiliations, or paint tuxedo-wearing habits, there are jokes for you. The following collection of jokes contains some age-old classics, passed down through the decades as well as new ones inspired by recent events. Some are a bit more risqué and raunchy, others tame but timeless. Some are short one-liners, others are long-form stories with a funny twist. You may not find all of these jokes funny, and that's your right as a sense-of-humor-wielding citizen of this planet. But without question, there are plenty of jokes here that will make you laugh more than you expected.

A man walks into a bar and orders a 12-year-old scotch. The bartender, believing that the customer will not be able to tell the difference, pours him a shot of the cheap three-year-old house scotch that has been poured into an empty bottle of the good stuff. The man takes a sip and spits the scotch out on the bar and reams the bartender: "This is the cheapest three-year-old scotch you can buy. I'm not paying for it. Now, give me a good 12-year-old scotch." The bartender, now feeling a bit of a challenge, pours him a scotch of much better quality, six-year-old scotch. The man takes a sip and spits it out on the bar. "This is only six-year-old scotch," he cries, "I won't pay for this, and I insist on a good 12-year-old scotch." The bartender finally relents and serves the man his best quality, 12-year-old scotch. An old drunk from the end of the bar, having witnessed the entire episode, walks down to the finicky scotch drinker and sets a glass down in front of him and asks, "What do you think of this?" The scotch expert takes a sip, and in disgust, violently spits out the liquid yelling, "Why, this tastes like piss!" The old drunk replies, "That's right, now tell me how old I am!"

Three pregnant women are sitting in a bar: A brunette, a redhead, and a blonde. The brunette says, "I know what baby I'm going to have." The other women ask how she knows. "Well, I was on top when I conceived, so I'll have a baby boy." The redhead says, "If your logic is correct, then I'll have a baby girl because I was on the bottom when I conceived." The blonde starts starts screaming, "PUPPIES, PUPPIES!"

What is a man's idea of a balanced diet?

A Coors Light in each hand!

What did the bartender say after Charles Dickens ordered a martini?

"Olive or twist?"

What did the bartender say after a book walked into the bar?

"Please, no stories!"

Why did God invent whiskey?

So the Irish would never rule the world!

What do Russians get when mixing holy water with Vodka?

The Holy Spirit!

You know what's fun about being sober?

Nothing

What did the man with a slab of asphalt under his arm order?

"A beer, please, and one for the road."

What has eight arms and an IQ of 60?

Four guys drinking Bud Light and watching a football game!

What's the difference between a G-Spot and a bottle of Jack Daniels?

A guy will actually SEARCH for a bottle of Jack Daniels.

How does a man show he's planning for the future?

He buys two cases of Miller Lite instead of one.

Why does Corona go through your system so fast?

Because it doesn't have to stop to change color.

What is the difference between a sofa and a man watching Monday Night Football?

The sofa doesn't keep asking for Bud Light!

What is the similarity between Corona and having sex in a rowboat?

They are both SO close to water!

Where do monkeys go to grab a beer?

The monkey bars!

What does a wet beer fart leave in your shorts?

A Bengal stripe

What do a shot of Everclear and a woman have in common?

Both of them make men start talking nonsense!

What happens when you cross a gynecologist drinking Pabst Blue Ribbon Beer and sexy blonde drinking Smirnoff Vodka?

A "Pabst Smir!"

What does a ghost drink?

BOOS

What is printed on the bottom of beer bottles in the south?

"Open other end."

A bee goes into a bar and comes out two hours later buzzing.

Boy: "I love you so much, I could never live without you."

Girl: "Is that you, or is that the beer talking?"

Boy: "It's me talking to the beer."

Give a man a fish and he'll eat for a day. Teach him how to fish, and he'll sit in a boat and drink beer all day.

Hear about the wall that went out on the town for its birthday?

It got plastered.

Mayan: Hey wanna beer?

Other Mayan: I'm working on this calendar, but I guess if I don't finish it won't be the end of the world.

Beer doesn't turn people into somebody they're not. It just makes them forget to hide that part of themselves.

A duck walks in to a bar and says, "Give me 200 beers." The bartender says, "How are you going to pay for that?" So the duck says, "Just put in on my bill!"

Life and beer are very similar: Chill for best results.

If you put root beer in a square cup, do you get beer?

When you get a hangover from wine, it's called the Grape Depression.

Warning! Beer will make your clothes shrink.

Money can't buy happiness. Just kidding! Yes it can, if that money is used to buy beer.

If life hands you lemons, make a whiskey sour!

Beer doesn't make you fat! It makes you lean...on tables, chairs, random people...

I don't drink to forget. I drink because beer is delicious. Forgetting is just a bonus.

I started drinking very young. My first DWI was on a Big Wheel.

I don't recycle because it makes me look like a huge alcoholic to my garbage man.

Some things are better left unsaid, but I'll probably get drunk and say them anyway.

The first thing on my bucket list is to fill the bucket with beer.

My body isn't a temple: It's a microbrewery with legs.

I was drinking at the bar last night, so I took a bus home. That may not be a big deal to you, but I've never driven a bus before.

A guy is sitting at a bar in a skyscraper restaurant high above the city skyline. He's slamming tequila left and right. He grabs one, drinks it, goes over to a window and jumps out. The guy who is sitting next to him can't believe that the guy has just done that. He is more surprised when, 10 minutes later, the same guy, unscathed, comes walking back into the bar and sits back down next to him. The astonished guy asks, "How did you do that? I just saw you jump out that window and we're hundreds of feet above the ground!" The jumper responds by slurring, "Well, I don't get it either. I slam a shot of tequila and when I jump out the window, the tequila makes me slow down right before I hit the ground. Watch." He takes a shot, slams it down, goes to the window, and jumps out. The other guy runs to the window and watches as the guy falls until right before the ground, slows down, and lands softly on his feet. A few minutes later, the guy walks back into the bar. The other guy has to try it too, so he orders a shot of tequila. He drinks it and goes to the window and jumps. As he reaches the bottom, he doesn't slow down at all: SPLAT! The first guy orders another shot of tequila and the bartender says to him, "You're really an asshole when you're drunk, Superman."

A bartender is wiping down barstools and getting ready to go home at the end of a long night. Just five minutes before closing, a man wearing a trench coat and sunglasses walks inside, holding a box wrapped in brown paper and tied together with string.

The man in the trench coat says: "I've been instructed to leave this box here for an associate. This box contains dangerous items that are incredibly valuable and could be lethal to the world if the box falls into the wrong hands. My associate will pick it up in exactly four days. Do not open the box, do not tell anyone you have the box, and for those four days, pretend that the box doesn't exist."

The man stands up and walks out of the bar, as the bartender quickly follows him outside. "Hey guy, you just can't leave your stuff here! Come back and—"

But the man has already disappeared into the night. The bartender is concerned and goes back inside to examine the box. He's deeply curious as to what's inside, but he's too worried to open it. So he holds on to the box, hoping nothing will happen.

Three days go by with the box safely placed behind the bar. The bartender is nervous to still be holding onto it, but is getting through the day, hour by hour. On the fourth and final day, though, a fight breaks out between a New England Patriots fan and an Atlanta Falcons fan. They throw punches and the Falcons fan picks up his New England enemy and throws him behind the bar. The opponent lands against some liquor bottles and falls down onto the box, flattening it, with the sound of something breaking inside. The bartender kicks everyone out of the bar, and drearily waits for the new associate to come back.

Five minutes to close, right on the dot, another mysterious man walks into the bar. He is also wearing a trench coat and sunglasses and commands the same respect and authority as the previous man. But when he sees the state of the box, he becomes concerned.

"My associate says that when he left the box here it was in pristine condition. This box looks severely damaged. What caused this?"

"There was a brawl here just a few hours before you showed up between an Atlanta Falcons fan and a Patriots fan. The Falcons guy picked up the Patriots fan, threw him behind the bar like a rag doll, and he landed on the box flattening it."

The mysterious man is quiet for a few moments before speaking. "So a Patriots fan flattened this box the very last day you had it?"

"Yeah, everything was going perfectly fine until that final day, even just a few hours ago."

The mysterious man is disappointed and silent again for a few seconds, then speaks. "Damn Patriots: Always screwing up everything in the fourth quarter."

A sullen-looking woman walks into a bar. She's wearing a black outfit and approaches the bar and somberly asks for two rum and cokes. The bartender tells the woman he doesn't serve more than one drink at a time to a customer. "Oh, it's not for me. When I turned 21, my Dad took me here for my first drink years and years ago. We each had a rum and coke, and every year after, we would always come back on my birthday to this bar, sit in these two stools, and have the same drink. But my father passed away last year, and this is my first birthday without him, so I figured I'd just keep up the tradition."

The bartender is touched by the story and agrees to let the woman have two drinks, and offers to pay for her Dad's. The woman graciously accepts the offer and walks out.

A year later, the woman comes back to the bar on her birthday and orders two drinks again, one for herself and one for her Dad. She doesn't look as sad this year, but still doesn't look like she's been fully over the grief either, and asks if it's OK if she has her Dad's drink this time. The bartender says yes and offers to pay for the Dad's drink. She graciously accepts again and walks out.

This keeps up for the next three years, the woman always coming in on her birthday, ordering two drinks, and the bartender offering them for free. One year, the bartender is sick on the woman's birthday and instructs his colleague to perform the same ritual for her. When the bartender is walking through town, he notices out of the corner of his eye that same woman who would come every year, sitting with an older man. The bartender approaches the two and introduces himself, with the woman clearly distressed.

"Oh hey! I'm actually sick today so I wasn't able to serve you, but noticed you from afar and just wanted to say hello. Who is this gentleman you're sitting with?"

"I'm her father," the man replies, the woman clearly embarrassed.

"Oh, you're her father? That's strange, because your daughter here has been coming to my bar every year to enjoy a memorial drink with her Dad. Apparently you had died five years ago, and having a drink with you on her birthday is the way she felt close to you after her death."

The older man is appalled and asks his daughter if this is true. Defeated, she admits her misdeed, and the older man is clearly disappointed and begins to scold her: "I'm so disappointed in you! What kind of daughter finds a bar that gives out two-for-one rum and cokes and doesn't invite her old man?"

A n older businessman walks into a bar. He's wearing a fine-tailored suit, has $1,000 Italian shoes and a luxury, diamond-encrusted watch. He clearly is doing well in life. But he looks incredibly depressed when he sits down next to one of the regular customers and orders a drink.

"What's the matter?" the bartender says. "You look like a guy who'd never be down on his luck."

"I used to be a billionaire. I would fly across the world, date beautiful supermodels, and stay at the finest hotels. I dined with Hollywood celebrities and global leaders, hell...I even was able to buy my own space shuttle and travel into space! There was nothing I couldn't do."

"Well what happened?" the bartender asks.

"My company lost all its money and I'm broke. The bank cancelled my credit cards, I lost my mansion, my model girlfriend broke up with me, and I just spent my last hundred bucks on a one-way ticket home to crash on my parent's couch. Everything I have is what you see here right now, and I'll probably have to sell it in the next few days to make ends meet."

The bartender empathizes with the man's story. "You'll bounce back, don't worry. It may take some time, but you seem like a smart enough guy, I wouldn't be surprised if you thought of the next big idea tomorrow and were on your way back to being rich."

The bartender can clearly see the businessman is hurting and goes around to give him a hug. After the businessman finishes his drink, the bartender shakes the businessman's hand and then wishes him well, reassuring him that he'll be just as successful as he once was. The customer seems a bit uplifted by this and walks out.

"Hey Mort, why were you so nice to that guy? You always said you hated rich people."

"I do, but I swiped that bastard's watch when he left the room."

Three billionaire supervillains are sitting at a bar, drinking extremely rare and expensive whiskey while discussing the best way to kill Lance Steele, the British secret agent who has always foiled all of their plans.

"I got it. Here's what we'll do: We'll kidnap Steele and leave him tied in a chair in a room full of impossibly hot lasers in one of my laboratories. The lasers will start at his feet, and then they'll slowly move up to his chest, burning his heart with 1,000 degrees and setting him on fire!"

"No no no," another supervillain says, "That's far too easy. What we'll do is tie Steel to a conveyor belt in one of my factories. The belt will move slowly, and he'll be tortured by all the machinery picking apart his insides. Then a giant wedge from overhead will flatten him like a pancake."

The third supervillain speaks up. "Pssh, a child could think of that! You need to think more deeply on what would hurt Steele not just physically but also emotionally. His parents were killed when they accidentally drove off a cliff and drowned. What you need to do is lock him in a car, push him off a cliff, and watch him die the same way his Mom and Dad did, like some cruel form of poetic justice."

As the supervillains speak, the bartender can't help but interrupt. "I'm sorry guys and I don't mean to eavesdrop, but all these plans sound needlessly convoluted. Steele could easily break free from all of your plans, he's way too smart, and he's had no issue with defeating you guys before."

The supervillains are displeased by a bartender barging in on their discussion. "Why, you're just nothing more than a glorified drink pourer! What makes you think that you're smarter than us, some of the most brilliant and evil supervillains who have ever lived?"

The bartender shoots back: "Well, Lance Steele has been sitting here on the other side of the bar for the entire time you've been here and you haven't managed to kill him yet!"

A zebra walks into a bar and looks depressed, even concerned for its own life. The bartender asks the animal what is wrong.

The zebra says: "I broke my leg last week and haven't been able to move as quickly. In the past, I never had a problem running away from any lions nearby, but I'm sure now if one shows up, God knows I'll be first to go. Those predators can smell weakness from a mile away."

Just as the zebra finishes its story, an antelope walks in wearing an eye-patch. The bartender asks him what's the matter.

The antelope says: "I recently got my eye infected and can't see a thing out of it. For us antelope, we need to be able to see everything around us at all times to make sure there aren't any pesky lions ready to pounce on us. But now I can only see things to the immediate left of me. God knows those lions love to eat antelope, and one needs to do is just wait until I'm looking in the wrong direction and I'm mincemeat."

Then a giraffe with a remarkably short neck walks into a bar and takes the last open seat. He too is clearly distressed, and the bartenders asks what's the matter.

The giraffe says: "For giraffes, our long necks are very useful in being able to see if any threats are coming our way. But for me, my neck is far too short, and if I ever saw a lion across the way looking for its next meal, there's nothing that would stop me from becoming dinner."

A lion then walks inside and orders a drink from the opposite side of the bar. He doesn't seem to notice the zebra, antelope, and giraffe who are sitting just five or six stools down from him, each paralyzed by fear. But the lion is too depressed to do anything about it. The lion complains to the bartender about being hungry and not having a decent meal for months.

The bartender says: "Now look at you! You're the king of the jungle, you're fierce and mighty, and you can eat anything that you want. Hell, you could eat the three of those the animals right now without them putting up a fight and have yourself a hearty meal. Why are you so sad?"

"That's just it," the lion says as he looks up. "I'm vegan."

A customer is sitting at a bar, having a heartfelt conversation with a bartender.

"Jack, I think I may be an alcoholic."

"Why do you say that?" Jack replies.

"Well, I drink at every chance I get."

"Lots of people drink throughout the day. That doesn't necessarily make you an alcoholic."

"Well, I spend every dollar I have on booze. Sometimes I can't even pay rent or buy groceries."

"Just because you can't control your spending doesn't make you an alcoholic."

"All my friends refuse to talk to because of my drinking. Heck, even my parents and siblings won't answer my calls."

"Just because they don't know how to have a good time doesn't make you an alcoholic."

"Huh, what do you know! Maybe I'm not an alcoholic after all," the man says.

"Oh, no, you're totally an alcoholic," Jack says.

"Why do you say that?"

"Because you haven't moved from that stool for five days straight!"

Four parents are sitting at a bar, with three of them beaming about what great students their kids are. The fourth parent is strangely silent and doesn't contribute to the stories at all.

"My son Timmy is the most brilliant math student that Rydell High has ever had," the first Mom says. "He might even be able to teach somewhere like Harvard or Oxford. I don't know where he gets it from!"

A Dad then chimes in: "You think that's impressive? My daughter Megan is an absolute whiz kid at science. There's no experiment or test or assignment that she hasn't gotten an A on. I wouldn't be surprised to hear that she cured some major illness or developed a pill that could cure world hunger or something like that."

The third parent, another beaming Mom, speaks: "Math and science are great and all, but my daughter Christine just has a way with words. She can pick apart the most complex themes that even some adults and literary geeks still can't wrap their heads around. Her teachers say she will be a brilliant poet or writer someday."

The fourth parent laughs at the other parents, clearly annoyed by their discussion.

"Hey, don't laugh at us just because your son isn't as gifted or talented as our kids," one of the parents says.

"Oh I'm not laughing at you," the fourth parent says. "I just can't wait to tell my boy who to cheat off of on his next exams!"

A woman traveling on business enters her hotel's bar late at night with only two other people there. The woman is enjoying a drink by herself when a suave-looking man comes up to introduce himself.

"Hello there. I couldn't help but notice you looked absolutely ravishing from my end of the bar, and I felt compelled to come up and introduce myself. I'm Jude."

Jude sits down next to the woman and they begin talking. The conversation starts off light, but after a few more drinks, the two of them start to loosen up and have a bit more fun. They end up having several more drinks before the man says he needs to change, and that he'll be in room 313 if the woman wants to drop by. In his absence, the bartender feels compelled to speak to the woman.

"Hey there, I see that you and Jude have been having quite a fun conversation. I just wanted to warn you though that he comes in here pretty much every night and does the same scheme with a woman who's travelling from out of town. He tries to woo them with a few compliments and a few drinks, and even reserves a different room at the hotel every night. He tells the girls he's going to travel to see them and all this stuff but they never hear from him again. It's really kind of gross, so just wanted to warn you and give you a quick heads-up."

"Oh, I know," the woman says. "In fact, I stayed at this hotel a year ago and he tried pulling the same thing on me. Honestly, I would have been surprised if he even remembered me a year later."

"So why haven't you just walked away or told him you wanted to be left alone?"

"Well if I did that, I wouldn't be able to find his room number to charge all of these drinks!"

Two teens, one standing on the other's shoulders, walk into a bar wearing a trench coat. The bartender quickly catches on to the ruse and decides to have some fun with the kids.

"What can I get you?"

"I'll have one beer please," the teen nervously says, his voice cracking.

"OK, one beer it is. Can I make a recommendation? We have over 100 beers here and I want to make sure you make the very best selection."

"Sure!" the teen says.

"Well our special this month is an imported beer from Italy called Grazie Tante. It's very delicious."

"I'll have that then."

The bartender goes to the other end and starts to pour a ginger ale mixed with lemon juice and a small bit of honey into a mug. He hands it back to the teen, who pays in cash and drinks it nearly in one gulp.

"Can I get another one, sir?" the teen asks, and the bartender goes and refills another glass with the same non-alcoholic beer concoction. The teen goes through three or four more and starts to think he's becoming inebriated.

The bartender is eating all of this up, but he knows that he has to come clean at some point. So when the kid gets ready to order his fifth beer.

"Listen, I know you aren't 21 years old, you're just two kids in a trench coat try-ing to drink for free. I haven't even been serving you beer at all, but a mixture of ginger ale, honey and lemon. I'm not angry, it's been pretty funny watch you pretend to get drunk. But now I think it's best that you leave."

The teen blushes and is embarrassed. He unbuttons his trench coat and his friend steps out, clearly exhausted from having to carry him all night. As they walk out the door, the friend beneath the trench coat begins to scold his friend.

"All you had to do is order a Coors but nooooooo, you just had to run up the tab with the fancy Italian import."

Two dogs walk into a bar and sit at the only available stools. They order a drink and as they sip, they notice the other people in the bar have become unwelcomingly quiet. The dogs look up and see how the entire bar is populated by malicious-looking cats.

"Well, my grandfather would be rolling over in his grave if he ever saw a couple of dogs sitting at the same bar he came to every day," one of the wily cats says. "There's a reason why dogs have their own bars, so they can get all that cheap kibble and bacon whiskey."

The other cats laugh as the dogs become uncomfortable. They don't feel ready to leave, but they just try to finish their drinks as fast as they can as another cat speaks.

"For the past 30 years I've been coming to this bar and I've never seen a dog strut on in here. Never a Dachshund, never a Pit Bull, hell, never even a Chihuahua-Pomeranian mix. I guess those mutts were wise enough to know that even if they did the doggie DNA test, they'd still never be welcome here."

Now fearful, the dogs pay for their drinks and get up to leave as a burly Maine Coon cat speaks.

"Hey now, just so you know, there's a really good dog bar down the street called Fido's, I reckon you should go there."

One of the dogs named Lucy has had enough and decides to speak up against the wishes of her dog friend, Max.

"And why's that? Why aren't we welcome here? Because we're dogs? I thought this is America!"

"This ain't the part of America you're from," one of the cats hollers and others laugh.

"Yeah, but it's still America. And as long as this bar is in America, we're going to sit here and enjoy our drinks."

The cats are stunned by the female dog's confidence and keep quiet. After the dogs have two more drinks, they leave for real this time, with the Maine Coon cat walking behind them outside.

"Hey now, we don't want any trouble, we're leaving," Max says.

"No no, I don't mean you any harm, I just wanted to apologize. My Dad had always hated dogs, and when I was growing up, he passed that on to me. But clearly he was from a different time, and I'm sorry for the way I acted back there."

Lucy and Max look at each other and accept the cat's apology as they walk down the street. The Maine Coon cat goes back inside and enjoy the rest of the night with his feline friends.

Walking in right behind him is the bar's owner, and as he gets inside, he yells at the bartender: "Dammit, Michael, how many times do I have to tell you to leave your pets at home?

RIDDLES

What is big, yellow, and comes in the morning to brighten parents' days?

A school bus

You will always find me in the past. I can be created in the present, but the future can never taint me. What am I?

History

What travels all around the world but stays in a corner?

A stamp

If a plane crashes in the ocean, where do you bury the survivors?

You don't bury survivors: They're still alive.

What is greater than God,

more evil than the devil,

the poor have it,

the rich need it,

and if you eat it, you'll die?

Nothing

There is a puzzle that can be asked all day with a different correct answer each time. What is the puzzle?

What did Donald Trump do this time?

An old man wants to leave all of his money to one of his three sons, but he doesn't know which one he should give it to. He gives each of them a few coins and tells them to buy something that will be able to fill their living room. The first man buys straw, but there is not enough to fill the room. The second buys some sticks, but they still do not fill the room. The third man buys two things that filled the room, so he obtains his father's fortune. What were the two things that the man bought?

A box of matches and a candle, so when he lit the candle, it would fill the room with light.

You are happy when I am gone, and not sad when I am further away. I am always willing to help, but you never wish I would stay. I always have advice, none of which you ever take. And every time I knock, it's your soul that is forsake. What am I?

A mother-in-law

A man can paint his house on either Wednesday or Friday. If he paints on Wednesday, he can only use red or blue paint, and if he paints on Friday, he can only use green or yellow. Will the man ever be able to paint his house purple, and if so, what day?

None of the days, because the Homeowner's Association won't allow it.

Two people are born at the same moment but have different birthdays. How is this possible?

They were born in different time zones.

You attack me, but I only seem to grow. When you deplete my life, you end up using more of me. You need me to live, but at the same time, too much of me will thwart your future. What am I?

Credit card debt

Before you is a picture of a man. I tell you: "Brothers and sisters I have none, but this man's father is my father's son."

Who is the man in the picture?

The man is my son

Two men are waiting for a bus in New York. The first man always arrives five minutes late, and if the bus isn't there in 10 minutes, he leaves to find another. The second man is always five minutes late, but always waits as long as necessary for the bus to arrive. Will the two men ever cross paths?

No, New Yorkers always avoid street contact with one another.

What's a seven-letter word containing thousands of letters?

Mailbox

Your friends have a version of me, but you don't have me at all. You've tried to get me, but for whatever reason, you failed. Your friend's version of me didn't cost money, but for you I do. People don't look down on your friends for their version of me, but they will for you. I come from a faraway place, but all your friends found me at home. Your friends' versions of me love them, but for me, it's your pockets I will roam. What am I?

A mail order bride

You're in a room with three monkeys. One monkey has a power drill, the other a calculator, and the last nothing. Who is the smartest primate?

You

In the dark, your feet always find me, but in the light, for your hands, I am never there. What am I?

A Lego™.

I start with a "v" and every woman has one. She can even use me to get what she wants. What am I?

Her voice

Over 1,000 people went down on me. I wasn't a maiden for long. Something really big and hard ripped me open. What am I?

The Titanic.

I lurk at all times, but you never see me. We usually meet only once a year, but you always hate me. I never contact you at all, but you always pay me. I screw you over, but you always end up following me. And if you don't, then you will go to jail for me. What am I?

The IRS

How do you find a blind man in a nudist colony?

It's not hard.

If you pay me, you get one freedom, but you lose another. I grow every year, but my fee is not worth my investment. What am I?

College tuition

Arnold Schwarzenegger's is really long. Michael J. Fox's is short. Daffy Duck's isn't human. Madonna doesn't have one. What am I?

A last name

Only great men and women have joined this society. You must go to great heights and get out of your comfort zone to join. It's definitely a risk and can even cause pain to loved ones and those near you, but if you join it, you will be a legend. What am I?

The Mile High Club

What gets longer when pulled, fits between breasts, slides neatly into a hole, has choked people when used improperly, and works best when jerked?

Seatbelts

You are always happy to have me when alone and am enjoyable with friends and family too, but you don't want to share me with someone you just met the night before. What am I?

Breakfast

You play with it at night before bed. You can't be seen fiddling with it at work. You only let very very special people touch it. What is it?

Your iPhone

You devote a significant amount of energy to maintaining and thinking about it, but you hate knowing that your parents are doing it. What is it?

Facebook

Sometimes a finger goes inside me. You fiddle with me when you're bored. The best man always has me first. What am I?

Your wedding band

There are ones that have always been real and others that are fake, and Dolly Parton has some big ones. It can cost you a lot of money for a good one, but at least you can pick the size and color. What am I?

A wig

You never think of me if something goes wrong. And when it does, I take far too long. You invite me into your home, but I am not a friend. And yet, you'll still have to see me time and time again. What am I?

Cable repair guy

If two's company and three's a crowd, what are four and five?

Nine

Men, both powerful and rich and helpless and poor, spend great dollars on me. I am all around the world but never in plain sight. You can find me during the day, but I am almost always better at night. You must have a certain wisdom to see me; I can be wise or dull. If you ever recognized me when you weren't expecting me not in my natural environment, it would be like you never saw me at all.

Strippers

You are awoken at 3 a.m. by a knock on your door. Your parents call you to let you know that they are there for breakfast. You are confused but quickly think of what food you have. You have bread, jam, butter, and eggs. What do you open first?

The door for your parents

If you have three apples and four oranges in one hand and four apples and three oranges in the other hand, what do you have?

Very large hands

What's made of rubber, handed out at some schools, and exists to prevent mistakes?

Erasers

I am known all over the world, but there is little of me to know at all. Some question if I am real, or if I even belong to my owner at all. To close ones, I'm a subject of sensitivity, but to others, a source of amusement. People have been talking about me for years, and much more recently, although the truth of me will never be revealed. What am I?

Donald Trump's hair

You only deal with me from time to time, but I am always a nuisance. My aims are noble, but intrusive. I can know anything about you, but you end up knowing nothing about me. My rules don't make sense, but you must obey them. I am not your friend, but you feel compelled to greet me with a smile. What am I?

The TSA

I have been known to cause great problems in the world, although by comparison, I am quite small. I am known for being uneducated, old, corrupt, and tasteless. People wish I would sail away, but I am stuck although water is all around me. What am I?

Florida

I give you shelter, but I am a prison. I help you in the future, but am now a burden. Not everyone deserves one of me, and if too many people have me, it can lead to great harm. What am I?

A mortgage

When you do not know what I am, then I am something. But when you know what I am, then I am nothing. What am I?

A riddle

POLITICS

President Donald Trump is sitting in the Oval Office, fuming over the latest White House leak to the Washington Post. No matter what he says or does, there's always a reporter who has the exact details down. Trump narrows the leaks down to three possible people in his staff, then concocts a full-proof plan to figure out which one of them is the rat. He gathers his first staff member, named Ben, into his office.

"Ben, you're one of my most trusted confidantes, so I'm telling only you this piece of information, and you can't tell anyone else. I'm going to go to Japan tomorrow and am going to tell the emperor that I'm never visiting their country again since they've treated me so poorly."

"You got it Mr. President, I won't tell a soul." Ben leaves the Oval Office, and the next staff member, Cindy, walks in.

"Cindy, I trust you with my life, and you can't reveal this to a single person, in or out of the White House. I'm flying to Mexico tomorrow and am going to tell the President, face-to-face, that I'm never stepping foot there again until his country treats me with more respect."

"Of course Mr. President, this stays between you and me." Cindy leaves, and Mark, the final staff member steps in.

"Mark, we need to make this quick. I'm hopping on a 16-hour flight to New Zealand tomorrow morning to meet with their Prime Minister and tell them that I will never contact them or step foot in their country until they start respecting me for the worldly leader that I am. You can't reveal this to anyone, it has to stay a secret."

"You got it Mr. President, my lips are sealed." Mark leaves the Oval Office, and Trump sits back in his chair, pleased that when tomorrow comes, he'll be able to finally learn which staff member has been going to the press behind his back.

The next morning, Trump is quickly rushed into a daily briefing and doesn't have time to watch cable news. His staff members are informing them about the latest events happening across the U.S., and Trump coyly asks if anything had happened internationally. His staff looks around concerned. One turns back and says, "Well Mr. Trump, there are no new threats, but strangely, the citizens of Mexico, Japan and New Zealand are all out in the streets celebrating something called 'No More Trump Day.'"

I don't approve of political jokes: I've seen too many of them get elected.

A government employee sits in his office, and out of boredom, decides to see what's inside his old filing cabinet. He pokes through the contents and comes across an old brass lamp. "This will look good on my mantel," he says, and he takes it home with him. While polishing the lamp, a genie appears and, as usual, grants him three wishes. "I would like an ice-cold Coke right now." He gets his Coke and drinks it. Now that he can think more clearly, he states his second wish. "I wish to be on an island with beautiful women, who find me irresistible." Suddenly, he's on an island with gorgeous women eyeing him lustfully. He tells the genie his third and last wish. "I wish I'd never have to work again." Instantly, he's back in his government office.

Three contractors are bidding to fix a broken fence at the White House. One is from Chicago, another is from Tennessee, and the third is from Minnesota. All three go with a White House official to examine the fence. The Minnesota contractor takes out a tape measure and does some measuring, then works some figures with a pencil. "Well," he says, "I figure the job will run about $900: $400 for materials, $400 for my crew, and $100 profit for me." The Tennessee contractor also does some measuring and figuring, then says, "I can do this job for $700: $300 for materials, $300 for my crew, and $100 profit for me." The Chicago contractor doesn't measure or figure, but leans over to the White House official and whispers, "$2,700." The official, incredulous, says, "You didn't even measure like the other guys! How did you come up with such a high figure?" The Chicago contractor whispers back, "$1000 for me, $1000 for you, and we hire the guy from Tennessee to fix the fence." "Done!" replies the government official. And that, my friends, is how the government works.

A little boy goes to his Dad and asks, "What is politics?" The Dad says, "Well son, let me try to explain it this way: I'm the breadwinner of the family, so let's call me capitalism. Your mother, she's the administrator of the money, so we'll call her the government. We're here to take care of your needs, so we'll call you the people. The nanny, we'll consider her the working class. And your baby brother, we'll call him the future. Now, think about that and see if that makes sense." The little boy goes off to bed thinking about what his father has said. Later that night, he hears his baby brother crying, so he gets up to check on him. He finds that the baby has soiled his diaper. The little boy goes to his parents' room and finds his mother sound asleep. Not wanting to wake her, he goes to the nanny's room. Finding the door locked, he peeks in the keyhole and sees his father in bed with the nanny. He gives up and goes back to bed. The next morning, the little boy says to his father, "Dad, I think I understand the concept of politics now." The father says, "Good, son, tell me in your own words what you think politics is all about." The little boy replies, "Well, while capitalism is screwing the working class, the government is sound asleep, the people are being ignored and the future is in deep shit."

Three Boy Scouts are fishing in a boat one day when they hear a lot of commotion. They follow the sounds and find another boat capsized as a man struggles to keep his head above water. Being Boy Scouts, they go to his aid and fish the man out.

The man is Donald Trump. The President towels himself off and catches his breath, and thanks the three Scouts. He asks if there is anything he can do for them.

"I'd sure like a tour of the White House," the first Scout says.

"No problem," says Trump. "How's next week?"

"I want to go for a ride in Air Force One," says the second Scout.

"We can do that next week, too," Trump replies.

"I'd like to be buried in Arlington National Cemetery," says the third.

"I'm sure we can arrange that," says Trump. "But son, you're awfully young to be worrying about that, aren't you?"

"You don't know my Dad," the scout replies. "When he finds out I helped save your life, he's gonna kill me!"

I asked Barack Obama if we could get together later, and he said Yes We Can!

A priest goes into a Washington, D.C., barbershop, gets his hair cut, and asks how much he owes. "No charge, Father," the barber says. "I consider it a service to the Lord." When the barber arrives at his shop the next morning, he finds a dozen small prayer booklets on the stoop along with a thank-you note from the priest. A few days later, a police officer comes in. "How much do I owe you?" the cop asks after his haircut. "No charge, officer," the barber answers. "I consider it a service to my community." The next morning the barber finds a dozen doughnuts on the stoop along with a thank-you note from the police officer. A few days after that, a Senator walks in for a haircut. "How much do I owe you?" he asks afterward. "No charge," the barber replies. "I consider it a service to my country." The next morning when he arrives at the shop, the barber finds a dozen Senators waiting on the stoop.

What's the difference between God and a conservative?

God knows He's not a Republican.

Donald Trump and the Pope both die on the same day. Due to a minor clerical error, the Pope goes to Hell, while Trump goes to Heaven. When the Pope arrives in Hell, everyone realizes the mistake. Due to an issue with the union, they can't swap the two until the next day, and the Pope has to spend the night in Hell, while Trump spends the night in Heaven. The next day, the paperwork gets worked out. On his way up to Heaven, the Pope runs into Trump. Trump asks the Pope, "How is your night in Hell?" "Very educational," the Pope responds. "I've learned a lot from the experience, but now I'm glad I'm going to Heaven. I've been waiting all my life to meet the Virgin Mary." "Ooh, sorry," says Trump, "you should have been there yesterday."

Little Billy wants $100 badly and prays for two weeks but nothing happens. Then he decides to write God a letter requesting the $100. When the postal authorities receive the letter addressed to "God, USA," they decide to send it to the President. The President is so impressed, touched, and amused that he instructs his secretary to send Billy a $5 bill. The President thinks this would appear to be a lot of money to a little boy.

Billy is delighted with the $5 and sits down to write a thank-you note to God, which reads:

Dear God,

Thank you very much for sending the money, however, I noticed that for some reason you had to send it through Washington, D.C., and, as usual, those crooks deducted $95.

Thanks,

Billy

Did you hear that the White House isn't displaying its Nativity scene this year? They couldn't find the three wise men!

George W. Bush goes to see the doctor to get the results of his brain scan. The doctor says: "Mr. President, I have some bad news for you. First, we have discovered that your brain has two sides: The left side and the right side." Bush interrupts, "Well, that's normal, isn't it? I thought everybody had two sides to their brain?" The doctor replies, "That's true, Mr. President. But your brain is very unusual because on the left side there isn't anything right, while on the right side there isn't anything left."

When Einstein dies and arrives at the gates of heaven, St. Peter won't let him in until he proves his identity. Einstein scribbles out a couple of his equations, and is admitted into paradise. And when Picasso dies, St. Peter asks, "How do I know you're Picasso?" Picasso sketches out a couple of his masterpieces. St. Peter is convinced and lets him in. When George W. Bush dies, he goes to heaven and meets the man at the gates. "How can you prove to me you're George W. Bush?" Saint Peter says. Bush replies, "Well heck, I don't know." St. Peter says, "Well, Albert Einstein showed me his equations and Picasso drew his famous pictures. What can you do to prove you're George W. Bush?" Bush replies, "Who are Albert Einstein and Picasso?" St. Peter says, "It must be you, George, c'mon on in."

I recently asked my friend's little girl what she wanted to be when she grows up. She said she wanted to be President someday. Both of her parents, liberal Democrats, were standing there, so I asked her, "'If you were President, what would be the first thing you would do?'"

She replied, "I'd give food and houses to all the homeless people."

Her parents beamed with pride.

"Wow, what a worthy goal," I told her. "But you don't have to wait until you're President to do that. You can come over to my house and mow the lawn, pull weeds, and sweep my yard, and I'll pay you $50. Then I'll take you over to the grocery store where the homeless guy hangs out, and you can give him the $50 to use toward food and a new house."

She thought that over for a few seconds, then she looked me straight in the eye and asked, "Why doesn't the homeless guy come over and do the work, and you can just pay him the $50?"

I said, "Welcome to the Republican Party."

YOU MIGHT BE A DEMOCRAT IF...

- You have a bold opinion about the tax code, but don't make enough money per year to actually be taxed.

- You've read extensive amounts of socialism philosophy and how the capitalist state is crushing the poor, but still can't bring yourself to take a job at the open bookstore.

- You write a letter to your office manager, complaining about how the Christmas party is offensive, and should be instead titled "non-denominational wintertime gathering."

- You advocate for free healthcare for all citizens across the country but don't pay attention to your own teenager doing drugs at home.

- You write letters to Congress asking to protect the environment, even though you can't be bothered to pick up the trash from your stoop.

- You write letters to local representatives complaining about the new Wal-Mart or Target closing independent stores in town but are still happy to shop there because they have a great discount on kale.

- You say that the government should help the homeless but you can't be bothered to give spare change from your espresso to a homeless person.

- You argue for a more robust public transportation system and for Americans to be less reliant on gasoline, but only when you're not too busy smoking a joint in your Toyota Prius.

- You book a ticket to Washington, D.C., and spend a month picketing in front of the White House to address global warming, all because the average temperature is two degrees above what the weatherman says on TV.

- You've donated hundreds of dollars to PETA but are in a scramble to get a reservation at the hot new luxury steakhouse that opened downtown.

- You don't actually listen to NPR or PBS but just donated so you could get the free tote bag.

A woman in a hot-air balloon realizes she's lost. She lowers her altitude and spots a man in a boat below. She shouts to him, "Excuse me, can you help me? I promised a friend I would meet him an hour ago, but I don't know where I am."

The man consults his portable GPS and replies, "You're in a hot air balloon, approximately 30 feet above a ground elevation of 2,346 feet above sea level. You are at 31 degrees, 14.97 minutes north latitude and 100 degrees, 49.09 minutes west longitude."

She rolls her eyes and says, "You must be a Republican."

"I am," replies the man. "How did you know?"

"Well," answers the balloonist, "everything you told me is technically correct. But I have no idea what to do with your information, and I'm still lost. Frankly, you've not been much help to me."

The man smiles and responds, "You must be a Democrat."

"I am," replies the balloonist. "How did you know?"

"Well," says the man, "you don't know where you are or where you are going. You've risen to where you are, due to a large quantity of hot air. You made a promise you have no idea how to keep, and you expect me to solve your problem. You're in exactly the same position you were in before we met, but somehow, now it's my fault."

A guy is visiting San Francisco and walks into a small store in Chinatown.

He notices a small bronze statue of a rat.

He asks the owner "How much?" and the owner replies, "Fifty dollars for the bronze rat, and $1,000 for the story behind it."

The guy says, "Forget the story," and buys the rat.

As he's walking down the street, he notices two live rats following him. As he continues to walk, more rats start following him.

He starts to get a little concerned and heads for the waterfront. By the time he gets there, thousands and thousands of rats are following him.

He walks up to the end of the pier and throws the bronze rat into the bay, and the rats all follow, leap off the pier, and drown.

The guy rushes back to the store and walks in. The owner says, "Ah! So you're back for the story."

The guys says, "No, I was wondering if you have any bronze Democrats?"

You might be a Republican if:

- You forget how many 0's you actually have sitting in your bank account.

- You spend the same more money flying to offshore tax havens and meeting with expert accountants to not pay taxes than you would actually paying your taxes.

- You think the best version of recycling is by not throwing away the PBR cans that have been lining your bathroom floor.

- You've gotten angry at a negative story written about Donald Trump in The New York Times, not because they attacked the candidate you preferred, but because you didn't know what any of the words in the article meant.

- You get angry at the sight of solar panels and wind turbines as you pump $4-a-gallon gas into your Hummer.

- You own a massive four-door SUV but have never had to take it out of first gear.

- You complain about minorities taking advantage of the welfare state but only when you're in line at the unemployment office.

- You argue on social media that marijuana is a dangerous drug destroying American lives as you take yet another swig of Jack Daniels.

- You get bored whenever going to the theater, opera, or symphony because there aren't enough Fox News graphics or Ted Nugent solos.

- You argue against food stamps being distributed to the poor but you live in your mother's basement.

- You voted for George W. Bush on the premise that he seemed like a good guy to have a beer with, but don't see the irony in that George W. Bush doesn't drink.

- You get angry when your hard-earned tax money gets spent on parks and public projects, even though you'll end up throwing a kegger there afterward.

- Your idea of travel is going to a different Lowe's store on the other side of town.

- You think global warming isn't real because it snowed once two years ago.

- You complain to your dealer at an Indian casino about how illegal immigrants are taking this country away from the true Americans.

- You own 12 different types of guns which you say are for safety, although you live in the nicest part of town.

- You have nothing against people of different ethnicities or religious backgrounds—just as long as those ethnicities are Caucasian and Christian.

B ernie Sanders is campaigning for the 2020 presidential race. Voters are invigorated by his energy and enthusiasm and his commitment to helping out the disenfranchised. As he's campaigning, Bernie meets with different officials from groups.

"Bernie, will you work to make sure that women have an equal say in the workplace as men, and that they are treated with respect, not just as second class citizens?"

"It is my dream to make sure that women's issues are addressed in every area of our society," Bernie says. The crowd roars, and another activist comes up to speak.

"Bernie, will you find a way to eradicate the country of student loan debt and find a more affordable way that people can get a higher education?"

"It is my dream to see every child and student be able to receive a high quality education and not have to pay hundreds of thousands of dollars in student loan debt," Bernie says. The crowd roars again, as another activist comes up to speak.

"Bernie, half of the country has no health insurance, and they can't pay their medical bills. People end up receiving terminal illnesses because they're too scared to go to a doctor for a simple checkup and how much that may cost. Will you give these needy people the healthcare they deserve?"

"It is my dream to see every American with full healthcare," Bernie says. The crowd erupts.

After his popular responses, Bernie ends up winning the election in a landslide. But a month into his term, his supporters are upset that he has not addressed any of their concerns.

"Bernie, what about women's issues, reducing student loan debt, and fixing healthcare?"

"Hey," Bernie says, "I just said it is my dream to do it, not that'd I'd actually do it!"

. . . .

Hillary Clinton is meeting with her campaign staff the day after she lost the election. She's pressing each of her staff members to figure out the specific reason why she lost.

"Well Madame Secretary, you didn't really have a strong pull in the South, even with your ties to Arkansas," one staffer says, unconvincingly.

Hillary says: "Well, those states have always been red, but that isn't the reason why we lost." She presses another staffer for an answer.

"Madame Secretary, you didn't really connect with voters in rural Pennsylvania and Ohio, and those were some big states that could've helped us win."

Hillary thinks this over for a moment: "Even without them, though, we still should have had enough electoral votes to clinch it."

Hillary's staffers are frustrated: They're giving her clear reasons why she lost, but she still doesn't seem to be listening to them. One more staffer speaks up.

"Mrs. Clinton, I think a reason why you may have lost, and I'm just spitballing here, might have been because your campaign lacked a clear coherent message on what you actually stood for, that you failed to incite any passion or drive for people to get out and campaign for you, that you, to many people, represent the very idea of nepotism and prestige politics, and even though your opponent is far worse in every single category, you failed to see why he became so popular among them in the first place, and you didn't do anything to reach out to them, you just felt that they would come to their senses. Maybe that's why you lost."

The other staff members are shocked by his forwardness, and they look at Mrs. Clinton, who is typing on her phone.

"Oh, did you say something?" she says. "I'm sorry, I was sending an email."

Vladimir Putin is drinking vodka with some of his cronies in Red Square. He's telling them all about Donald Trump and just how easy it is to tick him off and set any random new American policy into motion because he is so hotheaded. Putin asks one of his cronies to give him any topic or subject on their mind.

"How about Vodka being better than beer?" Putin smiles, agrees, and sends a text message to Trump: "Hey Don, I was talking with some brewery owners in the U.S. and they all say you're pretty dumb. The vodka makers disagree and say you're really smart."

"I can't believe they says that! I'll make those lousy beer drinkers pay!" Trump texts back. He then immediately declares that all beer in the U.S. is illegal and that Americans' drink of choice is now Vodka Tonics.

"Ooh ooh, how about Ferraris being better than Hondas?" another crony asks. Putin then texts Trump, "Hey Don, I heard the president of Honda say you were ugly, while the CEO of Ferrari says you're really handsome." "That jerk! I'll show him!" Trump texts back. The next day, Putin and his cronies laugh while watching the news, as Trump orders all Honda owners imprisoned and how all Americans will each get their own Ferrari.

One crony then has a really crazy idea: "Hey, what about someone in Congress saying that he really doesn't like his wife at all, but instead is in love with his daughter? That will really stir things up!" Putin is having too much fun to pass this up, so he then texts Trump, "Hey Don, Paul Ryan told me that you don't love Melania at all, but you're actually in love with Tiffany. Is that true?"

He gets back a text from Trump. "Putin, you and I both know that's a bald-faced lie."

"What do you mean? Ryan even said it to me yesterday," Putin texts back.

"Impossible, Ryan never says anything of the sort. Everyone knows that it's Ivanka I'm in love with, not Tiffany."

Barack Obama and Joe Biden are vacationing on a remote beach in Mexico. "You know Joe, I never really asked you what you're going to do now that you're no longer Vice President. Do you have any plans?"

"Well Barry, you know how you and Rahm Emanuel always talked about opening up a T-shirt shop in Hawaii, where you'd only have to sell one size of white T-shirt? I was actually really into that idea, but instead of just white T-shirts, we'd sell some with our faces on them, giving thumbs up with big goofy smiles. We'd call Barry and Joe's T-shirt-palooza shack, and if it became a big enough success, we'd expand to the other mainland states."

Obama laughs. "That's a real funny idea Joe, but that whole conversation me and Rahm had is really just a metaphor about not wanting to make as many decisions now that we're no longer in government life. And to be perfectly honest, white T-shirts would sell better than T-shirts with two old geezers on them. Hilarious idea, though."

"Yeah, you're right, that's too silly to ever work," Joe says with a laugh. The two return to their separate hotel rooms, where Joe then gets on the phone to make a call.

"Hey Jill? Yeah, it's Joe. I'm sorry, dear, but cancel our tickets to Hawaii, he didn't like the idea."

RELATIONSHIPS, DATING, & SEX

There are only three kinds of men who don't understand women: Young men, old men, and middle-aged men.

An elderly man wants to make his younger wife pregnant. So, he goes to the doctor to have a sperm count done. The doctor tells him to take a specimen cup home, fill it, and bring it back the next day. The elderly man comes back the next day: The specimen cup is empty and the lid is on it.

Doctor: "What is the problem?"

Elderly man: "Well, I tried with my right hand...nothing. So, I tried with my left hand...nothing. My wife tried with her right hand...nothing. Her left hand... nothing. Her mouth...nothing. Then my wife's friend tried. Right hand, left hand, mouth....still nothing."

Doctor: "Wait a minute. You mean your wife's friend tried too?!"

Elderly man: "Yeah, and we still couldn't get the lid off of the specimen cup!"

Online dating websites have all become niche. I'm starting my own called Fiber. It's just for people with their shit together.

I have another website that's for fans of the hip-hop group, NWA, it's called Eazy-Eharmony.

A man and his wife are dining at a table in a plush restaurant, and the husband keeps staring at a drunken lady swigging her drink as she sits alone at a nearby table.

The wife asks, "Do you know her?"

"Yes," sighs the husband, "She's my ex-girlfriend. I understand she took to drinking right after we split up seven years ago, and I hear she hasn't been sober since."

"My God!" says the wife, "Who would think a person could go on celebrating that long."

Three guys go to a ski lodge, and there aren't enough rooms, so they have to share a bed. In the middle of the night, the guy on the right wakes up and says, "I had this wild, vivid dream of getting a hand job!" The guy on the left wakes up, and unbelievably, he's had the same dream, too. Then the guy in the middle wakes up and says, "That's funny, I dreamed I was skiing!"

John lays down on his sofa after a long day at the office. The previous three months had been a depressing slump ever since his breakup from Miranda, but he decided it is time to move on. He set up an account on Tinder and started swiping.

He first swiped on girls who looked like Hollywood actresses, but to no avail. Then he opened up his pool a bit more, swiping on girls except for those who didn't share similar interests with him, or says something on their profile that stood out. He travelled 50 miles to the next city over, switched his pictures around a bit and copied verbatim an example of a successful profile online. But after travelling through the entire state of California, John didn't have a single match.

John showed up at the Tinder offices, demanding to speak to the CEO or someone who could help him. The office looked concerned, almost if they had seen him before or talked about him in private. A young 20-something receptionist that John recognized from the app told him to wait in the lobby until someone could speak with him.

"Hello, John? I'm Peter Donaghy, I'm the CEO and Chief Engineer of Tinder. Please come to my office so we can talk about your problem." John followed the CEO and they began to talk.

"So John, I understand you have a problem."

"Yeah I do, your stupid app isn't working. I literally swiped right on every single person in the state of California and had no matches. I even signed up for Tinder Plus but that didn't help at all. I think my profile might be bugged or my phone might have a virus or something."

"Well John, Tinder can't be 'bugged' or 'hacked,' and based on the way the app functions, it has nothing to do with your phone, or even the Facebook profile you use to login. From a technical standpoint, there is nothing wrong with the app whatsoever, and I should know, I was the one who designed it."

"What is it then? Why haven't I gotten any matches?"

Peter hunched back in his chair and took a deep breath before speaking.

"Well John, the truth is, you just…suck."

"I what? What did you say?"

"You suck. You really suck. Like you are just awful in every sense of the word. You are the single suckiest person in California."

"How dare you! I don't suck, I'm great! I have a job, I have my own apartment, I'm a dog owner."

"And that's all great John! Those are all great things to have and to be, but none of that can overturn your level of suckiness."

John is depressed, he had gotten a hard dose of reality he didn't care to hear, and is starting to accept it. "Well, what does that even mean that I suck? Why do I suck then?"

"Nobody here could explain it when they first saw your profile on the specific 'why' of your suckiness, but it is undeniable that there is one there. We researched for weeks to unearth what that indescribable sucky factor may be, and last week, we made a breakthrough. We discovered it, the root of your suckiness."

"Well, what is it?"

"John: You chew with your mouth open."

"I'm sorry, what? No I don't, that's not true."

"No it is true, it's the truest thing in the world. Look at all these pictures. In every single one of them, your mouth is slightly open while smiling, and you can see a tiny sliver of food."

Looking at the pictures on a phone, one wouldn't be able to notice John's open-mouth chewing tendencies, and the pictures would be too small to actually notice any food. But with them blown up large on the wall, it is apparent they were there.

"It's actually quite impressive, really. Only one of these photos is actually a situation that calls for eating food, this one here where you were at Chili's happy hour with a few of your work buddies, and you had a tortilla chip lodged in between your 13th and 14th molar, seen here. The single most unattractive, social pariah-inducing activity one can do is chew with their mouth open, with only bad body odor being a close second."

"Well, is there any hope?"

"Of course there is, just chew with your mouth closed. Once you truly learn to do that, take a few pictures of yourself, and you should find dozens of new matches. And if you need any help, don't hesitate to drop by."

Peter watches him as he walked away, and asks his receptionist about John.

"So what do you think? We finally figured out that guy's issue, he is chewing with his mouth open. He'll find love on Tinder in no time."

"Tough chance," the receptionist says, "that guy smells like shit."

I got a text message from a girl I had seen a few weeks back that says, "I'm late," which I thought was weird, because we didn't have any meetings set up.

A successful rancher dies and leaves everything to his devoted wife.
She is a very good-looking woman and is determined to keep the ranch, but she knows very little about ranching, so she decides to place an ad in the newspaper for a ranch hand.

Two men apply for the job. One is gay and the other, a drunk ex-con.

She thinks long and hard about it, and when no one else applies, she decides to hire the gay man, figuring it will be safer to have him around the house than the drunk.

He proves to be a hard worker who puts in long hours every day and knows a lot about ranching. For weeks, the two of them work, and the ranch is doing very well.

Then one day, the rancher's widow says to the gay man, "You have done a really good job, and the ranch looks great. You should go into town and kick up your heels."

The gay man readily agrees and goes into town one Saturday night. One o'clock comes, however, and he doesn't return. Two o'clock, and no sign.

He finally returns around two-thirty, and upon entering the room, he finds the rancher's widow sitting by the fireplace with a glass of wine, waiting for him.

She quietly calls him over to her.

"Unbutton my blouse and take it off," she says. Trembling, he does as she directs.

"Now take off my boots." He does as she asks, ever so slowly.

"Now take off my socks." He removes each gently and places them neatly by her boots.

"Now take off my skirt." He slowly unbuttons it, constantly watching her eyes in the firelight.

"Now take off my bra." Again, with trembling hands, he does as he is told and drops it to the floor.

"Now," she says, "take off my panties." By the light of the fire, he slowly pulls them down and off.

Then she looks at him and says, "If you ever wear my clothes into town again, you're fired!!"

Bernadette is a very buxom woman whose chest has earned glances and glares from men ever since her early twenties. She is always annoyed by the attention but doesn't really do that much about it until one day when she gets absolutely fed up. Bernadette purchases a T-shirt with the message "My eyes are up here" written on it. She wears the T-shirt and notices that any time guys try to look at her chest, they look away with embarrassment. Bernadette is happy with the new results until she notices a man still staring at her chest from 50 yards away, with a much more attentive gaze than any man has ever delivered. Bernadette approaches him and says, "Excuse me, can't you read what my shirt says?" and the man replies, "Yes, but I just wanted to see the message up close."

Joe wants to buy a motorbike. He doesn't have much luck until one day, he comes across a Harley with a For Sale sign on it. The bike seems even better than a new one, although it is 10 years old. It is shiny and in absolute mint condition. He immediately buys it and asks the seller how he kept it in such great condition for 10 years.

"Well, it's quite simple, really," says the seller, "whenever the bike is outside and it's going to rain, rub Vaseline on the chrome. It protects it from the rain."

And he hands Joe a jar of Vaseline. That night, his girlfriend, Sandra, invites him over to meet her parents. Naturally, they take the bike there. But just before they enter the house, Sandra stops him and says, "I have to tell you something about my family before we go in."

"When we eat dinner, we don't talk. In fact, the first person who says anything during dinner has to do the dishes."

"No problem," he says. And in they go. Joe is shocked. Right smack in the middle of the living room is a huge stack of dirty dishes. In the kitchen is another huge stack of dishes. Piled up on the stairs, in the corridor, everywhere he looks, dirty dishes. They sit down to dinner and, sure enough, no one says a word.

As dinner progresses, Joe decides to take advantage of the situation. So he leans over and kisses Sandra. No one says a word. So he reaches over and fondles her breasts. Still, nobody says a word.

So he stands up, grabs her, rips her clothes off, throws her on the table, and screws her right there, in front of her parents.

His girlfriend is a little flustered, her Dad is obviously livid, and her Mom is horrified when he sits back down, but no one says a word. He looks at her Mom.

"She's got a great body," he thinks. So he grabs the Mom, bends her over the dinner table, and has his way with her every which way right there on the dinner table. Now his girlfriend is furious and her Dad is boiling, but still, total silence. All of a sudden there is a loud clap of thunder, and it starts to rain. Joe remembers his bike, so he pulls the jar of Vaseline from his pocket.

Suddenly the father shouts: "I'll do the damn dishes!!!"

Two single women meet for coffee. They start talking about the men they're dating. The first woman says she's not seeing anyone special.

The second woman says she's very excited about a guy she's been dating for a month.

"Last night we went out for dinner, and afterward he says those four words I've been waiting all my life to hear from a man."

"Will you marry me?"

"No: 'Put your money away.'"

After an hour of gathering up his courage, a shy guy finally approaches the hot girl at the end of the bar. "Um, would you mind if I chatted with you for a while?"

She yells, "No, I won't sleep with you tonight, you pig!"

Everyone in the bar stops and stares. Completely embarrassed, the guy slinks back to his table with a red face.

After a few minutes, the woman walks over to him and apologizes. She smiles and says, "I'm sorry if I embarrassed you. I'm a graduate student in psychology, and I'm studying how people respond to embarrassing public situations."

To which the guy responds as loudly as possible, "What do you mean $200 for a BJ?"

A lady goes into a bar in Waco and sees a cowboy with his feet propped up on a table. He has the biggest boots she'd ever seen. The woman asks the cowboy if it's true what they say about men with big feet are well endowed. The cowboy grins and says, "Shore is, little lady. Why don't you come on out to the bunkhouse and let me prove it to you?" The woman wants to find out for herself, so she spends the night with him. The next morning she hands him a $100 bill. Blushing, he says, "Well, thank you, ma'am. I'm real flattered. Ain't nobody ever paid me for my services before." "Don't be flattered," she says. "Take the money and buy yourself some boots that fit."

Ronnie is a 25-year-old man who, while smart and friendly, has never had good luck with women. Every time he goes on a date, he's always too nervous or says something that causes the girl he's with to quickly lose interest. Ronnie complains to his friends, thinking that he'll always make a mistake and never find "the one." His friends come up with an idea, though: Wear a discreet earpiece and microphone, and then his friends will be able to listen to everything that goes on during the date, and feed him things to say through his earpiece.

His friends set him up on a date with a girl named Veronica, who like Ronnie, is also nice but shy and hasn't had much luck with the opposite sex. They go to dinner at a cozy restaurant downtown. Ronnie is nervous, but his friends start feeding him suggestions through the earpiece.

Ronnie then follows all of the instructions his friends give him and the date goes great. He and Veronica laugh, have a couple of drinks, and even order dessert. The date is going so well that they even agree to go back to Veronica's house afterward for coffee, with his friends still giving him instructions along the way.

Things became heated at Veronica's apartment, and she tells Ronnie to wait in the living room while she slips into something more comfortable. Ronnie is nervous but his friends are still cheering him on and boosting his confidence through the earpiece. But Ronnie has to go to the bathroom. As he stumbles through the hallway, he accidentally trips over a rug, falls to the floor, and as he tries to find something to hold onto, he opens the door to Veronica's room. He sees her unzipping her dress, with her own microphone and earpiece attached, revealing she also has been getting secret instructions from a group of friends on what to say and how to act during the date.

"What happened? What's going on?" the friends yell as Ronnie and Veronica look at each other with dumbfound shock.

"Well," Ronnie says, "my friends did tell me a girl loves a guy who knows how to listen."

John is a very ugly man by any conventional standard. Despite his charm and caring spirit, he cannot find a romantic partner who will look past his looks, and all he ever wanted to be is beautiful. To cheer himself up, John begins reading inspirational quotes and phrases on the Internet and comes across one that speaks to him and lifts his spirits. He then quits his high-paying job in finance and sells his home to open a bee sanctuary. John's friends know that he is having trouble in the romance department but are concerned about this latest career endeavor. When they ask him why, he refers back to the inspirational passage, saying, "You know what they say: 'Beauty is in the eye of the bee-holder'!"

One hot summer night in 1960, Steve has his first date with Susie.
He goes to pick her up and her Mom answers the door. She invites him in, and asks him what they plan to do on their date.

Steve replies that they'll probably see a movie, then get a burger.

Susie's Mom says, "Well, Susie really likes to screw."

Steve says, "Huh?"

Her Mom says, "Yes, she loves it. She could probably screw all night."

"OK, thanks!" replies Steve, mentally rearranging his plans for the night.

A few minutes later, Susie comes downstairs and they leave on their date.

About a half hour later, Susie comes running back in the house, her clothes disheveled, and yells:

"Mom, it's called the TWIST! The name of the goddamn dance is the TWIST!"

A group of friends is at the bar enjoying themselves, when sparks between two of the friends, Linus and Shirley, start to fly. They start kissing and eventually leave the bar, causing the rest of the group to cheer them on. They go back to Linus' house and start getting frisky.

When the moment comes, Shirley asks Linus if he has protection. He tells her that he can run to the store real quick and get back. Linus leaves and drives all over town, but all of the stores are closed or out of stock. He finally finds one on the furthest edge and makes his purchase before making the long drive home. When he gets back home, a couple of hours later, it's already dawn, and Shirley is getting ready to go to work.

Linus then meets up with his friends who ask Linus about how his night went with Shirley. Not wanting to lie but also not wanting to lose the admiration of his peers, Linus coyly replies, "Oh, I kept her up all night."

A guy and his girlfriend are kissing in the park.

Guy: I think I just swallowed your bubble gum!

Girl: No, honey, I just have the sniffles...

During the first date a guy tells a girl:

"You make me sleepy."

"Really?" she responds.

"Yes, we met three minutes ago, but I already want to take you to bed!"

Honey, would you like me to bring coffee to the bed?

No, darling, I will come to have breakfast with you.

Would you like to have scrambled eggs, my love?

Sure, kitty, two eggs, please.

Wait, you don't remember my name either, do you?

RELIGION

JUDAISM

According to Judaism, when does a fetus become a human?

When it graduates from law school.

A rabbi and a priest buy a car together and it's being stored at the priest's house. One day the rabbi goes over to use the car and he sees the priest sprinkling water on it. The rabbi asks, "What are you doing?" The priest responds, "I'm blessing the car." So the rabbi says, "OK, since we're doing that..." and he takes out a hacksaw and cuts two inches off the tail pipe.

A Jewish father is very troubled by the way his son turned out and goes to see his rabbi about it.

"Rabbi, I brought him up in the faith, gave him a very expensive Bar Mitzvah, and it cost me a fortune to educate him. Then he tells me last week, he's decided to be a Christian. Rabbi, where did I go wrong?"

The rabbi strokes his beard and says, "Funny you should come to me. I too, brought up my son as a boy of faith, sent him to university and it cost me a fortune, and then one day he comes to me and tells me he wants to be a Christian."

"What did you do?" asks the man of the rabbi.

"I turned to God for the answer," replies the rabbi.

"What did he say?" asks the man.

He says, "Funny you should come to me…"

A Chinese guy goes into a Jewish-owned establishment to buy black bras, size 38. The Jewish storekeeper, known for his skills as a businessman, says that black bras are rare and that he is finding it very difficult to buy them from his suppliers. Therefore he has to charge $50 for each pair. The Chinese guy buys 25 pairs.

He returns a few days later and this time orders 50 pair. The Jewish owner tells him that they have become even harder to get and charges him $60 per pair.

The Chinese guy returns a month later and buys the store's remaining stock of 50, and this time for $75 each. The Jewish owner is somewhat puzzled by the large demand for black size 38 bras and asks the Chinese guy, "Please tell me, what do you do with all these black bras?"

The Chinese guy answers: "I cut them in half and sell them as yarmulkes to you Jews for $200 each."

Did you hear about the Jewish Mother cash machine? When you take out some money, it says to you, "What did you do with the last $50 I gave you?"

A reporter goes to see a Jewish man who has been going to the Western Wall in Israel to pray once a day for 70 years, the reporter goes up to him and says, "Hello, I'm a television reporter and we know you're quite famous around this wall, so we were wondering if we could ask you a few questions." The man agrees and she asks, "So we were wondering: What have you actually been praying for, all these years?"

The man replies, "I have been praying for peace between the Jews and Arabs and for all world hatred and terrorism to stop, and for my children and grandchildren to grown up in a peaceful world."

The news reporter says, "Wow, that's truly beautiful. How do you feel after doing this for 70 years?"

The man replies, "I feel like I've been talking to a fucking brick wall."

A slacker teen is panicking while preparing for his Bar Mitzvah. The teen doesn't know how to read Hebrew, and he's spent the past three years in Hebrew school finding clever ways to get through all of his assignments without having to learn the language.

The synagogue's rabbi named Alexander is sure that Daniel is lying about how much he is studying, and so he asks him to bring a recording of him singing the portion to prove he knew it. Daniel provides a recording, but the voice on it is a bit strange. It sounds a little like Daniel, except the voice is much higher-pitched. The Rabbi is very skeptical, but he doesn't have any concrete evidence to prove the teen doesn't know his portion. With the Bar Mitzvah just a few days away, he agrees to let the teen go onstage, hoping that he has actually been studying during the time he says he is sick.

The day of the Bar Mitzvah arrives, and the teen is called up to recite his Torah portion. He knows nothing at all, but also knows that, except for the rabbi, nobody else in the synagogue actually understands Hebrew and won't know the actual Torah portion or what Daniel is saying. So the teen wings it, making up fake Hebrew words and just singing his heart out until stopping. Everyone in the synagogue is impressed, but the rabbi is furious, and he confronts the teen after the service ends.

"You know Daniel, I know that you weren't actually saying the Torah portion up there. I know that you hadn't been studying for all those months beforehand, that you just blew it off. I'm not going to tell anyone about this because I don't want you to look back decades from now on this day in shame. But I do want to say that I'm very disappointed in you."

"I'm sorry, rabbi, it was just so much work and I was afraid that even if I did study, I wouldn't do it right. I was just scared," Daniel says.

The rabbi can tell that Daniel feels bad and understands why he did it, but he isn't quite ready to forgive Daniel.

"Who did you get to record the portion for you?" the rabbi asks.

"I found the kid who had the same portion I did last year and they had it already recorded. I paid them $50 to use it when I was meeting with you. Apparently, they did the same thing from the kid before them last year."

The rabbi is confused. Last year's student, too, is like Daniel, a bit of a slacker who always tried to find ways to bypass the system. He then researches further and further back, how each year whoever read that Torah portion seemed to be a slacker. The young rabbi, still angry with Daniel, has to speak with an older retired rabbi from the synagogue and ask them where this might have started.

"Do you really not know who started this chain of cheating?" the older rabbi asks.

Alexander is puzzled, but then he has a moment of clarity. It is he who started the chain, years and years ago, when he was reciting the same Torah portion! Apparently the kid the year before Alexander is the very last one who actually bothered to learn it entirely. And every kid, years and years later, just paid the kid before him to use that tape.

"It is me! I can't believe it! I'm the very first one who kick-started this whole thing!"

"That must be very embarrassing for you Alexander," the wise older rabbi says.

"You, while now wise, were once a young man too looking for an easy way out. Perhaps it's time that you forgive young Daniel."

"You're right, rabbi, that I'm embarrassed, but not about that. I'm just upset that Daniel had to only pay $50 to get that recording. For me it was a cool $100."

....

B enjamin goes to see Rabbi Levy. "Rabbi," he says, "my life is in ruins. My Judith has left me and she's taken our children and our dog with her. She has also taken all my money and my car and as a result my business is in ruins. Please help me Rabbi, I don't know what to do."

After a few minutes thinking about the problem, Rabbi Levy replies, "OK, Benjamin, here is what you should do. Go home and open up your Bible to any page. Point randomly anywhere on that page and whatever it says, you must do. Do you understand?"

"Yes Rabbi," replies Benjamin, "I'll try."

So Benjamin goes home, takes his Bible from his bookcase, sits down with it, opens it to a random page, points and reads.

Six months later, Benjamin goes to see Rabbi Levy again. "Rabbi," he says, "since I saw you last, I've become a new man. I've remarried and become very successful in my business. I've even got a new dog and called it Levy after you. So I want to thank you Rabbi for the advice you gave me. It changed my life."

"If you don't mind me asking," says Rabbi Levy, "I've got a bad memory. What did I suggest you do that helped you so much?"

"Well Rabbi, you told me six months ago to open my Bible to any page, point, and to do what it says."

"So what did it say?" asks Rabbi Levy.

"Chapter 11," replies Benjamin.

CHRISTIAN

Why did God make Adam before Eve?
To give Adam a chance to speak

A drunken man staggers into a Catholic church and sits down in a confessional and says nothing. The bewildered priest coughs to attract his attention, but still the man says nothing. The priest then knocks on the wall three times in a final attempt to get the man to speak. Finally, the drunk replies: "No use knocking pal, there's no paper in this one either."

I think Jesus' stories would have translated better for me if they showed them to me like shows from the 1990s. I think the Holy Trinity would make the most fun sitcom family. The show could be the "Fresh Prince...Of Peace" I even wrote a theme song:

"In West Jerusalem, born and raised,

Walking on the seas is how I spent most of my days,

Chilling out relaxing, acting all cool

Making some tables at carpentry school

When a couple of Romans, who were up to no good,

Starting persecuting in my neighborhood

I did one little miracle and my Mom got scared,

She said, "I'm talking to your father... who's up in the air"

A little boy is afraid of the dark. One night his mother tells him to go out to the back porch and bring her the broom. The little boy turns to his mother and says, "Mama, I don't want to go out there. It's dark."

The mother smiles reassuringly at her son. "You don't have to be afraid of the dark," she explains. "Jesus is out there. He'll look after you and protect you."

The little boy looks at his mother real hard and asks, "Are you sure he's out there?"

"Yes, I 'm sure. He is everywhere, and he is always ready to help you when you need him," she says.

The little boy thinks about that for a minute and then goes to the back door and cracks it a little. Peering out into the darkness, he calls, "Jesus? If you're out there, would you please hand me the broom?"

Two little boys, ages 8 and 10, are excessively mischievous. They are always getting into trouble and their parents know all about it. If any mischief occurs in their town, the two boys are probably involved.

The boys' mother hears that a clergyman in town has been successful in disciplining children, so she asks if he would speak with her boys. The clergyman agrees, but he asks to see them individually. So the mother sends the eight-year-old first, in the morning, with the older boy to see the clergyman in the afternoon.

The clergyman, a huge man with a booming voice, sits the younger boy down and asks him sternly, "Do you know where God is, son?" The boy's mouth drops open, but he made no response, sitting there wide-eyed with his mouth hanging open. So the clergyman repeats the question in an even sterner tone, "Where is God?!" Again, the boy makes no attempt to answer. The preacher raises his voice even more and shakes his finger in the boy's face and bellows, "Where is God?!" The boy screams and bolts from the room, runs directly home, and dives into his closet, slamming the door behind him. When his older brother finds him in the closet, he asks, "What happened?" The younger brother, gasping for breath, replies, "We are in BIG trouble this time, dude. GOD is missing, and they think we did it!"

Four nuns die in a plane crash. Upon arrival at the Holy Gates, St. Peter meets them and says that they have to answer one question that will be verified in the Book Of Life before they can enter into the Heavenly kingdom. The question is: "Have you ever touched a man's privates?"

The first nun steps up and says No, but I've seen one in a book. St. Peter says for the nun to put some holy water on her eyes and she may enter.

The second nun steps up and the same question is asked of her. She says she once touched one for a second with her hand.

St. Peter tells the nun to put some holy water on her hand and she may enter.

Now the third and fourth nuns get into a fight about who will go next, and St. Peter asks what's the problem. The fourth nun says, "I want to wash my mouth out with that holy water before she puts her butt in it."

Once every four years, Pope Francis invites criminals and from all across the globe to the Vatican to forgive them for their sins. These people are among the worst of the worst menaces that society has ever encountered, but the Pope has never met a person he cannot forgive.

The Pope invites in his first guest, a well-dressed American man in his 40s.

"Your holy father, forgive me, for I have sinned. I am a Wall Street broker, and my firm is responsible in lending out bad mortgages for low-income families that had no reasonable way to pay them back all across the U.S. The loans were predatory and the people didn't know better, and I singlehandedly caused the evictions of more than 500 families, while also helping to plunge the country, and the world, into the worst financial disaster since the Great Depression. I want to be a better man and use my financial knowledge now to help people in Third World countries start businesses and better themselves. Holy Father, can you please forgive me?"

Pope Francis takes a moment to contemplate the man's story. His crimes are despicable, but he is showing true remorse. "You have been forgiven my son, please be on your way."

The next person comes in, a woman in her mid-30s from Great Britain.

"Your Holy Father, forgive me for I have sinned. I used to be a drug trafficker. I would take large quantities of narcotics in the United Kingdom and export them to poorer regions across the globe where there were very few health or governmental regulations to stop us. I always told myself that even if I wasn't selling the drugs to them, somebody else would. But that is a lie. I have now dedicated myself to creating drug rehabilitation facilities across the world. Oh Holy Father, through your endless wisdom and empathy, could you ever forgive me?

The Pope sits back in his chair and thinks harder on this case. The woman's crimes are great, but she does seem truly remorseful. "You have been forgiven, my daughter." The woman thanks the Holy Father, and when she steps out the door, an early 20-something man steps into the room. "What are your crimes, my son?" the Pope asks.

"Your Holy Father, I had just finished using the bathroom at my apartment when I noticed that there was no toilet paper left on the roll. I was really in a rush to meet someone and figured that I did not need to replace it right then and there. My roommate had to use the restroom after me but there was no toilet paper. Your Holy Father, is there any possible way you could forgive me?

The pope is stunned. "My son, this is the worst crime I have ever heard of. Have you tried to rectify it?"

"I bought 12 rolls that I left in the bathroom, and even hid a few extras under the sink as an emergency supply," the man says.

"My son, I don't believe that's enough. You did try to rectify the crime, but at the same time, the pain you inflicted on this young man is just far too great. No human, no matter how tortured his or her soul may be, should ever have to go through that horror. I'm sorry my son, I cannot forgive you. Please leave my home."

The young man is crushed, but he is compelled to ask the Pope another question.

"Holy Father, I don't want to question your holy wisdom, but there is something I have to ask."

"What is it my son? Are you still trying to seek forgiveness?"

"No Holy Father, I understand and respect your decision. But before I leave, can I use your restroom?"

A rich man is near death. He is very aggrieved because he had worked so hard for his money, and he wants to be able to take it with him to heaven. So, he begins to pray that he might be able to take some of his wealth with him.

An angel hears his plea and appears to him: "Sorry, but you can't take your wealth with you."

The man implores the angel to speak to God to see if He might bend the rules.

The man continues to pray that his wealth can follow him. The angel reappears and informs the man that God has decided to allow him to take one suitcase with him. Overjoyed, the man gathers his largest suitcase and fills it with pure gold bars and places it beside his bed.

Soon afterward, the man dies and shows up at the Gates of Heaven to greet St. Peter. Seeing the suitcase, Peter says, "Hold on, you can't bring that in here!"

But the man explains to him that he has permission and asks him to verify his story with the Lord. Sure enough, St. Peter checks and comes back saying, "You're right. You are allowed one carry-on bag, but I'm supposed to check its contents before letting it through."

Peter opens the suitcase to inspect the worldly items that the man found too precious to leave behind and exclaims, "You brought pavement?"

After describing his great travels, the twenty dollar bill asks the one dollar bill, "What about you? Where have you been?"

The $1 dollar replies, "Well, I've been to the Baptist church, the Methodist church, the Presbyterian church, the Episcopalian church, the Church of God in Christ, the Catholic church, the Mormon church, the church of the Latter Day Saints, the A.M.E. church, the Disciple of Christ church, the...

"WAIT A MINUTE! WAIT A MINUTE!!", shouts the twenty dollar bill to the one dollar bill. "What's a church?"

A man walking along a California beach is deep in prayer. All of a sudden he says out loud, "Lord, grant me one wish." Suddenly the sky clouds up above his head, and in a booming voice the Lord says, "Because you have tried to be faithful to me in all ways, I will grant you one wish." The man says, "Build a bridge to Hawaii so I can drive over any time I want to."

The Lord says, "Your request is very materialistic. Think of the logistics of that kind of undertaking. The supports required to reach the bottom of the Pacific! The concrete and steel it would take! I can do it, but it is hard for me to justify your desire for worldly things. Take a little more time and think of another wish, a wish you think would honor and glorify me."

The man thinks about it for a long time. Finally he says, "Lord, I wish that I could understand women. I want to know how they feel inside, what they are thinking when they give me the silent treatment, why they cry, what they mean when they say 'Nothing,' and how I can make a woman truly happy."

After a few minutes God says, "You want two or four lanes on that bridge?

A Jewish lady named Mrs. Feinberg is stranded late one night at a fashionable resort, one that does not admit Jews. The desk clerk looks down at his book and says, "Sorry, no room. The hotel is full."

The Jewish lady says, "But your sign says that you have vacancies."

The desk clerk stammers and then says curtly, "You know that we do not admit Jews. Now if you will try the other side of town..."

Mrs. Feinberg stiffens noticeably and says, "I'll have you know I converted to your religion."

The desk clerk says, "Oh, yeah? Let me give you a little test. How is Jesus born?"

Mrs. Feinberg replies, "He was born to a virgin named Mary in a little town called Bethlehem."

"Very good," replies the hotel clerk. "Tell me more."

Mrs. Rosenberg replies, "He was born in a manger."

"That's right," says the hotel clerk. "And why was he born in a manger?"

Mrs. Feinberg says loudly, "Because a jerk like you in the hotel wouldn't give a Jewish lady a room for the night!"

The Reverend Francis Norton wakes up Sunday morning and, realizing it is an exceptionally beautiful and sunny early spring day, decides he just has to play golf. So he tells the Associate Pastor that he is feeling sick and convinces him to say Mass for him that day. As soon as the Associate Pastor leaves the room, Father Norton heads out of town to a golf course about 40 miles away. This way he knows he won't accidentally meet anyone he knows from his parish.

Setting up on the first tee, he's alone. After all, it's Sunday morning and every-one else is in church!

At about this time, Saint Peter leans over to the Lord while looking down from the heavens and exclaims, "You're not going to let him get away with this, are you?" The Lord sighs, and says, "No, I guess not."

Just then Father Norton hits the ball and it shoots straight toward the pin, rolls up and falls into the hole. A 420-YARD HOLE IN ONE! St. Peter is astonished. He looks at the Lord and asks, "Why did you let him do that?" The Lord smiles and replies, "Who can he tell?"

A man, smelling like a distillery, flops down on a subway seat next to a priest. The man's tie is stained, his face is plastered with red lipstick, and a half-empty bottle of gin sticks out of his torn coat pocket. He opens his newspaper and begins reading.

After a few minutes the disheveled man turns to the priest and says, "Say, Father, what causes arthritis?"

"Mister," the priest says, "it's caused by loose living, being with cheap wicked women, too much alcohol, and a contempt for your fellow man."

"Well, I'll be damned," the drunk mutters, returning to his paper.

The priest, thinking about what he had says, nudges the man and apologizes. "I'm very sorry, I didn't mean to come on so strong. How long have you had arthritis?"

"I don't have it, Father. I was just reading that the Pope does."

[A-head]

Mormon

Why did Joseph Smith cross the road?

To get to the other bride

A cowboy, visiting Wyoming from Texas, walks into a bar and orders three mugs of beer. He sits in the back of the room, drinking a sip out of each one in turn. When he finishes them, he comes back to the bar and orders three more.

The bartender approaches and tells the cowboy, "You know, a mug goes flat after I draw it. It would taste better if you bought one at a time."

The cowboy replies, "Well, you see, I have two brothers. One is in Arizona, the other is in Colorado. When we all left our home in Texas, we promised that we'd drink this way to remember the days when we drank together. So I'm drinking one beer for each of my brothers and one for myself."

The bartender admits that this is a nice custom, and leaves it there. The cowboy becomes a regular in the bar and always drinks the same way. He orders three mugs and drinks them in turn.

One day, he comes in and only orders two mugs. All the regulars take notice and fall silent. When he comes back to the bar for the second round, the bartender says, "I don't want to intrude on your grief, but I wanted to offer my condolences on your loss."

The cowboy looks quite puzzled for a moment, then a light dawns in his eyes and he laughs.

"Oh, no, everybody's just fine," he explains, "it's just that my wife and I joined the Mormon Church and I had to quit drinking. Hasn't affected my brothers, though."

ISLAM

A man is taking a walk in Central park in New York. Suddenly he sees a little girl being attacked by a pit bull dog. He runs over and starts fighting with the dog. He succeeds in killing the dog and saving the girl's life. A policeman who is watching the scene walks over and says: "You are a hero! Tomorrow you can read it in all the newspapers: 'Brave New Yorker saves the life of little girl'!"

The man says, "But I'm not a New Yorker!"

The policeman answers: "Oh, then it will say in the newspapers in the morning: 'Brave American saves life of little girl'"

"But I am not an American!" says the man.

"Oh, what are you then?" The man says, "I am a Saudi!"

The next day the newspaper headline says: "Islamic extremist kills innocent American dog."

Two men are on a plane on a business trip when a Muslim couple boards the plane and are seated right in front of them. The two men, eager to have some fun, start talking loudly. "My boss is sending me to Saudi Arabia", the one says, "But I don't want to go: Too many Muslims there!" The Muslim couple hears and grows uncomfortable. The other guy laughs, "Oh, yeah, my boss wanted to send me to Pakistan but I refused: WAY too many Muslims!" Smiling, the first man says, "One time I was in Iran but I HATED the fact that there were so many Muslims!" The couple fidgets. The other guy responds, "Oh, yeah...you can't go ANYWHERE to get away from them. The last time I was in France, I ran into a bunch of them too!" The first guy is laughing hysterically as he adds, "That is why you'll never see me in Indonesia: WAY too many Muslims!" At this, the Muslim man turns around and responds politely, "Why don't you go to Hell! I hear there's not very many Muslims THERE!"

BUDDHISM

What did the Buddhist say to the hot dog vendor? "Make me one with everything." The hot dog vendor prepares it and gives it to the monk. The monk pays him and asks for the change. The hot dog vendor says: "Change comes from within."

The Buddha sees one of his followers meditating under a tree at the edge of the Ganges River. Upon inquiring why he is meditating, his follower states he is attempting to become so enlightened he may cross the river unaided. Buddha gives him a few pennies and says: "Why don't you seek passage with that boatman? It is much easier."

HINDUISM

One day two accountants, who are best friends, are walking together down the street. One is a Hindu and is constantly berating the other for eating meat. After stopping for a hot dog, the Hindu erupts, "Why do you eat meat? Do you even know what's in that hot dog? You know, you are what you eat!" The American replies, beating his chest, "I am what I eat: An uncontrollable vicious animal!"

As they step off the curb, a speeding car comes around the corner and runs the Hindu over. The American calls 911 and helps his injured friend as best he is able. The injured Hindu is taken to the hospital and is rushed into surgery. After a long and agonizing wait, the doctor finally appears. He tells the uninjured American, "I have good news, and I have bad news. The good news is that your friend is going to pull through. The bad news is that he's going to be a vegetable for the rest of his life."

ATHEISM

As the storm rages, the captain realizes his ship is sinking fast.

So he shouts out, "Anyone here know how to pray?"

Just one guy steps forward and says, "Aye, captain, I know how to pray."

"Good," says the captain, "You pray while the rest of us put on our life jackets: We're one short."

A young teacher explains to her class of third graders that she is a born-again Christian. She asks the class if any of them are born-again Christians too.

Not really knowing what it means to be born again, but wanting to please and impress their teacher, many of the children shoot their little hands into the air.

There's just one girl who doesn't raise her hand.

So the teacher asks her why she has decided to be different.

The girl says, "Because I'm not a Christian."

The teacher asks, "So what are you then?"

The girl replies, "I'm an atheist."

The teacher's a little perturbed now, her face slightly red. She asks the girl why she's an atheist.

The girl says, "It's just that my family isn't religious. My Mom's atheist, and my Dad's atheist, so I'm atheist."

The teacher is now angry. "That's no reason!" she says loudly. "What if your Mom is a moron, and your Dad is a moron. What would you be then?"

"Then," says the girl, "I'd be a born-again Christian."

One day the zookeeper notices that the orangutan is reading two books: *On the Origin of Species* and the *Bible.*

Surprised, he asks the orangutan, "Why are you reading both of those books?"

"Well," says the orangutan, "I just wanted to know if I am my brother's keeper or my keeper's brother."

An atheist is rowing on Loch Ness in Scotland one day, when suddenly the Loch Ness monster attacks and grabs him from his boat.

He panics and shouts "God help me!" and suddenly, the monster and everything around him just freezes.

A voice from the heavens booms, "You say you don't believe in me, but now you're asking for my help?"

The atheist looks up and says, "Well, 10 seconds ago I didn't believe in the Loch Ness Monster either."

PARENTING & FAMILY

A man speaks frantically into the phone, "My wife is pregnant, and her contractions are only two minutes apart!"

"Is this her first child?" the doctor asks.

"No, you idiot!" the man shouts. "This is her husband!

Two parents are living with their teenage son Jack, who has just started to go through puberty. Ever since his hormones kicked in, he's been reclusive and awkward, and avoids talking to his parents as much as possible. One time, when the Dad is walking by the bathroom, he hears his son in there, making a strange sound like a rapidly dripping faucet, and thought that maybe his son has finally developed those biological urges adults know all too well.

The Dad tells his Mom about what he heard, and the two decide to have a chat with Jack about what has been going on. They agree, though, to speak vaguely, as to not embarrass him or make him feel weird. After dinner, the Dad jumps into the conversation.

"Jack, your mother and I wanted to have a chat. We heard those noises from outside the bathroom. Don't worry, we don't want you to be alarmed or nervous or anything, we aren't upset or mad, but just wanted to let you know that what you're doing is perfectly normal."

"OK...," Jack says, a bit confused.

"Yeah honey, it's an urge you're getting right now, and I'm sure it's confusing and frustrating, but your Dad went through it at your age. Heck, even girls my age get those urges too."

"That's kind of weird," Jack says.

"It's not as weird as you think son," the Dad says. "Yeah, what we mean is that all teenagers do it, so you're far from the only person your age who's doing it right now. But if you have any other questions about what you're going through, or your body or any sudden urges or anything like that, we're here to talk. We love you."

The family finish eating dinner and Jack goes upstairs to talk to his friend on the phone.

"They were saying all this stuff like they know what I'm doing but they aren't mad, that they love me, that I'm normal, that my friends are doing it, and I'm just sitting here like, 'God, could you please stop talking so I can finally go back upstairs and finish fixing the broken faucet?'"

For two solid hours, the lady sitting next to a man on an airplane has been telling him about her grandchildren. She had even produces a plastic foldout photo album of all nine of the children.

She finally realizes that she has dominated the entire conversation.

"Oh, I've done all the talking, and I'm so sorry. I know you certainly have something to say. Please, tell me...what do you think of my grandchildren?"

A young punk gets on the cross-town bus. He's got spiked, multicolored hair that's green, purple, and orange. His clothes are a tattered mix of leather rags. His legs are bare and he's wearing worn-out shoes. His entire face and body are riddled with pierced jewelry and his earrings are big, bright feathers. He sits down in the only vacant seat that's directly across from an old man who glares at him for the next 10 miles. Finally, the punk gets self-conscious and barks at the old man, "What are you looking at you old fart! Didn't you ever do anything wild when you were young?" Without missing a beat, the old man replies, "Yeah, back when I was young and in the Navy, I got really drunk one night in Singapore, and screwed a parrot. I thought maybe you were my son."

A teenage boy is getting ready to take his girlfriend to the prom. First he goes to rent a tux, but there's a long tux line at the shop and it takes forever.

Next, he has to get some flowers, so he heads over to the florist and there's a huge flower line there. He waits forever but eventually gets the flowers.

Then he heads out to rent a limo. Unfortunately, there's a large limo line at the rental office, but he's patient and gets the job done.

Finally, the day of the prom comes. The two are dancing happily and his girlfriend is having a great time. But the girlfriend asks the boy to stand in line to take some pictures.

After the pictures are taken, the boy is frustrated and about to explode. His girlfriend asks him to get her some punch. So he heads over to the punch table and to his delight, there's no punch line!

With our second child on the way, my wife and I attend a pre-birth class aimed at couples who have already had at least one child.

The instructor raises the issue of breaking the news to the older child:

"Some parents," she says, "tell the older child, 'We love you so much we decided to bring another child into this family.' But think about that. Ladies, what if your husband came home one day and says, 'Honey, I love you so much I decided to bring home another wife'?"

One of the women speaks up immediately: "Does she cook?"

A man is at a popular theme park with his family who want to do nothing more than ride Log Mountain. It's the most popular attraction at the park and has a two-hour line. The man is a bit heftier than the other riders, but has had no problem getting into any of the other rides as the park. His family is convinced that he should have no problem getting in this one, but he still is a bit worried.

After hours of waiting, they finally reach their log. The staff looks worriedly at the man, skeptical about his chances of getting in the log. But they still let him try. He tries to shuffle into the back seat while his family looks embarrassed. After 10 minutes, the ride operators tell the man in the most polite way possible that he is just too big for the ride. His family then goes and rides it as the man sits depressed at the end of the line, waiting for them to finish.

When they get home from the park, the man decides that he's spent way too much of his life being overweight. He starts dieting and goes to the gym for two hours every day. He keeps at it for two months, and has dropped a whopping 100 pounds, now much more slim and agile and in significantly better shape. Wanting to prove that he can now go on Log Mountain, he drives to the theme park, with his family enthusiastically cheering him on in the back seat. They arrive just 30 minutes before the park is set to close, and there's not a person in sight in line for Log Mountain. The man rushes to the front with his family just inches behind them, and triumphantly sits in the log. They cheer him on that he is finally able to fit, and his wife and kids start to jump in to ride with him.

"Whoa wait, what are you doing?" the man says to his family. Confused, the wife replies "Well honey, we wanted to share your big moment with you, you finally are able to ride and we wanted to be part of that, you just seemed so sad your weight before so we're happy for you." The man laughs. "I wasn't happy that I can fit, I'm just happy that I can finally ride something alone by myself now!"

For weeks, a six-year old lad keeps telling his first-grade teacher about the baby brother or sister that is expected at his house.

One day the mother allows the boy to feel the movements of the unborn child. The six-year old is obviously impressed, but makes no comment. Furthermore, he stops telling his teacher about the impending event.

The teacher finally sits the boy on her lap and says, "Tommy, whatever has become of that baby brother or sister you were expecting at home?"

Tommy bursts into tears and confesses, "I think Mommy ate it!"

What is the difference between a pregnant woman and a light bulb?

You can unscrew a light bulb.

A woman is pregnant with twins, and shortly before they're due, she has an accident and falls into a coma. Her husband is away on business, unable to be reached. While the woman is in the coma, she gives birth to her twins, and the only person around to name her children is her brother.

When the mother comes out of her coma to find she had given birth and that her brother has named the twins, she becomes very worried, because he isn't a very bright guy. She is sure he has named them something absurd or stupid.

When she sees her brother, she asks him about the twins.

He says, "The first one is a girl."

The mother: "What did you name her?!?"

Brother: "Denise!"

Mom: "Oh, wow, that's not bad! What about the second one?"

Brother: "The second one is a boy."

Mom: "Oh, and what did you name him?"

Brother: "Denephew."

What is the most common pregnancy craving?

For men to be the ones who get pregnant

A country doctor goes way out to the boondocks to deliver a baby. It is so far out, there's no electricity. When the doctor arrives, no one is home except for the laboring mother and her five-year-old child. The doctor instructs the child to hold a lantern high so he can see, while he helps the woman deliver the baby.

The child does so, the mother pushes and after a little while, the doctor lifts the newborn baby by the feet and spanks him on the bottom to get him to take his first breath.

The doctor then asks the five-year-old what he thinks of the baby.

"Hit him again," the five-year-old says. "He shouldn't have crawled up there in the first place!"

Martin has just received his brand new driver's license. The family troops out to the driveway and climbs in the car, where he is going to take them for a ride for the first time. Dad immediately heads for the back seat, directly behind the newly minted driver.

"I'll bet you're back there to get a change of scenery after all those months of sitting in the front passenger seat teaching me how to drive," says the beaming boy to his father.

"Nope," comes Dad's reply, "I'm gonna sit here and kick the back of your seat as you drive, just like you've been doing to me all these years."

13-year-old Mary is having a tough day and has stretched herself out on the couch to do a bit of what she thought to be well-deserved complaining and self-pitying. She moans to her Mom and brother, "Nobody loves me. The whole world hates me!" Her brother, busily occupied playing a game, hardly looks up at her and passes on this encouraging word: "That's not true, Mary. Some people don't even know you."

Johnny, a very bright five-year-old, tells his Daddy he'd like to have a baby brother and, along with his request, he offers to do whatever he can to help. His Dad, a very bright 35-year-old, pauses for a moment and then replies, "I'll tell you what, Johnny, if you pray every day for two months for a baby brother, I guarantee that God will give you one!"

Johnny responds eagerly to his Dad's challenge and goes to his bedroom early that night to start praying for a baby brother. He prays every night for a whole month, but after that time, he begins to get skeptical. He checks around the neighborhood and finds out that what he thinks is going to happen has never occurred in the history of the neighborhood. You just don't pray for two months and then, whammo, a new baby brother. So, Johnny quits praying.

After another month, Johnny's mother goes to the hospital. When she comes back home, Johnny's parents call him into the bedroom. He cautiously walks into the room, not expecting to find anything, and there is a little bundle lying right next to his mother. His Dad pulls back the blanket and there is...not one baby brother, but two! His mother had twins! Johnny's Dad looks down at him and says, "Now aren't you glad you prayed?"

Johnny hesitates a little and then looks up at his Dad and says, "Yes, but aren't you glad I quit when I did?"

A woman has twins and gives them up for adoption. One of them goes to a family in Egypt and is named Amal. The other goes to a family in Spain, they name him Juan. Years later, Juan sends a picture of himself to his mum. Upon receiving the picture, she tells her husband that she wished she also had a picture of Amal. Her husband responds, "But they are twins. If you've seen Juan, you've seen Amal."

FAMOUS QUOTES

OSCAR WILDE

Life is much too important a thing ever to talk seriously about it.

The world has been made by fools that wise men should live in it.

There are few things easier than to live badly and to die well.

Give me the luxuries, and anyone can have the necessaries.

One should absorb the color of life, but one should never remember its details. Details are always vulgar.

Misfortunes one can endure—they come from outside, they are accidents. But to suffer for one's own faults—ah!—there is the sting of life!

In her dealings with man, Destiny never closes her accounts.

The world is a stage, but the play is badly cast.

Good taste is the excuse I've always given for leading such a bad life.

Be yourself; everyone else is already taken.

Always forgive your enemies; nothing annoys them so much.

I am so clever that sometimes I don't understand a single word of what I am saying.

Women are meant to be loved, not to be understood.

A good friend will always stab you in the front.

I don't want to go to heaven. None of my friends are there.

Anyone who lives within their means suffers from a lack of imagination.

I am not young enough to know everything.

Experience is merely the name men gave to their mistakes.

Everything in the world is about sex except sex. Sex is about power.

The very essence of romance is uncertainty.

Man is least himself when he talks in his own person. Give him a mask, and he will tell you the truth.

I think God, in creating man, somewhat overestimated his ability.

I never travel without my diary. One should always have something sensational to read in the train.

Some cause happiness wherever they go; others whenever they go.

I can resist anything except temptation.

A cynic is a man who knows the price of everything and the value of nothing.

All women become like their mothers. That is their tragedy. No man does, and that is his.

It is absurd to divide people into good and bad. People are either charming or tedious.

Crying is for plain women. Pretty women go shopping.

There is only one thing in the world worse than being talked about, and that is not being talked about.

I have nothing to declare except my genius.

Fashion is a form of ugliness so intolerable that we have to alter it every six months.

A man's face is his autobiography. A woman's face is her work of fiction.

After a good dinner, one can forgive anybody, even one's own relations.

Anybody can sympathize with the sufferings of a friend, but it requires a very fine nature to sympathize with a friend's success.

Whenever people agree with me, I always feel I must be wrong.

Life is far too important a thing ever to talk seriously about.

Morality is simply the attitude we adopt toward people we personally dislike.

To lose one parent may be regarded as a misfortune; to lose both looks like carelessness.

I choose my friends for their good looks, my acquaintances for their good characters, and my enemies for their good intellects.

A bore is someone who deprives you of solitude without providing you with company.

If you are not long, I will wait for you all my life.

There are only two kinds of people who are really fascinating: People who know absolutely everything, and people who know absolutely nothing.

The suspense is terrible. I hope it will last.

America is the only country that went from barbarism to decadence without civilization in between.

Everything in moderation, including moderation.

I may not agree with you, but I will defend to the death your right to make an ass of yourself.

One should never trust a woman who tells one her real age. A woman who would tell one that would tell one anything.

Hear no evil, speak no evil, and you won't be invited to cocktail parties.

I never put off till tomorrow what I can possibly do the day after.

Some things are too important to be taken seriously.

Friendship is far more tragic than love. It lasts longer.

WILLIAM SHAKESPEARE

Better a witty fool, than a foolish wit.

A young woman in love always looks like patience on a monument smiling at grief.

Journeys end in lovers meeting,

Every wise man's son doth know

Well, God give them wisdom that have it; and those that are fools, let them use their talents.

Foolery, sir, does walk about the orb like the sun; it shines everywhere.

Many a good hanging prevents a bad marriage.

Olivia: What's a drunken man like, fool?

Feste: Like a drowned man, a fool, and a madman: One draught above heat makes him a fool; the second mads him; and a third drowns him.

What kind o' man is he?

Why, of mankind.

Viola: I pity you.

Olivia: That's a degree to love.

If the skin were parchment and the blows you gave were ink,

Your own handwriting would tell you what I think.

If she lives till doomsday, she'll burn a week longer than the whole world.

Since mine own doors refuse to entertain me,

I'll knock elsewhere, to see if they'll disdain me

"I can see he's not in your good books."

"No, and if he were, I would burn my library."

I had rather hear my dog bark at a crow, than a man swear he loves me.

Some Cupid kills with arrows, some with traps.

When I says I would die a bachelor, I did not think I should live till I were married.

For which of my bad parts didst thou first fall in love with me?

I wish my horse had the speed of your tongue.

Silence is the perfectest herald of joy. I were but little happy if I could say how much.

Tax not so bad a voice to slander music any more than once.

I will live in thy heart, die in thy lap, and be buried in thy eyes—and moreover, I will go with thee to thy uncle's.

If her breath were as terrible as her terminations, there were no living near her, she would infect to the North star!

Well, everyone can master a grief but he that has it.

I cannot be a man with wishing, therefore I will die a woman with grieving.

For there is never yet philosopher that could endure the toothache patiently.

All this I see; and see that the fashion wears out more apparel than the man.

He wears his faith but as the fashion of his hat; it ever changes with the next block.

There's small choice in rotten apples.

If I be waspish, best beware my sting.

I see a woman may be made a fool,
If she had not a spirit to resist.

The poorest service is repaid with thanks.

The fool doth think he is wise, but the wise man knows himself to be a fool.

Do you not know I am a woman? When I think, I must speak.

I pray you, do not fall in love with me, for I am falser than vows made in wine.

Men have died from time to time, and worms have eaten them, but not for love.

Men are April when they woo, December when they wed.

Truly thou art damned, like an ill-roasted egg, all on one side.

We that are true lovers run into strange capers.

You and you are sure together,
As the winter to foul weather.

O, that's a brave man! He writes brave verses, speaks brave words, swears brave oaths, and breaks them bravely.

You are full of pretty answers. Have you not been acquainted with goldsmiths' wives and conned them out of rings?

ARISTOPHANES

Under every stone lurks a politician.

One must not try to trick misfortune, but resign oneself to it with good grace.

It is bad taste for a poet to be coarse and hairy.

Times change. The vices of your age are stylish today.

You will never make the crab walk straight.

Men of sense often learn from their enemies. It is from their foes, not their friends, that cities learn the lesson of building high walls and ships of war.

Prayers without wine are perfectly pointless.

An ancient tradition declares that every idiot blunder we pass into law will sooner or later redound to Athens' profit.

Mix and knead together all the state business as you do for your sausages. To win the people, always cook them some savory that pleases them.

The old are in a second childhood.

Wealth: The most excellent of all gods.

If a man owes me money, I never seem to forget. But if I do the owing, I somehow never remember.

Quickly, bring me a beaker of wine, so that I may wet my mind and say something clever!

Woman is adept at getting money for herself and will not easily let herself be deceived; she understands deceit too well herself.

A demagogue must be neither an educated nor an honest man; he has to be an ignoramus and a rogue.

An insult directed at the wicked is not to be censured; on the contrary, the honest man, if he has sense, can only applaud.

It should not prejudice my voice that I'm not born a man, if I say something advantageous to the present situation. For I'm taxed too, and as a toll provide men for the nation.

I would treat her like an egg, the shell of which we remove before eating it; I would take off her mask and then kiss her pretty face.

PLAUTUS

No guest is so welcome in a friend's house that he will not become a nuisance after three days.

According as men thrive, their friends are true; if their affairs go to wreck, their friends sink with them. Fortune finds friends.

One eyewitness weighs more than 10 hearsays. Seeing is believing, all the world over.

This is the great fault of wine; it first trips up the feet: It is a cunning wrestler.

Patience is the best remedy for every trouble.

It is well for one to know more than he says.

TERENCE

She ne'er was really charming till she died.

What a grand thing it is to be clever and have common sense.

They who love dancing too much seem to have more brains in their feet than in their head.

For you to ask advice on the rules of love is no better than to ask advice on the rules of madness.

You can take a chance with any man who pays his bills on time.

Benjamin Franklin

[Wine is] a constant proof that God loves us and loves to see us happy.

We are all born ignorant, but one must work hard to remain stupid.

In this world nothing can be said to be certain, except death and taxes.

To succeed, jump as quickly at opportunities as you do at conclusions.

Some people die at 25 and aren't buried until 75.

Any fool can criticize, condemn and complain—and most fools do.

A countryman between two lawyers is like a fish between two cats.

Tricks and treachery are the practice of fools that don't have brains enough to be honest.

Hunger is the best pickle.

A life of leisure and a life of laziness are two things. There will be sleeping enough in the grave.

A good conscience is a continual Christmas.

He that is good for making excuses is seldom good for anything else.

At 20 years of age the will reigns; at 30, the wit; and at 40, the judgment.

Guests, like fish, begin to smell after three days.

Three can keep a secret, if two of them are dead.

There are three faithful friends: An old wife, an old dog, and ready money.

I guess I don't so much mind being old, as I mind being fat and old.

MEN, WOMEN, & MARRIAGE

A doctor tells a group of patients, "The material we put into our stomachs is terrible. Red meat is awful. Soft drinks corrode your stomach lining. Chinese food is loaded with MSG. High-fat diets can be disastrous, and none of us realizes the long-term harm caused by the germs in our drinking water. But there is one thing that is the most dangerous of all. Can anyone here tell me what food it is that causes the most grief and suffering for years after eating it?" An old man raises his hand and says, "Wedding cake."

Four Catholic men and a Catholic woman are having coffee when one of the Catholic men tells his friends, "My son is a priest, when he walks into a room, everyone calls him 'Father.'"

The second Catholic man chirps, "My son is a Bishop. When he walks into a room people call him 'Your Grace.'"

The third Catholic gent says, "My son is a Cardinal. When he enters a room everyone says 'Your Eminence.'"

The fourth Catholic man then says, "My son is the Pope. When he walks into a room people call him 'Your Holiness.'"

Since the lone Catholic woman is sipping her coffee in silence, the four men give her a subtle, "Well....?"

She proudly replies, "I have a daughter, slim, tall, 38D breast, 24" waist and 34" hips. When she walks into a room, people say, 'Oh—My—God!'"

Two men at a bar have been enjoying a few drinks for the past couple of hours and are pretty drunk when one of them notices a beautiful woman sitting in the corner. One says to the other, "Jeez, I'd really like to dance with that girl."

The other man replies, "Well go ahead and ask her, don't be a chicken."

So the man approaches the lovely woman and says, "Excuse me. Would you be so kind as to dance with me?"

Seeing the man is totally drunk the woman says, "I'm sorry. Right now I'm concentrating on matrimony and I'd rather sit than dance."

So the man humbly returns to his friend.

"So what did she say?" asks the friend.

The drunk responded, "She said she's constipated on macaroni and would rather shit in her pants."

A woman goes to a discount store to purchase several items. When she finally gets to the checkout, she learns one of her items has no price.

She thinks she'll die of embarrassment when the checker gets on the intercom and booms out for all the store to hear, "Price check on lane thirteen. Tampax. Supersize."

But if that wasn't bad enough, the person looking for the price misunderstands the word "Tampax" for "Thumbtacks."

In a businesslike tone, a voice booms back over the intercom, "Do you want the kind you push in with your thumb or the kind you pound in with a hammer?"

A woman goes to a doctor and says Doctor, I have a problem. Every time I sneeze I have an orgasm. The doctor says, "Oh really, what have you been doing for it?"

The woman replies, "Snorting pepper."

A girl goes into the doctor's office for a checkup. As she takes off her blouse, the doctor notices an H on her chest. "How did you get that mark on your chest?" asks the doctor.

"Oh, my boyfriend goes to Harvard and he's so proud of it, he never takes off his Harvard sweatshirt, even when we make love," she replies.

A couple of days later, another girl comes in for a checkup. As she takes off her blouse, he notices a Y on her chest.

"How did you get that mark on your chest?" asks the doctor. "Oh, my boyfriend goes to Yale and he's so proud of it that he never takes off his Yale sweatshirt, even when we make love," she replies.

A couple of days later, another girl comes in for a checkup. As she takes off her blouse, he notices an M on her chest. "Do you have a boyfriend at Michigan?" asks the doctor.

"No, but I have a girlfriend at Wisconsin, why do you ask?"

Everyone is seated around the table as the food is being served. When little

Johnny receives his plate, he starts eating straight away.

"Johnny, wait until we've says our prayer," his mother reminds him.

"I don't have to," the little boy replies.

"Of course you do," his mother insists. "We say a prayer before eating at our house."

"That's at our house," Johnny explains, "but this is Grandma's house and she knows how to cook."

An enormously wealthy 65-year-old man falls in love with a young woman in her 20s and is contemplating a proposal.

"Do you think she'd marry me if I tell her I'm 45?" he asks a friend.

"Your chances are better," says the friend, "if you tell her you're 90."

A woman is leaving a convenience store with her morning coffee when she notices a most unusual funeral procession approaching the nearby cemetery.

A long black hearse is followed by a second long, black hearse about 50 feet behind the first one. Behind the second hearse is a solitary woman walking a pit bull on a leash. Behind her, a short distance back, are about 200 women walking single file.

The woman is so curious that she respectfully approaches the woman walking the dog and says, "I am so sorry for your loss, and I know now is a bad time to disturb you, but I have never seen a funeral like this. Whose funeral is it?"

"My husband's."

"What happened to him?"

The woman replies, "My dog attacked and killed him."

She inquires further, "Well, who is in the second hearse?"

The woman answers, "My mother-in-law. She was trying to help my husband when the dog turned on her."

A poignant and thoughtful moment of silence passes between the two women.

"Can I borrow the dog?"

"Get in line."

A woman's husband has been slipping in and out of a coma for several months, yet she has stayed by his bedside every single day. One day, when he comes to, he motions for her to come nearer. As she sits by him, he whispers, eyes full of tears, "You know what? You have been with me all through the bad times. When I got fired, you were there to support me. When my business failed, you were there. When I got shot, you were by my side. When we lost the house, you stayed right here. When my health started failing, you were still by my side. You know what?" "What dear?" she asks gently, smiling as her heart begins to fill with warmth. "I think you're bad luck."

A woman goes to her doctor's office. She is seen by one of the new doctors, but after about four minutes in the examination room, she bursts out screaming and runs down the hall. An older doctor stops her and asks what the problem is, and she explains. He has her sit down and relax in another room. The older doctor marches back to the first and demands, "What's the matter with you? Mrs. Terry is 63 years old, she has four grown children and seven grandchildren, and you tell her she's pregnant?" The new doctor smiles smugly as he continues to write on his clipboard. "Cured her hiccups though, didn't it?"

One day an old woman walks into a shop and gets some dog food. She goes to pay for it and the cashier says, "You can't buy that dog food. We need evidence that you have a dog." So the woman brings in her dog and she gets the dog food. The next day the same old lady goes to get some cat food and the cashier says, "You can't have that cat food. We need evidence that you have a cat." So she goes home and gets her cat and she gets the cat food. Next day, the same old lady goes in again and she has a box. She tells the cashier to put her finger in it, so she does. She says it feels warm and soft, and the little old lady says, "Now you're satisfied! Can I have some toilet paper, please!"

The CIA has an opening for an assassin. After all of the background checks, interviews, and testing are done, there are three finalists: Two men and a woman. For the final test, the CIA agent takes one of the men to a large metal door and hands him a gun.

"We must know that you will follow your instructions, no matter what the circumstances. Inside of this room, you will find your wife sitting in a chair. Kill her!" The man says, "You can't be serious. I could never shoot my wife." The agent says, "Then you're not the right man for this job."

The second man is given the same instructions. He takes the gun and goes into the room. All is quiet for about five minutes. Then the man comes out with tears in his eyes. "I tried, but I can't kill my wife." The agent says, "You don't have what it takes. Take your wife and go home."

Finally, it's the woman's turn. She is given the same instructions, to kill her husband. She takes the gun and goes into the room. Shots are heard, one shot after another. They hear screaming, crashing, banging on the walls. After a few minutes, all is quiet. The door opens slowly and there stands the woman. She wipes the sweat from her brow, and says, "This gun is loaded with blanks. I had to beat him to death with the chair."

An airplane is about to crash. A female passenger jumps up frantically and announces, "If I'm going to die, I want to die feeling like a woman." She removes all her clothing and asks, "Is there someone on this plane who is man enough to make me feel like a woman?" A man stands up, removes his shirt and says, "Here, iron this!"

A group of 3rd, 4th, and 5th graders, accompanied by two female teachers, go on a field trip to the local race track to learn about thoroughbred horses and the supporting industry, but mostly to see the horses.

When it's time to take the children to the bathroom, it's decided that the girls will go with one teacher and the boys will go with the other.

The teacher assigned to the boys is waiting outside the men's room when one of the boys comes out and tells her that none of them can reach the urinal. Having no choice, she goes inside, helped the boys with their pants, begins hoisting the little boys up one by one, and holds onto their wee-wees to direct the flow away from their clothes.

As she lifts one, she couldn't help but notice that he is unusually well en-dowed. Trying not to show that she is staring, the teacher says, "You must be in the 5th."

"No, ma'am," he replies, "I'm in the 7th, riding Silver Arrow, but thanks for the lift."

A couple lay in bed. The man says, "I am going to make you the happiest woman in the world." The woman says, "I'll miss you."

"It's just too hot to wear clothes today," Jack says as he steps out of the shower. "Honey, what do you think the neighbors will think if I mow the lawn like this?"

"Probably that I married you for your money," she replies.

A group of girlfriends go on vacation and see a five-story hotel with a sign that reads "For women only." Since they are without their boyfriends, they decide to go in.

The doorman, a very attractive guy, explains to them how it works. "We have five floors. Go up floor by floor, and once you find what you're looking for, you can stay there. It's easy to decide, since each floor has signs telling you what's on that floor. The only rule is, once you leave a floor, you can't return to it."

The women talk it over and decide to go for it.

They start going up, and on the first floor the sign reads, "All the men here are horrible lovers, but they are kind and sensitive."

The friends laugh and without hesitation move on to the next floor.

The sign on the second floor reads, "All the men here are wonderful lovers, but they generally treat women badly."

This wasn't going to do, so again they head for the stairs.

The friends move up to the third floor where the sign reads, "All the men here are great lovers and sensitive to the needs of women."

This is good, but there are still two more floors so...

So on to the fourth floor, and this sign seems perfect. "All the men here have perfect builds; are sensitive and attentive to women; are perfect lovers; they are also single, rich and straight."

The women are really pleased, but they decide that they would rather see what the FIFTH floor has to offer before they settle.

When they reach the fifth floor, there is only a sign that reads: "There are no men here. This floor is built only to prove that there is simply no way to please a woman."

How many divorced men does it take to change a light bulb?

Who cares? They never get the house anyway.

One day a group of husbands and wives go to a scientific program. The doctor there is showing them brains from real people and is explaining how expensive it would be to buy one. He says it is five million dollars for a female brain and 10 million dollars for a male brain. The men snicker, thinking they know why. One of the women says, "Well, why is that, sir?" The doctor answers, "The men's brains cost more, for they have never been used."

Two young lovers go up to the mountains for a romantic winter vacation. When they get there, the guy goes out to chop some wood. When he gets back, he says, "Honey, my hands are freezing!" She says, "Well, put them here between my thighs and that will warm them up." After lunch he goes back out to chop some more wood and comes back and says again, "Man! My hands are really freezing!"

She says again, "Well, put them here between my thighs and warm them up." He does, and again that warms him up. After dinner, he goes out one more time to chop some wood to get them through the night. When he returns, he says again, "Honey, my hands are really, really freezing!"

She looks at him and says, "For crying out loud, don't your ears ever get cold?"

A tough looking group of hairy bikers are riding when they see a girl about to jump off a bridge, so they stop. The leader, a big burly man, gets off his bike and says, "What are you doing?" "I'm going to commit suicide," she says. While he doesn't want to appear insensitive, he also doesn't want to miss an opportunity, so he asks, "Well, before you jump, why don't you give me a kiss?" She does, and it is a long, deep, lingering kiss. After she's finished, the tough, hairy biker says, "Wow! That is the best kiss I've ever had! That's a real talent you're wasting. You could be famous. Why are you committing suicide?" "My parents don't like me dressing up like a girl."

A man is sitting at a bar enjoying a cocktail when an exceptionally gorgeous, sexy, young woman enters. The man can't stop staring at her. The young woman notices this and walks directly toward him. Before he can offer his apologies for being so rude, the young woman says to him, "I'll do anything you want me to do, no matter how kinky, for $100, with one condition." Flabbergasted, the man asks what the condition is. The young woman replies, "You have to tell me what you want me to do in just three words." The man considers her proposition for a moment, withdraws his wallet from his pocket, and hands the woman five $20 bills. He looks deeply into her eyes and slowly says, "Paint my house."

A couple is celebrating their 30 years of marriage. The husband asks his wife: "We have raised 12 kids. But Johnny is different from the rest. Please, tell me honestly, I will forgive you, but I wanna know: Have you cheated on me?

The wife replies: "Yes, I did. Johnny is your real son."

Two friends are chatting. John tells his friend: "You know, once I came home from work and I found my wife sitting on a chair dressed in transparent underwear. And she tells me: "Tie me up and do whatever you want." So I tied her up and went fishing."

There are three guys talking in the pub. Two of them are talking about the amount of control they have over their wives, while the third remains quiet.

After a while, one of the first two turns to the third and says, "Well, what about you, what sort of control do you have over your wife?"

The third fellow says, "I'll tell you. Just the other night my wife came to me on her hands and knees."

The first two guys were amazed. "What happened then?" they ask. "She says, 'Get out from under the bed and fight like a man!'"

What is a man's idea of helping with the housework?

Lifting his leg so you can vacuum

What are the two reasons why men don't mind their own business?

1. No mind. 2. No business.

Why is it so hard for women to find men who are sensitive, caring, and good looking?
Because those men already have boyfriends

Why do bachelors like smart women?

Opposites attract.

How can you tell soap operas are fictional?

In real life, men aren't affectionate out of bed.

Why do little boys whine?

Because they're practicing to be men.

Why are married women heavier than single women?

Single women come home, see what's in the fridge, and go to bed. Married women come home, see what's in bed, and go to the fridge.

How does a man show he's planning for the future?

He buys two cases of beer instead of one.

What should you give a man who has everything?

A woman to show him how to work it

Why do female black widow spiders kill the males after mating?

To stop the snoring before it starts

A 15- year-old Amish boy and his father are in a mall. They are amazed by almost everything they see, but especially by two shiny, silver walls that can move apart and then slide back together again. The boy asks, "What is this, Father?" The father, never having seen an elevator, responds, "Son, I have never seen anything like this in my life, I don't know what it is." While the boy and his father are watching with amazement, a fat old lady in a wheelchair moves up to the moving walls and presses a button. The walls open, and the lady rolls between them into a small room. The walls close, and the boy and his father watch the small numbers above the walls light up sequentially. They continued to watch until it reaches the last number, and then the numbers begin to light in the reverse order. Finally the walls open up again and a gorgeous 24-year-old blonde steps out. The father, not taking his eyes off the young woman, says quietly to his son, "Go get your mother."

A man is on his deathbed with his family surrounding him, all of his children and grandchildren, his extended nephews and nieces, but at the front of the group is his loving wife who's been by his side for decades. The man says goodbye to each member of his family with a hug and kiss, but then asks his wife to stick around for a moment as they all leave the room. He is about to go at any minute, but there's something he has to say to his dear wife before he passes on.

"Muriel, I don't know how to tell you this, or even if there's a right way to tell you, but I must before I pass away. Before I met you, I had another wife. Her name is Sharon, we were married for 15 years and had three children. We were very much in love, and had the perfect life. Or what I thought was perfect, until I met you. The moment I saw you at that café, I knew I had to have you in my life. I've always thought about the best way to tell you, but the timing was never right, and I was afraid you'd leave if you knew the whole truth."

Muriel is in shock. The man who she is endlessly devoted to has been lying to her for years. And he is about to pass away! She is heartbroken but also angry, and is silent for a few seconds until finally speaking up.

"Why tell me this now? Are you looking for redemption or something? Are you hoping that I forgive you? What do you want me to do with this new information? Do you want me to make amends with them, and incorporate their children into our life?

The man looks back at her, and with renewed energy says, "Jesus no, I want you to call them! It's been 45 years since I went out to get milk, they're probably worried sick!"

A husband and wife in their 60s are coming up on their 40th wedding anniversary. Knowing his wife loves antiques, he buys a beautiful old brass oil lamp for her. When she unwraps it, a genie appears. He thanks them and gives each of them one wish. The wife wishes for an all expenses paid, first class, around the world cruise with her husband. Shazam! Instantly she is presented with tickets for the entire journey, plus expensive side trips, dinners, shopping, etc. The husband, however, wishes he had a female companion who is 30 years younger. Shazam! Instantly he turns 93 years old.

A stranger walks up to an Egyptian man at the Cairo bazaar and offers to sell him contraband Viagra for 100 Egyptian pounds.

The Egyptian man says, "No, not worth it."

The stranger says, "How about 20?"

The Egyptian man says, "No, not worth it."

The stranger says, "How about 10?"

The Egyptian man says, "No, not worth it."

The stranger says, "Listen, these pills cost $10 each in the U.S. How can you say they're not worth it?"

The Egyptian man says, "Oh, the pills are worth it—my wife isn't."

Two engineers named Bob and Steve get shipwrecked on an island. They try every method of escaping the island to make contact with the outside world but to no avail. The resourceful men figure out how to build an electronic generator that can power their cell phones and even generate a small but reachable signal to the outside world. After using the device for a week, they are having no luck. Steve has an idea: Turn off the machine, and someone will find them. Bob says that is idiotic, that the device is their only chance to be found, but Steve says just to trust him. They turn off the machine and go to bed. The next morning, the men awake to Coast Guard boats on the island and Steve's clearly disgruntled wife looking over them. Bob wonders how Steve could have possibly known that's how they would be found. And Steve replies, "My wife always manages to find me when my cell phone is off."

A college math professor and his wife are both 60 years old. One evening, the wife comes home and finds a note from her husband that says, "My dear, now that you are 60 years old, there are some things you no longer do for me. I am at the Holiday Inn with my 20-year-old student. Don't bother waiting up for me."

He returns home late that night to find a note from his wife: "You, my dear, are also 60 years old and there are also things I need that you're not giving me. So I am at the Motel 6 with one of your 20-year-old students. Being a math professor, I'm sure you know that 20 goes into 60 more times than 60 goes into 20. So, don't you wait up for me."

What do you do when you see your husband staggering in the back yard?

Shoot him again.

A woman meets with her lover, who is also her husband's best friend. They make love for hours. Afterward, as they lie in bed, the phone rings. Since it's the woman's house, she picks up the receiver. The best friend listens, only hearing her side of the conversation:

"Hello? Oh, hi...I'm so glad that you called. Really? That's wonderful. Well, I'm happy to hear you're having such a great time. Oh, that sounds terrific. Love you, too. OK. Bye-bye."

She hangs up the telephone and her lover asks, "Who is that?"

"Oh," she replies, "That was my husband telling me about the wonderful time he's having on his fishing trip with you."

What is the fastest way to determine the sex of a chromosome?

Pull down its genes

Matt and Samantha are the best pilots that NASA ever had, and the married couple is also hopelessly in love. They are confident but not egocentric. For an upcoming mission to Mars, the romantic duo is chosen, with NASA hoping they could generate a bit more publicity for the mission and the space program at large through their married couple astronauts story.

Seven crew members in total comprise the shuttle on its mission to Mars. The journey will take six months to get there and six months back. Frankly, there isn't enough work to be done while drifting through the empty vacuum of space, so crew will spend time in cryogenic sleep while one astronaut will stay awake for a month at a time, just making sure that nothing goes awry on the journey. Except for Matt and Samantha: They are both allowed to share their month awake together. They have the last month's shift until arriving at Mars, and things are going swimmingly at first. But things go sour during the last week of their month after the couple finish dinner.

"Um, Samantha, why are the empty vacuum food bags still sitting on the table?"

"Oh, I just wanted to watch an episode of *It's Always Sunny in Philadelphia* real quick, NASA uploaded the new season, I was going to throw them away after."

"OK, well you know that we can't just leave these around, they might float off and get stuck in something and clog the instruments."

"I know, that's why I was going to do it after."

"OK, but that's a really big threat, and I can't be expected to do it for you, even though were married, NASA wants each of us to do our specific duties on this mission, I can't pick up your slack just like you can't pick up mine."

"I wasn't expecting you to, that's why I was going to do it after my TV episode. And don't talk to me like a child, Matt, I damn well know what my duties on this mission are."

The small bickering quickly turns into a full-blown argument, with screaming and shouting that lasts for hours. With no one to vent to, those harsh feelings grow and grow. The couple doesn't speak for the nearly a week, and finally the day comes when the shuttle is set to arrive at Mars, and it is Matt and Samantha's turn to wake up their crew and prep them for arrival. Out of the five crew members sleeping, two are men and three are women. Matt and Samantha go to wake each of them up.

"I'm glad you're awake guys, it's just, I need to talk to you guys about Samantha."

"What's wrong? Did she contract some sort of illness?" asks Mark, the shuttle's chief botanist.

"No no, nothing like that, she's just being suuuuuuuuccch a pain in my ass."

Over on the other side of the shuttle, Samantha is giving the women crew her side of the story.

"And then he says 'Well why can't you pick them up now?' And I was like 'It doesn't matter, I was going to pick them up later, there's no difference if I did it now, it's not like they're going to fly off into space and cause the shuttle to spiral out of control."

"Well, Samantha," says Rachel, the shuttle's physician, "unless Matt isn't performing his required duties, or if he is stopping you from completing yours, this seems like something the two of you need to work out."

"Ugh, you guys always take his side!"

The crew hears non-stop complaining for the next couple of hours until Captain Nicole orders everyone into the dining area of the shuttle.

"Clearly, something happened between the two of you, but we're about to be the first humans who ever stepped foot on the red planet, and there is no room in our cargo bin to be carrying any negativity. Be adults about this, the world is counting on us."

Matt and Samantha look at each other reluctantly, but then embrace and share a kiss before thanking the crew and leaving the cabin. With the couple finally gone, Rachel speaks up.

"Holy shit, it was so awkward having to pretend to be asleep when they were fighting."

Three brilliant scientists have been colleagues ever since their days in university. One of the scientists, though, is a complete hipster. Even through all of their successes and acclaim, nothing ever seems to impress the hipster scientist, to the annoyance of his peers.

But the other two scientists finally feel their latest invention will be the thing that elicits a true emotional, non-apathetic response from the hipster. They've developed a laser so powerful and so state-of-the-art that it can cut down components to their smallest levels. They decide to try the laser out in front of other prestigious scientists, cutting a banana under a microscope.

The laser cuts the banana into halves, then fourths, then eighths, and then continues until they are looking at an exponentially small portion of a banana cell. The other scientists in the audience clap and cheer at the invention: They have never seen anything like it before. The hipster scientist, though, crosses his arms and rolls his eyes, clearly judging the people in the audience. His peers have had enough.

"What's your problem? We've been working really hard on this, it's a great invention. Jesus, look at how small we were able to cut that banana! What about that doesn't amaze you?!"

The hipster scientist hisses. "Psh. I liked it better before it was a molecule."

There are two types of people in this world: Those who can extrapolate from incomplete data and

A proton, a neutron, and helium walk into a bar and order three beers. The bartender appears with three beers and asks the proton, "Are you sure you're over 21?" The proton replies, "I'm positive." So the bartender gives him the first beer. He gives the second beer to the neutron and says, "For you, no charge."

He throws the third beer in helium's face. Helium doesn't react.

Heisenberg and Schrödinger are driving along the freeway when they are stopped by a police officer. The cop says to Heisenberg, who is driving, "Do you know how fast you were going?!" Heisenberg says, "No, but I knew where I was." "OK, smart guy," says the cop, "I'm going to search your car." So he does, and then comes back to the window. "Did you know you have a dead cat in a box in the trunk?" Schrödinger says, "No, but I do now."

Two atoms are walking along. One of them says: "Oh, no, I think I lost an electron." "Are you sure?" "Yes, I'm positive."

The teacher asks, "Flora, what part of the human body increases 10 times when excited?" Flora blushes and says, "That's disgusting, I won't even answer that question." The teacher calls on Johnny: "What part of the human body increases 10 times when excited?" "That's easy," says Johnny. "It's the pupil of the eye." "Very good, Johnny," responds the teacher. "That's correct." She then turns to Flora and says, "First, you didn't do your homework. Second, you have a dirty mind. And third, you're in for a BIG disappointment."

One day after sleeping badly, an anatomist goes to his frog laboratory and removes from a cage one frog with white spots on its back. He places it on a table and draws a line just in front of the frog. "Jump frog, jump!" he shouts. The little critter jumps two feet forward. In his lab book, the anatomist scribbles, "Frog with four legs jumps two feet."

Then, he surgically removes one leg of the frog and repeats the experiment. "Jump, jump!" The frog leaps forward 1.5 feet. He writes down, "Frog with three legs jumps 1.5 feet."

Next, he removes a second leg. "Jump frog, jump!" The frog manages to jump a foot. He scribbles in his lab book, "Frog with two legs jumps one foot."

Not stopping there, the anatomist removes yet another leg. "Jump, jump!" The poor frog somehow manages to move 0.5 feet forward. The scientist writes, "Frog with one leg jumps 0.5 feet."

Finally, he eliminates the last leg. "Jump, jump!" he shouts, encouraging forward progress for the frog. But despite all its efforts, the frog doesn't budge. "Jump frog, jump!" he cries again. It's no use; the frog doesn't respond. The anatomist thinks for a while and then writes in his lab book, "Frog with no legs goes deaf."

A male frog telephones the Psychic Hotline and is told, "You are going to meet a beautiful young girl who will want to know everything about you."

The frog is thrilled, "This is great! Will I meet her in a bar?"

"No," says the psychic, "in her biology class."

Why are men sexier than women?

You can't spell sexy without xy.

Albert Einstein is just about finished with his work on the Theory of Special Relativity, when he decides to take a break and go on vacation in Mexico. So he hops on a plane and heads to Acapulco. Each day, late in the afternoon, sporting dark sunglasses, he walks in the white Mexican sand and breathes in the fresh Pacific sea air. On the last day, he pauses during his stroll to sit down on a bench and watch the sunset. When the large orange ball is just disappearing, a last beam of light seems to radiate toward him. The event brings him back to thinking about his physics work. "What symbol should I use for zee speed of light?" he asks himself. The problem is that nearly every Greek letter has been taken for some other purpose. Just then, a beautiful Mexican woman passes by. Albert Einstein just has to say something to her. Almost out of desperation, he asks, as he lowers his dark sunglasses, "Do you not zink zat zee speed of light is very fast?" The woman smiles at Einstein and replies, "Si."

A photon checks into a hotel. The bellhop asks, "Can I help you with your luggage?" The photon replies, "I don't have any. I always travel light."

A small piece of sodium that lives in a test tube falls in love with a Bunsen burner. "Oh Bunsen, my flame," the sodium pines. "I melt whenever I see you." The Bunsen burner replies, "It's just a phase you're going through."

What is the difference between a physicist, an engineer, and a mathematician? If an engineer walks into a room and sees a fire in the middle of the room and a bucket of water in the corner, he takes the bucket of water and pours it on the fire and puts it out. If a physicist walks into a room and sees a fire in the middle of the room and a bucket of water in the corner, he takes the bucket of water and pours it around the fire and lets the fire put itself out. If a mathematician walks into a room and sees a fire in the middle of the room and a bucket of water in the corner, he convinces himself there is a solution and leaves.

Three people apply for the same job. One is a physicist, one is a statistician, and one is an accountant. The interviewing committee first calls in the physicist. They say, "We have only one question. What is 500 plus 500?" The physicist, without hesitation, says "1,000." The committee sends him out and calls in the statistician. When the statistician comes in, they ask the same question. The statistician ponders the question for a moment, and then answers, "1,000. I'm 95% confident." He is then also thanked for his time and sent on his way. When the accountant enters the room, he is asks the same question: "What is 500 plus 500?" The accountant replies, "What would you like it to be?" They hire the accountant.

PICK-UP LINES

Tonight, this Han doesn't want to fly Solo.

You look exactly like my future ex-wife.

If we had a garden, I'd put my tulips and your tulips together.

My Mom thinks I'm gay, can you help me prove her wrong?

I'm in a boy band called Wrong Direction.

Did you fart? Because you just blew me away.

Hey, tie your shoes! I don't want you falling for anyone else.

Can I take a picture with you? I want to show Santa what I want for Christmas.

Did you sit in a pile of sugar? Because you have a sweet ass.

Girl, is your name wifi? Because I'm feeling a connection!

Is that a mirror in your pocket? Cause I can see myself in your pants!

Hey, my name's Macintosh, can I crash at your place tonight?

Are you from Georgia? Because you're looking mighty peachy.

I'd offer you a cigarette, but you're already smoking hot.

What's a nice girl like you doing in a dirty mind like mine?

So, come back to my place, and if you don't like it, I swear I'll give you a full refund.

If you were a Transformer, you'd be Optimus Fine.

You must be Jamaican, because Jamaican me crazy.

Are you a parking ticket? Because you've got 'fine' written all over you.

Are you from Tennessee? Because you're the only ten I see.

You must be tired from running around in my head all night.

Would you like gin and platonic, or do you prefer scotch and sofa?

It's handy that I have my library card because I'm totally checking you out.

How much does a polar bear weigh? Enough to break the ice! Hi, I'm ____

They call me "the fireman" because I turn the hoes on.

You're hot. I'm ugly. Let's make average babies.

Do you believe in love at first sight, or should I walk by again?

Are you an interior decorator? Because when I saw you, the entire room became beautiful.

Did it hurt when you fell from heaven?

I feel like Richard Gere because I'm standing next to a Pretty Woman.

That's a nice shirt. Can I talk you out of it?

Are you my appendix? Because I have a funny feeling in my stomach that makes me feel like I should take you out.

Do you have a Band-Aid? I just scraped my knee falling for you.

The word of the day is 'legs.' Let's go back to my place and spread the word.

Do you drink a lot of Snapple? Because you look like you're made from the best stuff on earth.

If you were a basketball, I'd never shoot because I'd always miss you.

Do you work for FedEx? Because I could have sworn I saw you checking out my package.

I'm fighting the urge to make you the happiest woman on earth tonight.

Let's go back to my room and do some math: Add a bed, subtract our clothes, divide your legs, and multiply.

Was your dad a boxer? Cause you're a knockout!

If being sexy was a crime, you'd be guilty as charged!

Do you have a map? 'Cause I just got lost in your eyes.

My name isn't Elmo, but you can tickle me any time you want.

If you were a vegetable, you'd be a cute-cumber.

Guess what my shirt is made out of? Boyfriend/Girlfriend material.

Roses are red, violets are blue, and how would you like it if I came home with you?

I lost my phone number. Can I have yours?

Is your dad a baker? Because you've got some nice buns.

There is something wrong with my cell phone. It doesn't have your number in it.

If I had to rate you on a scale of one to ten, I'd give you a nine, because I'm the one you are missing.

Some people say that Disneyland is the happiest place on earth. Those people, however, have never been in your arms.

Two bachelors sit talking. Their conversation drifts from politics to cooking. "I got a cookbook once," says the first, "but I could never do anything with it."

"Too much fancy cooking in it, eh?" asks the second. "You said it. Every one of the recipes began the same way: 'Take a clean dish and....'"

A little old lady sits at the café counter and orders a hamburger. A huge guy behind the counter bellows, "One burger!"

Whereupon the chef grabs a huge hunk of chopped meat, stuffs it in his bare armpit, pumps his arm a few times to squeeze it flat, and then tosses it on the grill.

"That's the most disgusting thing I've ever seen," the old lady says.

"Yeah?" says the counterman. "You should be here in the morning when he makes the doughnuts."

A young boy wants to bake a cake for his mother's birthday as a surprise. His Dad is on board for the idea and gives the boy a recipe for red velvet cake to work from. He gets the materials from the refrigerator ready for the cake: Eggs, frosting, cake mix, flour, chocolate, etc. But as he tries to carry the materials, he drops them all on the floor, causing a huge mess.

The boy is distraught. Not only does he have to clean up the mess, but there aren't enough materials left for a cake. So the boy improvises. Instead of eggs, he uses dog doo from the backyard. Instead of frosting, he uses lasagna noodles with ketchup on top. And instead of flour, he cuts up some flowers from outside their home. The boy mixes all the items together, sticks it in the oven, and the whole house reeks of something awful as the Mom gets home.

Excited to show his creation, the boy invites his Mom to the dining room table and asks her to take a bite. The Mom agrees, not wanting to disappoint her son, but her distaste is evident.

"Honey, what type of cake is this? It tastes…interesting."

"Oh, well, it's red velvet cake, but I used different ingredients, like some of the dog doo in the back yard, and some lasagna, and ketchup."

The Mom looks terrified and wipes a crumb from her mouth.

"OK, and then you put this in the oven?"

"Yeah, for 30 minutes."

The Mom puts down the fork and decides to come clean to her son. "I'm sorry, but this cake isn't very good. I really appreciate what you did for me on my birthday, but next time, please remember, you have to keep the cake in the oven for at least 45 minutes: That way, the dog doo has some time to properly bake."

One day, young Sarah girl is watching her mother make a roast sirloin of beef. She cuts off the ends, wraps it in string, seasons it, and sets it in the roasting dish.

Sarah politely asks her Mum why she cut off the ends of the roast. Mum replies, after some thought, that that's the way that her mother had done it.

That night, Grandma comes to dinner and Sarah and her mother ask why she has cut the end off of the roast before cooking. After some thought, Grandma replies that she cooks the meat the way her mother had done it.

Now Great-Grandma is quite old and lived in a nursing home, so Sarah, her Mum and Grandma go to visit her and again, they ask the very same question.

Great-Grandma looks at them a bit surprised and says, "So it would fit in the roasting dish, of course."

A preacher goes to a nursing home to meet an elderly parishioner. As he sits there, he notices this bowl of peanuts beside her bed and takes one. As they talk, he can't help himself and eats one after another. By the time they are through talking, the bowl is empty. He says, "Ma'am, I'm sorry, but I seem to have eaten all of your peanuts."

"That's OK," she says. "They would have just sat there. Without my teeth, all I can do is suck the chocolate off and put them back."

Early one morning, the Mole family awakes and Daddy mole climbs to the top of the mole hole and sniffs the air. "I smell bacon frying," he says.

Momma mole crowds in beside him and sniffs the air: "I smell eggs cooking," she says. Baby mole tries and tries to get to the top but there is no room left, so he says, "All I can smell is molasses!"

How to eat soup with a fork

1. Prepare your delicious soup of choice.

2. Once you discover you only have forks, do not fear!

3. Write a polite note to your roommate describing how the dishes in the sink are his and you would appreciate him handling it.

4. Use the fork to collect chicken, noodles, etc., into an island in the middle of your bowl.

5. You remember that you left a note to your roommate in the past and nothing came of it, so replace the note with more passive aggressive language.

6. Use a bowl like a cup and sip the soup into your mouth. Use the fork to fend off chicken, noodles, etc., from hitting you in the eye.

7. Put all dirty dishes in your roommate's bed.

8. Clean the fork after use.

A tourist on a farm asks the farmer why one pig has a wooden leg.

The farmer says, "That pig is the bravest pig I ever saw."

"So why does he have a wooden leg?" the tourist asks.

"One night, our house caught on fire, and he came inside and woke us all up."

The tourist asks again, "So, why does that pig have a wooden leg?"

"You can't eat a pig that brave all at once!"

What do you get when you mix beans and onions?

Tear gas

Why couldn't the sesame seed leave the gambling casino?

Because he was on a roll

Many years ago, a baker's assistant called Richard the Pourer, whose job it was to pour the dough mixture in the making of sausage rolls, noted that he was running low on one of the necessary spices, so he sent his apprentice to the store to buy more.

Unfortunately, upon arriving at the shop, the young man realized that he had forgotten the name of the ingredient. All he could do was to tell the shopkeeper that it was: "For Richard the Pourer, for batter for wurst."

My wife has not spoken to me in three days.

I think it has something to do with what happened on Sunday night when she thought she heard a noise downstairs.

She nudged me and whispered, "Wake up, wake up!"

"What's the matter"? I asked.

"There are burglars in the kitchen. I think they're eating the tuna casserole I made tonight."

"That'll teach them!" I replied.

A man goes into a restaurant where all the waitresses are gorgeous. A particularly voluptuous waitress wearing a very short skirt comes to his table and asks, "What would you like, sir?"

He looks at the menu, scans her beautiful frame top to bottom, and then answers, "A quickie."

The waitress turns and walks away in disgust.

After she regains her composure she returns and asks again, "What would you like, sir?"

Again the man thoroughly checks her out and again answers, "A quickie, please."

This time her anger takes over, she reaches over and slaps him across the face with a resounding SMACK! and storms away.

A man sitting at the next table then leans over and whispers, "Um, I think it's pronounced 'quiche.'"

A man is dining alone in a fancy restaurant and there's a gorgeous redhead sitting at the next table. He has been checking her out since he sat down, but he lacks the nerve to talk with her.

Suddenly she sneezes, and her glass eye comes flying out of its socket toward the man. He reflexively reaches out, grabs it out of the air, and hands it back.

"Oh my, I am so sorry," the woman says, as she pops her eye back in place. "Let me buy your dinner to make it up to you."

They enjoy a wonderful dinner together, and afterward they go to the theatre, followed by drinks. They talk, they laugh, and she shares her deepest dream and he shares his. She listens to him with interest.

After paying for everything, she asks him if he would like to come to her place for a nightcap and stay for breakfast. They have a wonderful time.

The next morning, she cooks a gourmet meal with all the trimmings.

"You know," he says, "you are the perfect woman. Are you this nice to every guy you meet?"

"No" she replies. "You just happened to catch my eye."

A couple go for a meal at a Chinese restaurant and order the "Chicken Surprise."

The waiter brings the meal, served in a lidded cast iron pot.

Just as the wife is about to serve herself, the lid of the pot rises slightly and she briefly sees two beady little eyes looking around before the lid slams back down.

"Good grief, did you see that?" she asks her husband.

He hasn't, so she asks him to look in the pot.

He reaches for it and again the lid rises, and he sees two little eyes looking around before it slams down.

Rather perturbed, he calls the waiter over, explains what is happening, and demands an explanation.

"Please sir," says the waiter, "what did you order?"

The husband replies, "Chicken Surprise."

"Ah! I'm sorry," says the waiter, "I brought you the Peeking Duck!"

A friend and I are standing in line at a fast-food restaurant, waiting to place our order.

There's a big sign posted: "No bills larger than $20 will be accepted."

The woman in front of us, pointing to the sign, remarks, "Believe me, if I HAD a bill larger than $20, I wouldn't be eating here."

A man goes to the nursing home to visit his 84-year-old father. While there, he notices the nurse is giving his father hot chocolate and Viagra. The man asks, "Why are you doing that? I mean, at his age what will it do for him?" The nurse explains, "The hot chocolate will help him sleep." The man says, "And the Viagra?" "It keeps him from falling out of bed."

A man finds a magic lamp on the beach. He rubs it and out pops a genie, who gives the man three wishes. The man wishes for a million dollars, and poof! There's a million dollars. Then he wishes for a convertible, and poof! There's a convertible. And then, he wishes he could be irresistible to all women. Poof! He turns into a box of chocolates.

Two attorneys go into a diner and order two drinks. Then they produce sandwiches from their briefcases and start to eat. The waiter becomes quite concerned and marches over to tell them, "You can't eat your own sandwiches in here!" The attorneys look at each other, shrug their shoulders, and then exchange sandwiches.

Don't spell "part" backward. It's a trap.

I was going to make a dubstep joke...but I dropped it.

I've accidentally swallowed some Scrabble tiles.
My next crap could spell disaster.

Did you hear about the guy who got hit in the head with a can of soda?
He's lucky it's a soft drink.

Did you hear about the restaurant on the moon?
Great food, but no atmosphere

Thieves had broken into my house and stolen everything except my soap, shower gel, towels, and deodorant.
Dirty bastards!

The store keeps calling me to come back and buy more furniture...but all I really wanted was a one-night stand.

When I get naked in the bathroom, the shower usually gets turned on.

What kind of shoes does a pedophile wear?
White vans

I have a few jokes about unemployed people, but it doesn't matter: None of them work.

Yesterday I accidentally swallowed some food coloring. The doctor says I'm OK, but I feel like I've dyed a little inside.

A man enters a local paper's pun contest. He sends in 10 different puns, in the hope that at least one of the puns would win. Unfortunately, no pun in 10 did.

This girl says she recognizes me from the vegetarian club, but I'd never met herbivore.

Vagina jokes aren't funny. Period.

I found a rock that measures 5,280 feet in length. Must be some kind of milestone.

Two antennas meet on a roof and get married. The wedding is OK, but the reception is incredible.

Did you hear about the guy whose whole left side is cut off? He's all right now.

I wondered why the baseball is getting bigger. Then it hit me.

I'm reading a book about anti-gravity. It's impossible to put down.

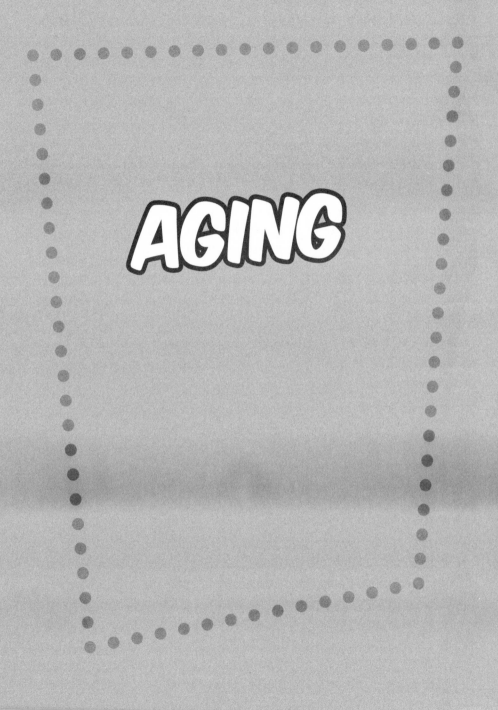

Regular naps prevent old age, especially if you take them while driving.

A woman goes to visit his 80-year-old grandfather and while they're eating breakfast, the woman notices that his plate is dirty. So she asks, "Grandfather, are these plates clean?"

Her grandfather replies, "Those plates are as clean as cold water can get them, so go on and finish your meal."

That afternoon, while eating the hamburgers her grandfather made for lunch, she notices many little black specks around the edge of his plate, so again she asks, "Grandfather, are you sure these plates are clean?"

Without looking up from his burger, the grandfather says, "I told you those dishes are as clean as cold water can get them, now don't ask me about it anymore."

Later that day, the man decides to go visit some friends in the area. As he leaves the house, the Grandfather's dog, who is lying on the floor, starts to growl and won't let him pass.

"Grandfather, your dog won't let me out," complains the granddaughter.

Without diverting his attention from the football game he is watching, his grandfather shouts, "Coldwater, get your butt out of the way!"

N ow that I'm older, I realize that my imaginary friend is really nothing more than an imaginary acquaintance.

A fter retiring, I went to the Social Security office to apply for Social Security. The woman behind the counter asks me for my driver's license to verify my age. I look in my pockets and realize I've left my wallet at home. I tell the woman that I'm very sorry, but I have to go home and come back later.

The woman says, "Unbutton your shirt." So I open my shirt, revealing my curly silver hair. She says, "That silver hair on your chest is proof enough for me" and she processes my Social Security application.

When I get home, I excitedly tell my wife about my experience at the Social Security office. She says, "You should have dropped your pants. You might have gotten disability, too."

Two old men in a retirement village are sitting in the reading room and one says to the other, "How do you really feel? I mean, you're 72 years old, how do you honestly feel?"

"Honestly, I feel like a newborn baby. I've got no hair, no teeth, and I just wet myself."

I have the body of a 25-year-old supermodel, but it takes up too much space in my freezer.

Two elderly ladies have been friends since their 30s. Now in their 80s, they still get together a couple of times a week to play cards. One day they're playing gin rummy and one of them says, "You know, we've been friends for many years and, please don't get mad, but for the life of me, I can't remember your name. Please tell me what it is."

Her friend glares at her. She continues to glare and stare at her for at least three minutes. Finally, she says, "How soon do you need to know?"

Few women admit their age; few men act it.

Wine improves with age. I improve with wine.

How can you speed up the heart rate of your 60-year-old husband?

Tell him you're pregnant.

How can you avoid getting wrinkles?

Take off your glasses.

No, seriously. How can I get rid of these crow's feet and all the wrinkles on my face?

Go braless. It usually pulls them out.

What is the most common remark made by 60-year-olds when they browse an antique store?

"I remember these!"

You are so old, when you were a kid, rainbows were black and white.

Where can a man over 60 find a younger, good-looking woman who is interested in him?

Try the bookstore under Fiction.

What can a husband do when his wife is going through menopause?

Keep busy. If he's handy with tools, he can finish the basement. Then when he's finished, he'll have a place to live.

An elderly woman from Brooklyn decides to prepare her will and make her final requests. She tells her rabbi she has two final requests. First, she wants to be cremated, and second, she wants her ashes scattered over Bloomingdale's.

"Bloomingdale's!" the rabbi exclaims. "Why Bloomingdale's?"

"Then I'll be sure my daughters visit me twice a week."

Why should senior citizens use valet parking?

The valet won't forget where he parked your car.

Is it a common problem for seniors to have trouble with memory storage?

No. Memory storage is not the problem. Memory retrieval is.

Do people sleep more soundly as they get older?

Yes, but it's usually in the afternoon.

Where should old people look for glasses?

On their forehead

A cop on a horse says to little girl on bike, "Did Santa get you that?" "Yes," replies the little girl.

"Well, tell him to put a reflector light on it next year!" and fines her $5. The little girl looks up at the cop and says, "Nice horse you've got there. Did Santa bring you that?" The cop chuckles and replies, "He sure did!" "Well," says the little girl, "Next year tell Santa that the dick goes under the horse, not on top of it!"

Police Officer: "How high are you?"

Pothead: "No officer, it's 'Hi, how are you?'"

A man goes to the police station wishing to speak with the burglar who had broken into his house the night before. "You'll get your chance in court." says the Desk Sergeant. "No, no, no!" says the man. "I want to know how he got into the house without waking my wife. I've been trying to do that for years!"

A police officer pulls over a driver and informs him that he has just won $5,000 in a safety competition, all because he is wearing his seat belt. "What are you going to do with the prize money?" the officer asks. The man responds, "I guess I'll go to driving school and get my license." His wife says, "Officer, don't listen to him. He's a smart aleck when he's drunk." The guy in the back seat pops up out from under the blanket and says, "I knew we wouldn't get far in this stolen car." Just then a knock comes from the trunk and a voice calls out, "Are we over the border yet?"

A police officer pulls over this guy who had been weaving in and out of the lanes. He goes up to the guy's window and says, "Sir, I need you to blow into this breathalyzer tube." The man says, "Sorry, officer, I can't do that. I am an asthmatic. If I do that, I'll have a really bad asthma attack." "OK, fine. I need you to come down to the station to give a blood sample." "I can't do that either. I am a hemophiliac. If I do that, I'll bleed to death." "Well, then we need a urine sample." "I'm sorry officer, I can't do that either. I am also a diabetic. If I do that I'll get really low blood sugar." "Alright then, I need you to come out here and walk this white line." "I can't do that, officer." "Why not?" "Because I'm too drunk to do that."

A woman and a man are involved in a car accident, a bad one. Both of their cars are totally demolished but amazingly neither of them is hurt. After they crawl out of their cars, the woman says, "So you're a man, that's interesting. I'm a woman. Wow, just look at our cars! There's nothing left, but fortunately we are unhurt. This must be a sign from God that we should meet and be friends and live together in peace for the rest of our days." The man replies, "I agree with you completely." "This must be a sign from God!" the woman continues, "and look at this, here's another miracle. My car is completely demolished but this bottle of wine didn't break. Surely God wants us to drink this wine and celebrate our good fortune." Then she hands the bottle to the man. The man nods his head in agreement, opens it and drinks half the bottle and then hands it back to the woman. The woman takes the bottle, immediately puts the cork back in and hands it back to the man. The man asks, "Aren't you having any?" The woman replies, "No. I think I'll just wait for the police."

A police officer comes upon a terrible wreck where the driver and passengers have been killed. As he looks upon the wreckage, a little monkey comes out of the brush and hops around the crashed car. The officer looks down at the monkey and says, "I wish you could talk." The monkey looks up at the officer and shakes his head up and down. "You can understand what I'm saying?" asks the officer. Again, the monkey shakes his head up and down. "Well, did you see this?" "Yes," motions the monkey. "What happened?" The monkey pretends to have a can in his hand and turns it up by his mouth. "They were drinking?" asks the officer. "Yes." "What else?" The monkey pinches his fingers together and holds them to his mouth. "They were smoking marijuana?" "Yes." "Now wait, you're saying your owners were drinking, and smoking marijuana before they wrecked?" The monkey nods. "What were you doing during all this?" "Driving" motions the monkey.

The local sheriff is looking for a deputy, so Gomer—who is not exactly the sharpest nail in the bucket—goes in to try out for the job. "OK," the sheriff drawls, "Gomer, what is 1 and 1?" "11" he replies. The sheriff thinks to himself, "That's not what I meant, but he's right." "What two days of the week start with the letter 'T'?" "Today and tomorrow." He is again surprised that Gomer supplied a correct answer that he had never thought of himself. "Now Gomer, listen carefully: Who killed Abraham Lincoln?" Gomer looks a little surprised

himself, then thinks really hard for a minute and finally admits, "I don't know."
"Well, why don't you go home and work on that one for a while?" So, Gomer
wanders over to the pool hall where his pals are waiting to hear the results of
the interview. Gomer is exultant: "It went great! First day on the job and I'm
already working on a murder case!"

An old lady is speeding down the highway while she is knitting. A cop sees this and speeds up alongside her vehicle. "Pull over!" the cop says. "No!" the woman replies, "It's a cardigan!

A farmhand is driving around the farm, checking the fences. After a few
minutes, he radios his boss and says, "Boss, I've got a problem. I hit a
pig on the road and he's stuck in the bull-bars of my truck. He's still wriggling.
What should I do?" "In the back of your truck there's a shotgun. Shoot the
pig in the head and when it stops wriggling you can pull it out and throw it in
a bush." The farm worker says OK and signs off. About 10 minutes later he
radios back. "Boss, I did what you says: I shot the pig and dragged it out and
threw it in a bush." "So what's the problem now?" his boss snaps. "The blue
light on his motorcycle is still flashing!"

A couple of young, entrepreneurial prostitutes are riding around town with
a sign on the top of their car that reads: "Two Prostitutes: $50." A police
officer, seeing the sign, pulls the ladies over and advises that they will have to
remove the sign or go to jail. Right about that time, a minivan passes by with
a sign on the side of it that reads: "Jesus Saves." "How come you don't stop
them?" asks one of the girls. "Well, that's a little different," the officer replies,
"their sign pertains to religion." The two ladies of the night pout a bit, but they
take their sign down and drive off peacefully. The following day, the same
police officer is running radar when he notices the same two young ladies

driving around with another sign on their car. Figuring he has an easy arrest, he flips his lights on and begins to catch up when he notices what the new sign reads: "Two Fallen Angels Seeking Peter: $50."

A blonde woman is speeding in a 35 MPH zone when a police officer pulls her over and walks up to the car. The officer also happens to be a blonde woman, and she asks for the blonde's driver's license.

The driver searches frantically in her purse for a while and finally says to the blonde policewoman, "What does a driver's license look like?"

Irritated, the blonde cop says, "You dummy, it's got your picture on it!"

The blonde driver frantically searches her purse again and finds a small, rectangular mirror down at the bottom. She holds it up to her face and says, "Aha! This must be my driver's license!" and hands it to the blonde policewoman.

The blonde cop looks in the mirror, hands it back to the driver and says, "You're free to go. And, if I had known you were a police officer too, we could have avoided all of this."

Two rednecks, Bubba and Earl, are driving down the road drinking a couple of bottles of beer.

The passenger, Bubba, says, "Lookey thar up ahead, Earl, it's a police roadblock!! We're gonna get busted fer drinkin' these here beers!!"

"Don't worry, Bubba," Earl says. "We'll just pull over and finish drinkin' these beers then peel off the label and stick it on our foreheads, and throw the bottles under the seat."

"What fer?", asks Bubba.

"Just let me do the talkin', OK?," says Earl.

Well, they finish their beers, throw the empties out of sight and put a label on each of their foreheads.

When they reach the roadblock, the sheriff says, "You boys been drinkin'?"

"No, sir," says Earl, pointing at the labels. "We're on the patch."

The Los Angeles Police Department, the FBI, and the CIA are all trying to prove that they are the best at apprehending criminals. The President decides to give them a test. He releases a rabbit into a forest and each of them has to catch it.

The CIA goes in.

They place animal informants throughout the forest. They question all plant and material witnesses. After three months of extensive investigations, they conclude that rabbits do not exist.

The FBI goes in.

After two weeks with no leads, they burn the forest, killing everything in it, including the rabbit, and they make no apologies. The rabbit had it coming.

The LAPD goes in.

They come out two hours later with a badly beaten bear.

The bear is yelling: "OK! OK! I'm a rabbit! I'm a rabbit!"

A driver is pulled over by a police officer for speeding. As the officer writes the ticket, she notices several machetes in the car.

"What are those for?" she asks suspiciously.

"I'm a juggler," the man replies. "I use those in my act."

"Well, show me," the officer demands.

So he gets out the machetes and starts juggling them, first three, then more, finally seven at one time, overhand, underhand, behind the back, putting on a dazzling show and amazing the officer.

Another car passes by. The driver does a double take, and says, "My God. I've gotta give up drinking! Look at the test they're giving now."

A man is speeding down an Alabama highway, feeling secure in a gaggle of cars all traveling at the same speed. However, as they pass a speed trap, he gets nailed with an infrared speed detector and is pulled over.

The officer hands him the citation, receives his signature and is about to walk away when the man asks, "Officer, I know I was speeding, but I don't think it's fair. There were plenty of other cars around me who were going just as fast, so why did I get the ticket?"

"Ever go a-fishin'?" the policeman asks the man.

"Ummm, yeah...," the startled man replies.

The officer grins: "Did you ever catch 'em all?"

T here once was a sheriff who, no matter what the situation, always said, "It could have been worse" after viewing the scene of the crime. It drove his two deputies absolutely crazy.

One day, the two deputies in the Sheriff's Office answer an emergency call at a farmhouse. When they walk in, they find the nude bodies of a man and a woman in the bedroom. They both have been shot to death. When the deputies go to the living room, they find the body of a man with a gun at his side.

"No doubt about it," one deputy says to the other. "This is a double murder and suicide. This guy came home and found his wife in bed with somebody else and shot them both. Then he shot himself."

"You're right," the other deputy replies. "Double murder and suicide. But I'll bet you when the sheriff gets here, he's going to say 'It could have been worse' as he always does!"

"No way. How could it be worse? There are three people in the house, and all of them have been shot to death. It couldn't be worse. You're on," says the first deputy.

About that time, the old sheriff arrives at the scene. He walks into the bedroom and sees the two nude bodies. He then walks into the living room and sees the man on the floor with the gun by his side. "No doubt about it," the sheriff says, shaking his head. "It's a double murder and suicide. This guy came home and found his wife in bed with somebody else and shot them both. Then he shot himself."

After hesitating for a moment, the old sheriff looks his deputies squarely in the eyes. "But, you know," he says, "it could have been worse."

The deputy who lost the bet jumps up and shouts, "Sheriff, how could it have been worse? There are three people in this farmhouse, and all three of them are dead. It couldn't have been worse!!"

"Yes it could," the sheriff retorts. "You see that guy there on the floor? If he had come home yesterday, that would be me in there in that bed!"

An elderly Florida lady does her shopping, and upon returning to her car, finds four males in the act of leaving with her vehicle. She drops her shopping bags and draws her handgun, proceeding to scream at the top of her voice, "I have a gun, and I know how to use it! Get out of the car!" The four men don't wait for a second invitation. They get out and run like mad. The lady, somewhat shaken, then proceeds to load her shopping bags into the back of the car and get into the driver's seat. She is so shaken that she can't get her key into the ignition. She tries and tries, and then it dawns on her why. A few minutes later, she finds her own car parked four or five spaces farther down! She loads her bags into the car and then drives to the police station. The sergeant to whom she tells the story nearly tears himself in two with laughter. He points to the other end of the counter, where four pale men are reporting a carjacking by a mad, elderly woman described as white, less than five feet tall, glasses, curly white hair, about 75, and carrying a large handgun.

A policeman sees a car weaving all over the road and hits his flashing lights. He walks up to the driver's window and sees a good-looking woman behind the wheel. There is a strong smell liquor on her breath.

He says, "I'm going to give you a breathalyzer test to determine if you are under the influence of alcohol."

She blows up the balloon and he walks it back to his patrol unit. After a couple of minutes, he returns to her car and says, "It looks like you've had a couple of stiff ones."

She replies, "You mean it shows that, too?"

A man is flying to New York. He decides to strike up a conversation with his seatmate. "I've got a great policeman joke. Would you like to hear it?" "I should let you know first that I am a policeman." "That's OK. I'll tell it really slow!"

ADVICE
LETTERS

Dear Justin,

I've been married to my darling wife Evelyn for nearly 20 years. We met in college in psychology class. We were both from the west attending a school in the northeast, and weren't too accustomed to the cold. I was wearing an oversized red sweater and her a massive green cardigan, while our classmates poked fun at our wintertime weather cautiousness. But when I saw my wife in that moment, I knew I never wanted to be with anyone ever again.

Now, two decades later, that spark and passion seems to have faded away from our marriage. Our newlywed days were filled with laughter, pranks and jokes, but now it's just routine hellos, goodbyes, kisses on the cheek, and maybe one night of intimacy out of the year. We're both really busy with work, and with two kids to look after, we're lucky if we can get an hour of alone time in the day, by which point we just want to use for sleep anyways.

I want to bring back that spark and life to our marriage, but I'm not sure how I can do it since we're both so busy. What should I do?

Sincerely,

Rocky Marriage in Rhode Island

Dear Rocky Marriage,

When it comes to writing advice columns, there are certain times when I must admit that I do not know or have personal experience in a particular subject. In your example, I must say I know nothing about marriage. I'm not married, nor do I ever plan to marry. This may seem as something that could discredit me from giving you advice, but at the same time, my ability to look at the institution of marriage with an outside lens actually makes me the perfect person to speak about your issue.

Let's look at the facts here. When you were younger, your relationship was new, you had very few personal commitments except maybe to study and occasionally call your parents. Now that you're older, you've become buried in responsibility, with the act of even trying to have fun on your own being seemingly selfish. I've seen couples have similar issues like you have with your wife, and a way they have addressed it is by scheduling a periodic, fun activity together, something like a weekly cooking class, or swing dancing lessons at the rec center. Rocky Marriage, I must say, this is the WRONG way to go. Learning to cook will be a useless skill by the time automated robots take care of preparing all our meals, and swing dancing is really only applicable if you're planning to go to one of Jay Gatsby's lavish parties.

I suggest you don't do anything different and just proceed through each day. Finding new ways to spark excitement in a relationship takes a lot of work, and that's time instead you could spend relaxing or watching TV. Plus, the fact that you have so little to say to each other now means you'll have to think of significantly less topics to talk about. And who out there can honestly say they like small talk? Lack of communication and passion is your recipe for success, my friend.

-Justin

Dear Justin,

I'm a 45-year-old electrician living in Sarasota, Florida. I have a loving husband, two adorable kids, my own home, and friends and family who are willing to take a bullet for me. But even with everything a man could ask for, I am still unhappy. I want to be an actor. It isn't necessarily something that I've wanted to do my whole life, and I don't really have any professional theater or performing arts experience. Heck, the last play I actually saw was Joseph and the Amazing Technicolor Dreamcoat when I was still a kid. But after realizing that this is my dream, I feel that I can't just limit my life and not pursue it.

Right now, I'm the main provider for my family, my husband is in school, and our kids will be going to college in a few years, so it isn't necessarily feasible that I pack up my bags and head straight to Los Angeles without a steady income source for my family. But I don't want to wake up 30 years from now filled with regret that I didn't follow my dreams. What should I do?

Your friend,

Starstruck in Sarasota

Dear Starstruck,

Your story struck a familiar chord with me, because it's pretty similar to a recent life crisis my friend Jen found herself in. See, Jen too had big Hollywood dreams but a lot of commitments to take care of, she was a single mother with lots of student loan debt, and when one of her parents got sick, she needed to be there to help through their medical procedures. But in-between all of those commitments, Jen auditioned for a part in the local theater's production of Death of a Salesman. She ended up getting the role of Linda Loman, the female lead. I saw Jen perform on the closing night of the production, and after all the turmoil she had recently faced in her life, it was the first time I saw her smile.

Starstruck, I must tell you, that production of Death of a Salesman was the worst piece of garbage I've ever seen. It was hackneyed and contrived, and Jen honestly couldn't act her way out of a cardboard box if her life depended on it. I think she is only happy because she didn't know how terrible she was, and frankly I would have asked for my money back if the show itself wasn't free. See, Jen made the mistake of finding a fulfilling creative pursuit to work at in the midst of all her responsibilities, when she should have just moved to L.A. from the get-go. She has siblings who can help with her parents, and her daughter is like 16 anyways, she can take care of herself.

Starstruck, the moment you stop reading this, buy a plane ticket first class to L.A. The money you'll lose from your electrician job will be chump change compared to the millions you'll make on your first blockbuster movie. Bring your family with you and try to get them into acting too. Because hey, the only thing better than a movie star-sized mansion is four movie star-sized mansions. Good luck, and remember to thank me in your Oscar acceptance speech.

-Justin

Dear Justin,

I've been working at my manufacturing company for about eight years now, and while it isn't necessarily my "dream job," it's something that I mostly enjoy going to on day-to-day basis. I was pretty happy with my salary, and never really concerned myself with how much other people on my team made, I usually thought it was none of my business. When I was rearranging a few things in the copy room, I came across one of my co-worker's paystubs. I couldn't help myself from looking, and I was shocked at what I saw: My co-worker, who is 10 years younger than me, doesn't have a master's degree, and has been at the company for only two years, makes $15,000 more a year than I do.

I must say, I was pretty furious about this, especially after all the time and energy I've devoted to the company over the years. While I get yearly raises, I never would have imagined someone else made so much more than me. I want to bring it up to my boss to increase my own salary, since I do deserve it, but I also don't want to reveal how I found out that information or say the wrong thing. The last thing I would need is to lose my job because I was being nosey. What should I do?

Yours truly,

Salaried in Saskatchewan

Dear Salaried,

Your story reminds me of when I was a little kid, running my first lemonade stand in the cruel heat of summer. I had my lemonade, cups, and a cute, rickety stand positioned right in the middle of our neighborhood, and was selling cups for fifty cents apiece. I'd walk home every day with at least $5 in my pocket, which at that time felt like a million bucks. But one day, when I took a break from my stand, I went to another part of the neighborhood and saw a kid who had his own lemonade stand, except he was selling cups for $1 each, and he had a line down the street. His lemonade wasn't nearly as good as mine (between you and me, it tasted a bit sour), but customers still loved him.

You know what that other child was better at than I? Marketing. See, Timmy on the other side of the neighborhood, just by advertising his lemonade for $1 a cup, created the impression that his lemonade was worth $1 a cup, and there-fore, higher quality. My lemonade, while cheaper and tastier, wasn't deemed as valuable, and thus wasn't as popular.

Do you see where I'm getting at here? Your co-worker, just simply stating that they are worth more, inherently makes them worth more money. If you're applying to a job and say that you need $10 minimum an hour, and there's another person who needs $15 minimum an hour, that person asking for $15 is going to get the job, because the store owner is going to see that they don't come cheap, and that means that they're worth something.

So your particular example, here's what I suggest you do. Schedule a 10-min-ute meeting with your boss, politely ask them not to reply until you get done saying what you need to say, and gently bring up the issue of your inexperi-enced co-worker making more than you. Then bring in doctored financial re-ports and photos showing your co-worker has been embezzling money from the company and is using their work computer to traffic drugs on their lunch break. Your co-worker will be fired, and you'll receive praise and recognition for keeping the company's best interest at heart. Wait a few days until the steam blows over, and ask for a raise to what your co-worker was making. And if your boss still balks, just offer them a nice cup of lemonade.

-Justin

Dear Justin,

I'm a man in his early twenties who's caught up in a little bit of a love triangle with two girls, whom I'll call Jessica and Melissa. Jessica is jaw-droppingly gorgeous, a talented athlete, and incredibly intelligent. But every time I try to get Jessica's attention, she turns me down. When I shoot her a text message asking her to hang out, she always says that she is busy, or sometimes doesn't even reply at all.

Melissa though, is the exact opposite. Melissa is always there for me, and we always have a great time hanging out with each other. We have the same sense of humor, and every time I'm ever feeling down or need a shoulder to cry on, she's the first out of anybody to volunteer. Me and Melissa started off as friends, but now things have started to heat up between us and have hinted at going to a romantic level.

Here's the thing though. Right when my friendship with Melissa started becoming more of a mutual crush, Jessica started showering me in attention. She now texts me all the time, is always writing cutesy messages to me on social media, and anytime I actually see her in public, she becomes increasingly physical, things like playing with my hair, hugging me when no situation calls for it, things like that.

I really like Melissa a lot, but now it seems like I have a shot with Jessica too. Which one should I go after?

Regards,

Lovesick in Louisville

Dear Lovesick,

When I was a 10-year-old, I got a Nintendo for my birthday. My little brother was eight, and wanted to play with it all the time, but I didn't let him. For countless weeks, I would do nothing but play Nintendo, and my brother would get all upset that I wasn't letting him play. (I would lie sometimes and say a game was only one player, when it was really two, just so I could keep going by myself.) I must admit, I got an equal amount of joy from telling my brother that he couldn't play as much as actually playing it myself.

When my Mom saw how upset my brother was, she decided to buy him a bike. It was a pretty beat-up thing she found at Goodwill, but my little brother loved that bike. He would ride it down our street, go down to the ice cream store and get a scoop, and be back just in time for dinner. After a while, he didn't even care about playing the Nintendo anymore since he was having so much fun on his bike. I think you can guess what happened next: I got bored of playing Nintendo, and I really wanted to borrow my brother's bike after seeing it how happy it made him.

Humans have a natural tendency to want things that we can't have. With Jessica, it looks like she only wanted you when you didn't have any interest in her anymore. And now if you go back to pursuing her again, she may end up not liking you again, since you're no longer the "forbidden fruit," so to speak. From what you say about Melissa though, it seems like she definitely appreciates you, she's not buying into these "I only like him when he doesn't like me/I don't like him when he does like me" games. There seems to be a genuine, honest, connection between the two of you, and something like that is very rare.

My advice? Stick with Jessica. If Melissa really does care about you that much, she'll still care even if you pursue Jessica again. Plus your emotions will be in constant flux, and you'll feel passionate and alive of all the "Does she like me?" paranoia going on in your head. The funny thing about love games? They can be just as fun as Nintendo ones.

-Justin

Dear Justin,

I recently won a sizable amount of cash while playing the lottery, and now I never have to work again. But just as the saying goes, "more money, more problems," I have found myself in a bit of a financial, and familial, dilemma.

See, I haven't spoken to my cousins on the mother's side of my family for about 10 years. There was actually a pretty infamous falling out between us at a Thanksgiving dinner way back when, and just those harsh emotions from that night haven't really ever let up. But after they heard I won the lottery, they immediately contacted me through every possible method: Phone, email, letter, telegram, heck, even one of those planes that writes messages in the sky.

I finally gave in and responded, and they filled me in with how they're in financial troubles and could really use a slice of the money. And they're stressing because we're family, that it's only "right" I give some of it to them.

I find myself in between a rock and a hard place. My Mom, who's no longer with us, did love those cousins, but she also didn't know about what caused our Thanksgiving fallout. My cousins still are my blood, but at the same time, I think if they really cared about me, they would have tried to make contact with me besides just when I made a bunch of money. I still feel bad though, I did win a lot from my lottery prize and have more than I could ever ask for, and could give some to them without it causing me any significant financial stress. But just something about it doesn't really seem morally "right" I guess you could say. Any thoughts?

Cheers,

Jackpot in Jacksonville

Dear Jackpot,

Congratulations on winning! Mind cutting me a bit of that payout? It's only fair since I'm giving you advice and all. I kid, I kid.

Your story reminds me of a situation I found myself in about three years ago. My friend had invited me to the local shopping mall, where they were having a lot of sports themed-contests and promotions, things like make a basket from half court and win a gift card to the mall's food court. My friend is really good at hockey, and wanted to try this one competition where if you shot a puck into this small area known as a "piehole," you'd win 100 bucks to the sporting goods store there. I had never played hockey before, but my friend still encouraged me to go along with him and try just for fun.

He was a bit overconfident though when taking his shot, and boy, did it miss the pie hole by a mile. He was definitely upset, even demanded a re-do, but the staff wouldn't let him. When it was my time to shoot, I accidentally dropped the stick first since it was the first time I ever handled one. But when I shot it, lo and behold, the puck went straight into the pie hole. I was ecstatic!

When they handed me the $100 gift card, my friend congratulated me and jokingly asked what I was going to buy him. Or rather, I thought he was joking at the time. See, in my friend's mind, he felt that since he had invited me to the contest, and even though he didn't win, that he still could claim a portion of my winnings. Right then and there, I asked myself three questions:

1. Do I personally feel that I owe my friend any of this gift card?

2. Does my friend actually believe that he rightfully deserves part of this, and is not just putting pressure on me, hoping that I acquiesce and give him some?

3. If me and my friend had swapped roles, would he do the same for me and give a portion of his winnings?

For each of those questions, I found myself saying no, and ultimately didn't give him any. He didn't talk to me for very long after, but I discovered it wasn't that much of a loss since he wasn't really that good of a friend in the first place.

For you, Jackpot, you need to ask yourself those same three questions, but replace the gift card with your lottery winnings. If you can't honestly say yes to all three of them, then your family members don't deserve that money. But if you can say yes to all three, just fake your own death, set up a trust where family can't touch it, and then after enough time they'll forget about you, and just resume your life under a new identity and official name so they can't find you again. Find a nice piehole to keep that money safe and secure.

-Justin

GYM & FITNESS

I forgot to post on Facebook I was going to the gym. Now this whole workout is a waste of time.

One day while jogging, a middle-aged man notices a tennis ball lying by the side of the walk.

The ball being fairly new and in good condition, he picks the ball up, puts it in his pocket and proceeds on his way.

Waiting at the cross street for the light to change, he notices a beautiful blonde standing next to him smiling.

"What do you have in your pocket?" she asks.

"Tennis ball," the man says, smiling back.

"Wow," says the blonde, looking upset. "That must hurt. I once had tennis elbow and the pain was unbearable!"

Jack, decidedly overweight, and not at all bright, asks Doctor Mayo at Portchester Health Centre, for help in losing weight. The doctor advises Jack to run 10 miles a day for 30 days. This, she promises, will help Jack lose as much as 20 pounds in a month. Jack, naturally very excited, follows Doctor Mayo's advice to the letter, and, after 30 days, he is delighted to find that he has, indeed, lost 20 pounds.

Delighted, Jack phones Doctor Mayo and thanks her profusely for the wonderful advice that has produced such a tremendous result.

At the end of the conversation, however, he asks one last question: "How do I get home now, Doctor, since I'm 300 miles away?"

No one ever gives Tarzan credit for being the first vine celebrity.

Did you know people are getting paid to mention products in their Snapchat posts? That's as crazy as the discounts at Merv's Mattress and Futon Warehouse.

Jane has to move back home with her Mom after not being able to find a job after college. Jane's Mom always gets on her case, but she is also very gullible, the type who always believes rumors and conjectures and always buys into a conspiracy theory, no matter how bizarre or untruthful it may be. Many of the rumors and stories she sees are on Facebook, which she then shares and comments on with outrage: Things like "Congress is giving ISIS members a seat in the Senate" or "Solar energy panels are actually devices that are sending our personal bank info to criminals in Eastern Europe." But Jane has a brilliant idea: She will make her own website that looks like that of a professional newspaper or TV station, and then she can write articles about how tough the job market is that her Mom won't be able to help herself from sharing.

Jane starts to write a few articles with headlines like "Job market at its lowest point for post-grads in decades" that she shares on Facebook, hoping her Mom will buy into it. Her Mom, though, doesn't take the bait, saying that the articles are a bunch of baloney and that kids today are just lazy. Jane then tries making her articles a bit more salacious and tantalizing, hoping that extra edge will be the thing that gets her Mom to share. She writes one with the headline "College grads unable to find jobs after President Obama raised minimum work age to 23." She publishes it just a few minutes before their family dinner, and just like clockwork, her Mom starts ranting and raving about President Obama and how the Democrats are trying to keep graduates from working.

When she isn't busy filling out applications, Jane spends her other hours during the day writing nonsensical articles to help her get out of chores. When her Mom asks that she vacuum the house, Jane quickly writes a short article titled "Vacuum cleaner industry has deep ties to Osama Bin Laden," and she then sees her Mom throw out their family vacuum cleaner not too long after. She keeps this ruse up for several months as she looks for work while living rent-free, but doesn't expect that thousands of people will read them and then millions, with Jane collecting a nice bit of advertising revenue. No topic is too taboo: Everything from "Surgeries lead to chances of home break-ins" to "Republicans are the descendants of the Illuminati" generates massive traffic. Soon Jane is spending more time during the day on the fake articles, more than she did ever looking for a job, and then she stops looking for a job altogether.

But one day, Jane's Mom trips while carrying groceries up the stairs and breaks her hip. Jane calls 911 and rides in an ambulance with her Mom to the hospital, but her Mom refuses any painkillers or help from the paramedics, saying that she read online that morphine is known to cause mad cow disease in patients. When doctors tell her she needs to have her hip replaced, Jane's Mom rebukes their claims, referencing an article she read online that hip replacements are just procedures that fuel the black market organ trade in southeast Asia.

Jane is ravaged with guilt, her writing these articles has caused her Mom to refuse medical treatment she direly needed, and she's afraid that her stubbornness will lead to her Mom's death. Instead, Jane comes clean and tells her Mom everything, that she had written everything that got her Mom riled up. Her Mom is understandably upset, but is also impressed by the money that she earned, and ends up agreeing to the surgery.

After wishing her Mom luck as she goes into the operating room, the doctor approaches Jane with a few forms to sign. "You know, I was afraid your Mom wasn't going to make it earlier," the doctor says. "Yeah, I'm glad she finally came to her senses." "And just in the nick of time too. I read this article earlier that patients who don't jump into surgery right away are more likely to experience home break-ins."

I have divorced parents, which only means that I can't participate in Throwback Thursday. That's because I don't know who has my childhood photos and I think it would be rude if I asked the wrong parent because it would just sound like I was asking, "Hey, do you have any of those memories of that life that you didn't want to live? I was hoping to post them on the Internet and think about the good times I thought we were having."

A King enrolls his donkey in a race and wins.

The local paper reads: KING'S ASS WINS.

The king is so upset with this kind of publicity that he gives the donkey to the queen.

The local paper then reads: QUEEN HAS THE BEST ASS IN TOWN.

The king faints.

The Queen sells the donkey to a farmer for $10.

The next day, the paper reads: QUEEN SELLS HER ASS FOR $10.

The queen faints.

The next day, the King orders the Queen to buy back the donkey and set it free in jungle.

The local paper reads: QUEEN ANNOUNCES HER ASS IS FREE & WILD.

MILITARY

A soldier runs up to a nun. Out of breath he asks, "Please, may I hide under your skirt? I'll explain later." The nun agrees. A moment later, two Military Police run up and ask, "Sister, have you seen a soldier?" The nun replies, "He went that way." After the MPs run off, the soldier crawls out from under her skirt and says, "I can't thank you enough, Sister. You see, I don't want to go to Syria." The nun says, "I understand completely." The soldier adds, "I hope I'm not rude, but you have a great pair of legs!" The nun replies, "If you had looked a little higher, you would have seen a great pair of balls. I don't want to go to Syria either."

At one Army base, the annual trip to the rifle range is canceled for the second year in a row, but the semi-annual physical fitness test is still on as planned. One soldier muses, "Does it bother anyone else that the Army doesn't seem to care how well we can shoot, but they are extremely interested in how fast we can run?"

Airman Jones is assigned to the induction center, where he advises new recruits about their government benefits, especially their GI insurance. It isn't long before Captain Smith notices that Airman Jones is having a staggeringly high success rate, selling insurance to nearly 100% of the recruits he advises. Rather than ask about this, the Captain stands in the back of the room and listens to Jones' sales pitch. Jones explains the basics of the GI Insurance to the new recruits, and then says: "If you have GI Insurance and go into battle and are killed, the government has to pay $200,000 to your beneficiaries. If you don't have GI insurance, and you go into battle and get killed, the government only has to pay a maximum of $6000. Now," he concludes, "which group do you think they are going to send into battle first?"

The sergeant-major growls at the young soldier, "I didn't see you at camouflage training this morning." "Thank you very much, sir."

A crusty old Sergeant Major finds himself at a gala event, hosted by a local liberal arts college. There is no shortage of extremely young, idealistic ladies in attendance, one of whom approaches the Sergeant Major for conversation. She says, "Excuse me, Sergeant Major, but you seem to be a very serious man. Is something bothering you?" "Negative, ma'am," the Sergeant Major says, "Just serious by nature." The young lady looks at his awards and decorations and says, "It looks like you have seen a lot of action." The Sergeant Major's short reply is, "Yes, ma'am, a lot of action." The young lady, tiring of trying to start up a conversation, says, "You know, you should lighten up a little. Relax and enjoy yourself." The Sergeant Major just stares at her in his serious manner. Finally the young lady says, "You know, I hope you don't take this the wrong way, but when is the last time you had sex?" The Sergeant Major looks at her and replies, "1955." She says, "Well, there you are. You really need to chill out and quit taking everything so seriously! I mean, no sex since 1955! Isn't that a little extreme?" The Sergeant Major, glancing at his watch, says in his matter-of-fact voice, "You think so? It's only 2130 now."

General Baldwin had barely arrived in the forward area when a sniper's bullet removes a button from his shirt. He throws himself to the ground in terror. The men stand around with the greatest unconcern. The general yells at a passing sergeant: "Hey, isn't somebody going to kill that damned sniper?" The sergeant looks down at the general and replies: "I guess not, General. We're scared that if we kill him, the enemy will replace him with somebody who really knows how to shoot."

On some air bases, the Air Force is on one side of the field and civilian aircraft use the other side of the field, with the control tower in the middle. One day the tower receives a call from an aircraft asking, "What time is it?" The tower responds, "Who is calling?" The aircraft replies, "What difference does it make?" The tower replies, "It makes a lot of difference. If it is an American Airlines flight, it is 3 o'clock. If it is an Air Force plane, it is 1500 hours. If it is a Navy aircraft, it is 6 bells. If it is an Army aircraft, the big hand is on the 12 and the little hand is on the 3. If it is a Marine Corps aircraft, it's Thursday afternoon."

A young lieutenant is passed by a private, who fails to salute. The lieutenant calls him back, and says sternly: "You did not salute me. For this you will immediately salute 200 times."

At this moment the General comes up.

"What's all this?" he exclaims, seeing the poor private about to begin.

The lieutenant explains. "This ignoramus failed to salute me, and as a punishment, I am making him salute 200 times."

"Quite right," replies the General, smiling. "But do not forget, sir, that upon each occasion, you are to salute in return."

The sergeant-major has the reputation of never being at a loss for an answer. A young officer makes a bet with a brother officer that he will, in less than 24 hours, ask the sergeant-major a question that will baffle him.

The sergeant-major accompanies the young officer on his rounds, in the course of which the cook-house is inspected. Pointing to a large copper kettle of water just commencing to boil, the officer asks: "Why does that water only boil round the edges of the copper and not in the center?"

"The water round the edge, sir," replies the veteran, "is for the men on guard; they have their breakfast half an hour before the remainder of the company."

T he officer of the day, during his tour of duty, pauses to question a sentry who is a new recruit.

"If you should see an armed party approaching, what would you do?" asks the officer.

"Turn out the guard, sir."

"Very well. Suppose you saw a battleship coming across the parade ground, what would you do?"

"Report to the hospital for examination, sir," is the prompt reply.

P rivate Simpkins has returned from the front, to find that his girl has been walking out with another young man, and naturally he asks her to explain her frequent promenades in the town with the gentleman.

"Well, dear," she replies, "it is only kindness on his part. He just took me down every day to the library to see if you were killed."

A n officer on board a warship is drilling his men.

"I want every man to lie on his back, put his legs in the air, and move them as if he were riding a bicycle," he explains. "Now commence."

After a short effort, one of the men stops.

"Why have you stopped, Murphy?" asks the officer.

"If ye plaze, sir," Murphy says, "Oi'm coasting."

During a dust storm at one of the army camps, a recruit seeks shelter in the cook's tent.

"If you put the lid on that camp kettle, you would not get so much dust in your soup."

"See here, my lad, your business is to serve your country."

"Yes," replies the recruit, "but not to eat it."

NEW YORK

Here's to New Yorkers for being tolerant of everyone except anyone directly in their path.

A New York City birthday party: Where you are put on a "guest list" of a bar you usually frequent anyway.

"How do I get to Carnegie Hall?" "Practice, practice!"

Four guys are walking down the street: A Saudi, a Russian, a North Korean, and a New Yorker.

A reporter comes running up and says, "Excuse me, what is your opinion about the meat shortage?"

The Saudi says, "What's a shortage?"

The Russian says, "What's meat?"

The North Korean says, "What's an opinion?"

The New Yorker says, "Excuse me? What's 'Excuse me'?"

CALIFORNIA

What's the only thing that grows in Los Angeles?

The crime rate

What happens when blondes move from Oregon to California?

Both states become smarter!

A Texan, a Californian, and a Nevadan are out riding their horses. The Texan pulls out an expensive bottle of whiskey, takes a long draught, then another, and then suddenly throws it into the air, pulls out his gun and shoots the bottle in midair.

The Californian looks at the Texan and says, "What are you doing? That was a perfectly good bottle of whiskey!!" The Texan replies, "In Texas, there's plenty of whiskey and bottles are cheap."

A while later, not wanted to be outdone, the Californian pulls out a bottle of Champagne, takes a few sips, throws the half full Champagne bottle into the air, pulls out his gun, and shoots it in midair.

The Nevadan can't believe this and says, "What the heck did you that for? That was an expensive bottle of Champagne!!" The Californian replies, "In California, there is plenty of Champagne and bottles are cheap."

A while later, the Nevadan pulls out a bottle of Sierra Nevada Pale Ale. He opens it, takes a sip, takes another sip, then chugs the rest. He then puts the bottle back in his saddlebag, pulls out his gun, turns, and shoots the Californian.

The shocked Texan says, "Why in the hell did you do that?"

The Nevadan replies, "Well, in Nevada, we have plenty of Californians and bottles are worth a nickel."

Where in L.A. can a deer hunter find does in season year round?

Venison Beach

How many Californians does it take to screw in a light bulb?

Eleven. One to change it and 10 to follow the trend.

TEXAS

What's the real difference between a New York Zoo and a Texas Zoo?

In a zoo in New York, the plaque will have the name of the animal as well as information about it. In Texas, the plaque at the zoo has the name of the animal and then will have the name of the animal and the recipe.

Why did Texas change their field from grass to artificial turf?

To keep the Longhorns cheerleaders from grazing the field at halftime

What did the Texas female say after sex?

Get off me, Dad, you're crushing my smokes!

Why is Texas officially changing its name to Tex?

Because the ass is in Washington

FLORIDA

A man walks into a Florida bar with his alligator and asks the bartender:
"Do you serve lawyers here?"
"Sure."
"Good. One beer for me and a lawyer for my alligator."

ITALIAN

Why did the Mafia cross the road?

Fugeddaboudit

What's a four-letter word in Italian for goodbye?

"BANG"!

Why are Polish jokes so short?

So the Italians can understand them.

Why did Pope Francis have reservations about accepting his papacy?

It meant moving to an Italian neighborhood!

What does FIAT stand for?

Frenzied Italian At Traffic-lights

How does an Italian get into an honest business?

Usually through the skylight

How do Italian girls shave their legs?

They lie down outside and have someone mow them.

What do you get when you cross an Italian and a Polish person?

A guy who makes you an offer you can't understand

How is the Italian version of Christmas different?
One Mary, one Jesus, and 32 Wise Guys

A wealthy American man has been having an affair with an Italian woman for a few years. One night, during a rendezvous, she confides to him that she is pregnant. Not wanting to ruin his reputation or his marriage, he tells her he will pay her a large sum of money if she will go to Italy to have the child.

If she stays there, he will also provide child support until the child turns 18.

She agrees, but wonders how he will know when the baby is born.

To keep it discreet, he tells her to mail him a postcard, and write "Spaghetti" on the back. He will then arrange for child support.

One day, about nine months later, he comes home to his confused wife.

"Honey," she says, "you received a very strange postcard today."

"Oh, just give it to me and I'll explain it later," he says.

The wife does as she is asked, and she watches as her husband reads the card, turns white and faints.

On the card is written: "Spaghetti, spaghetti, spaghetti. Two with meatballs, one without."

An old Italian woman is riding the elevator in a very lavish New York City office building. A young and beautiful woman gets into the elevator and, smelling like expensive perfume, turns to the old Italian woman and says arrogantly, "Giorgio Beverly Hills, $100 an ounce!"

The next young and beautiful woman gets on the elevator and also very arrogantly turns to the old Italian woman and says, "Chanel No. 5, $150 an ounce!"

About three floors later, the old Italian woman has reached her destination and is about to get off the elevator. Before she leaves, looks both beautiful women in the eye, she bends over, and passes gas.

"Broccoli! Forty-nine cents a pound."

What language do the Vatican Police speak?

Pig Latin

GERMAN

Happiness is a German cook who doesn't.

Why wasn't Jesus born in Germany?

God couldn't find three wise men or a virgin.

Did you hear about the winner of the German beauty contest?

Me neither.

What do you call a Blind German?

A Not See

A Dutchman and German man sit next to each other on an airplane. The German takes off his shoes and then stands up to get a drink. He asks the Dutchman if he'd like him to fetch him a cola too. The Dutchman says that would be very nice. While the German man is getting the drinks, the Dutchman spits into the German man's shoes. Toward the end of the flight, the German put his shoes back on and then realizes what the Dutchman had done. He says to him, "Why do we always have this hostility between our two countries? Spitting in one another's shoes and weeing in each other's drinks!"

IRISH

An Englishman, an Irishman, and a Scotsman are confessing their secret vices to each other. "I'm a terrible gambler," says the

Englishman.

"I'm a terrible drinker," says the Scotsman.

"My vice is much less serious," says the Irishman, "I just like to tell tales about my friends."

How would you recognize an Irish pirate?

He's the one with patches over both eyes.

Did you hear about the Irish woman with five legs?

Her knickers fitted her like a glove.

What's the difference between God and Bono?

God doesn't wander around Dublin thinking he's Bono.

One night, Mrs. McMillen answers the door to see her husband's best friend, Paddy, standing on the doorstep.

"Hello Paddy, but where is my husband? He went with you to the beer factory!"

Paddy shakes his head. "Ah, Mrs. McMillen, there was a terrible accident at the beer factory: Your husband fell into a vat of Guinness stout and drowned!"

Mrs. McMillen starts crying. "Oh don't tell me that, did he at least go quickly?"

Paddy shakes his head. "Not really. He got out three times to pee!"

A Texan walks into a pub in Ireland and clears his voice to the crowd of drinkers. He says, "I hear you Irish are a bunch of hard drinkers. I'll give

$500 American dollars to anybody in here who can drink 10 pints of Guinness back-to-back."

The room is quiet and no one takes up the Texan's offer. One man even leaves. Thirty minutes later, the same gentleman who left shows back up and taps the Texan on the shoulder. "Is your bet still good?" asks the Irishman.

The Texan says yes and asks the bartender to line up 10 pints of Guinness. Immediately the Irishman tears into all 10 of the pint glasses drinking them all back-to-back. The other pub patrons cheer as the Texan sits in amazement.

The Texan gives the Irishman the $500 and says, "If ya don't mind me askin', where did you go for that 30 minutes you were gone?"

The Irishman replies, "Oh, I had to go to the pub down the street to see if I could do it first."

A n Englishman, a Frenchman, and an Irishman are in a pub talking about their children.

"My son was born on St George's Day," remarks the Englishman, "So we obviously decided to call him George."

"That's a real coincidence," observes the Frenchman. "My daughter was born on Valentine's Day, so we decided to call her Valentine."

"That's really incredible," drawled the Irishman, "Exactly the same thing happened with my son Pancake!"

AUSTRALIAN

What is the Australian animal that most resembles the Australian male?

The wombat, because he eats, roots, and leaves.

What's an Australian's idea of foreplay?

You awake?

What's a Tasmanian's idea of foreplay?

You awake, mum?

An Australian is someone who thinks that the three major political parties in Australia are Labor, Liberal, and Cocktail.

What's the difference between an Australian and a computer?

You only have to punch information into a computer once.

Why do so many Australian men suffer premature ejaculation?

Because they have to rush back to the pub to tell their mates what happened!

A Kiwi and an Aussie go fishing one afternoon and decide to have a couple of cold beers. After a while, the Aussie says to the Kiwi, "If I were to sneak over to your house and make wild passionate love to your wife while you are at work, and she gets pregnant and has a baby, would that make us related?" The Kiwi after a great deal of thought, says, "Well, I don't know about related, but it sure would make us even."

Three Aussie guys, Shane, Ricky and Jeff, are working on a high-rise building project in Wagga Wagga. Unfortunately, Shane falls off the scaffolding and is killed instantly.

As the ambulance takes the body away, Ricky says, "Someone should go and tell his wife."

Jeff says, "OK, I'm pretty good at that sensitive stuff, I'll do it."

Two hours later, he comes back carrying a case of Foster's.

Ricky says, "Where did you get that, Jeff?"

"Shane's wife gave it to me."

Ricky continues, "That's unbelievable! You told the lady her husband is dead and she gave you beer?"

"Well not exactly," Jeff says. "When she answered the door, I said to her, 'You must be Shane's widow.' She says, 'No, I'm not his widow.' And I said, 'I'll bet you a case of Foster's you are.'"

SCOTTISH

An Englishman, Irishman, Welshman, Scotsman are captured while fighting in a far-off foreign land, and the leader of the captors says, "We're going to line you up in front of a firing squad and shoot you all in turn. But first, you each can make a final wish."

The Englishman responds, "I'd like to hear 'God Save The Queen' just one more time to remind me of the old country, played by the London Boys Choir. With Morris Dancers dancing to the tune."

The Irishman replies, "I'd like to hear 'Danny Boy' just one more time to remind me of the old country, sung in the style of Daniel O'Donnell, with Riverdance dancers skipping gaily to the tune."

The Welshman answers, "I'd like to hear 'Men Of Harlech' just one more time to remind me of the old country, sung as if by the Treorchy Male Voice Choir."

The Scotsman says quickly, "I'd like to be shot first."

BRITAIN

Ronald, an Englishman, goes to Spain on a fishing trip. While there, Ronald hires a Spanish guide to help him find the best fishing spots. Since Roland is learning Spanish, he asks the guide to speak to him in Spanish and to correct any mistakes of usage.

Together they are hiking on a mountain trail when a very large, purple and blue fly crosses their path. The Englishmen points at the insect with his fishing rod, and announces, "Mira el mosca."

The guide, sensing a teaching opportunity to teach Ronald, replies, "No, señor, 'la mosca' es feminina."

Ronald looks at him in amazement, then back at the fly, and then says, "Good heavens! You must have incredibly good eyesight."

One day an Englishman, a Scotsman, and an Irishman walk into a pub together. They each buy a pint of Guinness. Just as they're about to enjoy their creamy beverage, a fly lands in each of their pints and are stuck in the thick head. The Englishman pushes his beer away in disgust. The Scotsman fishes the fly out of his beer and continues drinking it as if nothing has happened. The Irishman, too, picks the fly out of his drink, holds it out over the beer, and starts yelling, "Spit it out! Spit it out, you bastard!"

Why did the Siamese twins move to England?

So the other one could drive!

What's the difference between England and a tea bag?

The tea bag stays in the cup longer.

What does the Loch Ness monster eat?

Fish and ships

Why were the two whores travelling in London pissed off?

Because they found out that Big Ben is a clock!

What time was it when the monster ate the British prime minister?

Eight P.M.

An English man, Irishman, and a Scot are sitting in a pub full of people. The Englishman says, "The pubs in England are the best. You can buy one drink and get a second one free." Everyone in the pub agrees and gives a big cheer. The Scot says,"Yeah, that's quite good, but in Scotland, you can buy one drink and get another two for free." Again, the crowd in the pub gives a big cheer. The Irishman says, "Your two pubs are good, but they're not as good as the ones in Ireland. In Ireland you can buy one pint, get another three for free, and then get taken into the backroom for a shag."

The English says, "WOW! Did that happen to you?" and the Irishman replies, "No, but it happened to my sister."

MEXICO

What do you call a Mexican with a rubber toe?

Roberto

Did you hear about the Mexican racist?

He joined the que que que.

A big tough Mexican man marries a good-looking Mexican lady and after the wedding, lays down the following rules:

"Honey, I'll be home when I want, if I want and at what time I want, and I don't expect any hassle from you. I expect a great dinner to be on the table unless I tell you otherwise. I'll go hunting, fishing, boozing, and card-playing when I want with my old buddies and don't you give me a hard time about it. Those are my rules! Any comments?"

His lovely new bride says, "No, that's fine with me. Just understand that there will be sex here at eight o'clock every night, whether you're here or not."

Two entrepreneurs, Jack and John, decide to start a bungee-jumping business south of the border. They go to Casa del Sol, Mexico, build a huge platform, and open for business. By noon the first day, they both notice that while everyone is watching, no one is buying tickets. Jack tells John to go up and jump, so everyone could see how much fun it is, and then they will buy tickets and try it. John jumps, almost reaches the ground, and springs back up. Jack sees that his shirt is torn and his hair is mussed. John goes down again and springs back up. This time he has several bruises and his clothes are ripped to shreds. The third time down and back up, he has several open wounds, a broken arm, and is bruised over most of his body. Jack quickly raises John to the platform and asks him what in the world is going on. John replies, "I'm not sure. Do you know what 'piñata' means?"

CANADIAN

A Canadian is walking down the street with a case of beer under his arm. His friend Doug stops him and asks, "Hey Bob! Whatcha get the case of beer for?"

"I got it for my wife, eh?" answers Bob.

"Oh!" exclaims Doug. "Good trade."

An American, a Scot, and a Canadian are in a terrible car accident. They are all brought to the same emergency room, but all three of them die before they arrive. Just as they were about to put the toe tag on the American, he stirs and opens his eyes. Astonished, the doctors and nurses present ask him what happened.

"Well," says the American, "I remember the crash, and then there was a beautiful light, and then the Canadian and the Scot and I were standing at the gates of heaven. St. Peter approached us and said that we were all too young to die, and that for a donation of $50, we could return to the earth. So of course I pulled out my wallet and gave him the $50, and the next thing I knew I was back here."

"That's amazing!" says one of the doctors, "but what happened to the other two?"

"Last I saw them," replies the American, "the Scot is haggling over the price and the Canadian is waiting for the government to pay for his."

Three men are traveling in Europe and happen to meet at a bar in London. One man is from England, one is from France and one is from Canada. They get acquainted and start talking about their problems with their wives.

The guy from England begins by saying: "I told my wife in no uncertain terms that from now on she would have to do the cooking. Well the first day after I told her, I saw nothing. The second day I saw nothing. But on the third day when I came home from work, the table was set, a wonderful dinner was prepared with wine, and even dessert."

Then the man from France speaks up: "I sat my wife down and told her, that from now on she would have to do all the shopping, and also do the cleaning. The first day I saw nothing. The second day I saw nothing. But on the third day when I came home, the whole house was spotless, and in the pantry, the shelves were filled with groceries."

The fellow from Canada is married to an enlightened woman from the prairies. He sits up straight on the bar stool, pushes out his chest and says: "I gave my wife a stern look and told her, that from now on she would have to do the cooking, shopping and housecleaning. Well the first day I saw nothing. The second day I still saw nothing. But on the third day I could see a little bit out of my left eye..."

A Canadian couple is strolling through Hyde Park in London and sits down on a bench next to an elderly Briton.

The Brit notices their lapel pins sporting the Canadian flag and, to make conversation, says, "Judging by your pins, you must be Canadians."

"Indeed we are," replies the Canadian gentleman.

"I hope you won't mind my asking," says the Brit, "but what do the two red bars on your flag represent?"

"Well," replies the Canadian gentleman, "one of the bars stands for the courage and hardiness of our people in settling the cold expanses and broad prairies of our country. The other is for the honesty and integrity for which Canadians are known."

The Brit mulls this over and nods. Having poor eyesight at his advanced age, and not being familiar with maple leaves, he then asks, "And what's that six-pointed item in the middle of your flag?"

"Oh, that's to remind us of the six words of our national motto," the Canadian lady pipes up.

The Brit then asks, "And what are those six words?"

The Canadian smiles and replies, "They are 'Don't blame us: We're not Americans.'"

FRENCH

D uring one of the many wars that the French and the British fought and the French usually lost, the French just happen to capture a British Major. An officer brings the Major to the French general for interrogation. The French general begins ridiculing the Major for wearing "that stupid red tunic." The French general says, "Why do you wear that red uniform, it makes it easy for us to shoot you." The British major replies, "If I do get wounded, the blood will not show, and my soldiers will not get scared." The French general says, "That is a very good idea," Then he turns to his orderly and says, "From now on, all French officers will wear brown pants."

Why did the French send Lady Liberty to America?

A. They had no use for her anyway.

B. They didn't want the tired, poor, huddled masses to come to France, for God's sake.

C. She wouldn't put out.

D. To be a constant reminder of the help they gave to defeat the British. As if WE'RE the ones with the short memory.

E. They wanted to remind future generations that they once had the balls to do what is right.

F. All of the above.

How do you keep a French person from crashing your party?

Put a sign up that says "no nudity"

Why do French people eat snails?

Because they don't like fast food!

What is the French national anthem?

I give up.

What's the difference between Frenchmen and toast?

You can make soldiers out of toast.

RUSSIAN

A large group of Russian soldiers in the border area in 1939 are moving down a road when they hear a voice call from behind a small hill: "One Finnish soldier is better than 10 Russians!" The Russian commander quickly orders 10 of his best men over the hill, whereupon a gun battle breaks out and continues for a few minutes, then silence. The voice once again calls out: "One Finn is better than 100 Russians!" Furious, the Russian commander sends his next best 100 troops over the hill and instantly a huge gun fight commences. After 10 minutes of battle, again silence. The calm Finnish voice calls out again: "One Finn is better than 1,000 Russians!" The enraged Russian commander musters 1,000 fighters and sends them to the other side of the hill. Rifle fire, machine guns, grenades, rockets and cannon fire ring out as a terrible battle is fought...then silence. Eventually one badly wounded Russian fighter crawls back over the hill and with his dying words tells his commander, "Don't send any more men...it's a trap! There's two of them!"

A Frenchman, an Englishman, and a Russian are admiring a painting of Adam and Eve in the Garden of Eden.

The Frenchman says, "They must be French, they're naked and they're eating fruit."

The Englishman replies with, "Clearly they're English. Observe how politely the man is offering the woman the fruit."

The Russian then notes, "They are Russian of course. They have nothing to wear, nothing to eat, and they think they are in paradise."

Stalin is giving a long speech at an event, naturally in front of a huge audience. While he's in full flow, somebody near the front of the hall sneezes. Stalin stops and surveys the crowd.

"Who sneezed?" he asks.

Deathly silence.

"I repeat," says Stalin, "who sneezed?"

Not a peep.

"Very well," says Stalin. "First row, stand up!" Everyone in the first row stands up. "Guards! Open fire!"

A few seconds later, the entire first row of the audience is lying in bloody heaps on the ground.

"Now, who sneezed?" Still not a whimper. "Second row, stand up! Guards! Open fire!" The second row writhes and breathes its last.

"Now, comrades: Who sneezed?" Absolute silence. "Third row! Stand up! Guards! Op...."

"Wait! Wait!" From the sixth row a man rises, shaking so hard with fear that he can barely stay on his legs. "Please! Comrade Stalin! It was me. I sneezed."

Stalin fixes his eye on the wretch. The entire audience watches, paralyzed.

"You sneezed?"

"Yes, Comrade Stalin, yes. It is me."

"Bless you, comrade!"

A Russian party official arrives late at night to his hotel, in Russia. He is not surprised to find that his reservation has been mislaid but he is more than a little peeved that his status in the party isn't enough to get him a good room anyway. However, the clerk insists, the only bed they have left is the fourth bunk in a four-bed dorm: He'll have to make do with that. The Russian grumbles but eventually he picks up his suitcase and heads for the dorm. On his way, he meets a chambermaid and, thinking he might as well try to make friends with his room-mates, he asks her to bring them four cups of tea.

As he enters the dorm, he finds that the other three guests are Polish. They are having a fairly wild party and they're very drunk. They also ignore him from the moment he enters. After sitting there for several minutes, he realizes he can't stand them anymore and decides to pull a joke on them. He stands up, grasps a floor lamp and speaking into the light bulb as if it were a microphone he says: "Comrade Colonel, we would like four cups of tea to our room immediately!"

The Poles stare at him in disbelief, which turns to horror as the chambermaid knocks on the door and delivers the tea a few minutes later. In about 30 seconds the Poles have all packed their bags and fled the hotel. Our Russian gets the entire room to himself. He sleeps very soundly. The next morning, however, as he's checking out and is about to leave, the desk clerk calls after him: "By the way, Sir, the Comrade Colonel says to tell you he appreciated your little joke last night!"

What is 150 yards long and eats potatoes?

A Moscow queue waiting to buy meat

A new Russian comes in to buy a car. He tells the salesman he wants a grey BMW. The salesman finds him exactly the car he wants, and the man pays cash for it. As he is about to leave, the salesman asks him, "Didn't you buy a car just like this from us last week?" "Oh, yes, I did," replies the new Russian, "but the ashtray got full."

ANTI-JOKES

A dyslexic man walks into a bra...

If you die and have five cents in your pocket, does the toast still land jelly side down?

Roses are red

Violets are blue

I have a gun

Get in the van

What's green and has wheels?

Grass. I lied about the wheels.

What's brown and sticky?

A stick!

What's red and smells like blue paint?

Red paint

What did one French man say to the other?

I don't know, I don't speak French.

Why is six afraid of seven?

Because seven is a registered six-offender.

What do you call a Hispanic woman flying a plane?

A pilot, you fucking racist!

A guy walks into a bar…and he breaks down in tears over how his crippling alcoholism has consumed his life.

Knock Knock!

Who's there?

Banana.

Banana who?

Knock Knock!

Who's there?

Banana.

Banana who?

Knock Knock!

Who's there?

Orange.

Orange who?

Orange you glad I didn't say juvenile diabetes? Because that's not funny.

Chuck Norris walks into a bar… and is greeted with smiles and handshakes, because he's a respected actor.

What's the difference between a blonde and a tennis ball?

A blonde is a human being and a tennis ball is used in a recreational sport.

What do you tell a woman with two black eyes?

"I'm concerned for your safety in this relationship and think you should seek help."

Knock Knock!

Who's there?

Dave.

Dave who?

Dave proceeds to break into tears, as his grandmother's Alzheimer's has progressed to the point where she can no longer remember him.

There's an Irishman, a homosexual, and a Jew standing at a bar. What a fine example of an integrated community.

A duck walks into a bar, the bartender says, "What'll it be?" The duck doesn't say anything because it's a duck.

Haikus are easy,

But sometimes they don't make sense.

Refrigerator.

Roses are grey. Violets are grey. I am a dog.

I like my coffee like my women…**without a penis.**

A horse walks into a bar and the bartender asks "Why the long face?" The horse replies, "My wife is dying of terminal cancer."

Why are black people so good at basketball?

Dedication and hard work

What did the farmer say when he lost his tractor?

Where's my tractor?

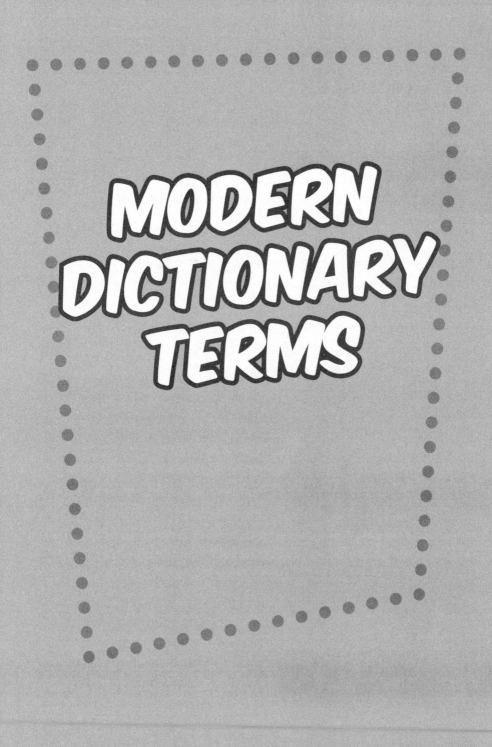

MODERN DICTIONARY TERMS

Perennial one-upper: A person who tries to supersede any accomplishment you make or story you tell with a superior accomplishment or story they made in order to gain attention

While Janet is excited to talk about her recent week-long trip to London with her co-worker, Gloria, a perennial one-upper, says you can really only see the city when you've lived there for a year, like she did.

Tenuis peni: The term for a person who owns an exotic sports car and drives aggressively without regard for safety

Bernie wasn't sure if the driver of the Maserati next to him was a tenuis peni, but when he hit the gas pedal and zoomed to 60 in a school zone with the stereo blasting, his belief was confirmed.

Yelp abuser: A person who leaves lengthy and erroneously inaccurate reviews of businesses on Yelp, despite it being their fault for the infraction they caused in the first place

In her eyes, it didn't matter that Jennifer wasn't at home to accept her delivery in the scheduled time frame. She is a Yelp abuser, and left a scathing review on IKEA's page on how "poorly" she was treated.

Perennially late texter: A person who is always on their phone whenever you see them, but takes three hours to respond to texts whenever you try to reach out to them.

Chris says he didn't have his phone on him when Bill texted him three hours earlier. Bill knew that is a lie, as Chris, a perennially late texter, can't go five minutes without looking at Instagram.

The third wheel: The third car that carelessly turns left after a light turns red

The drivers on the other side of the street were prepared for the red Prius and blue Sonata to turn left just after the light turned red. But when the yellow Camry, followed after them, it became a much disliked third wheel.

Fått nog: The immense, painful frustration one feels when trying to assemble furniture purchased by IKEA

Despite following all of the necessary instructions and keeping his supplies in a tidy place, Mark's Swedish cabinet fell apart on the floor. He is furious: He is Fått nog.

Telemarketer-nesis: The gifted ability to frustrate a telemarketer so much that you can physically hear their anger rising through the volume of their keyboard clicks.

AT&T didn't listen to Sharon's first three requests to stop calling her. So she employed some bona fide telemarketer-nesis by talking about her family for 30 minutes as the AT&T rep was forced to listen.

Unparental-like conduct: A parent who becomes overly invested in the outcome of a youth sports game, with the penalty for such behavior being inversely related to age of children participating in the sport

Roxanne's complaints at the hockey game would have been understandable if the players were teens or young adults. But since the kids participating were only five years old, her screaming obscenities and flipping the bird at referees was a gross display of unparental-like conduct.

Eater's remorse: The empty feeling of receiving the wrong entrée at a restaurant but not having enough time to have the staff fix it and get what you originally ordered

Peter wasn't a big fan of tuna or mayonnaise. But with only 10 minutes to eat lunch before he had to return back to work, he sorrowfully ate the sandwich with eater's remorse.

Crying conspiracy: A belief held by some parents that a baby only cries when it knows you're out of the room and can annoy you most

Even after spending three hours in the baby's room without hearing a peep, when the baby started crying the moment they walked down the hall, they couldn't help believe that it was a crying conspiracy.

Parental misguidance: When a parent provides unsolicited child-rearing advice to another, despite serious qualms about their own ability to raise a child

Even though his son had already been arrested three times before the age of 15, that didn't stop Ziggy from giving parental misguidance to other fathers on the proper way to raise their kids.

Meter vulture: A police officer who lurks around the corner from a parking meter, waiting until the meter is officially one minute past expiration date to issue a ticket

It was literally just two minutes after two when Yoni got back to his car, but it didn't matter. Officer McHewitt is a meter vulture and happily gave the young teen a ticket.

Parallel Parkour: The extensive lengths one goes through to fit into a tight parking spot in a busy part of town

It doesn't matter that she has less than an inch of room on either side of her car. It is impossible to find an open spot in San Francisco during rush hour and Bethany is happy to spend 30 minutes to parallel parkour.

Miracle gallon: When you only have a gallon of gas left in you tank but it lasts for a hundred miles

Proper usage: "Thank be to the lord in heaven for blessing our Hyundai Elantra with a miracle gallon."

Sunk soda cost: When you repeatedly purchase Cokes from the vending machine even though you could save money by purchasing a 12-pack from the grocery store

Miranda didn't mind paying for the sunk soda cost of her Diet Dr. Pepper, as driving to the store on her miracle gallon would be unnecessary.

Netflixistential crisis: The feeling of dread and emptiness that consumes one's soul when after hours of binging, there is nothing suitable to watch on Netflix

The thought of re-watching "The Michael Scott Paper Company" episode of The Office *for the 15th time put Peter into a debilitating Netflixistential crisis.*

Couch doubloons: The hidden treasure one discovers underneath their sofa or bed when moving

Even though they could no longer afford the rent, Sean and Steven took solace in the quarters, lighters, and other couch doubloons they could now take to their new apartment.

Size X-asperated: When folding a T-shirt or button down shirt during laundry, and after becoming too tired, throwing a wrinkled shirt into a drawer instead of ironing it out

Working off only two hours sleep, Shelly didn't care that the shirt was from the fancy department store at the mall, she just settled on it being Size X-asperated so laundry could be over with.

Broken bromance: When your male best friend starts dating someone new and they don't have as much time to hang out with you anymore

Tommy and James had gone to every minor league wrestling tournament in the K-Mart parking lot for the past six years. But when James started dating the girl with the afternoon shift from work, Tommy found himself with a broken bromance.

Uberlemma: When you had an ok but not great but not awful Uber ride and you're deliberating whether to leave a tip

Jeff is in an Uberlemma if the five-minute ride to the concert venue really called for a $1 tip.

Neighbor theater: When the walls are thin enough at your apartment that you can hear your neighbor talking but too thick that you can't understand what they're saying, so you concoct a make-believe theater show that they're unwittingly the star of

After the couple next door got in a fight late at night on Tuesday, Mark dealt with his insomnia through an entertaining round of Neighbor Theater.

Trainxiety: The dread one feels when riding crowded public transportation in a major city and accidentally makes eye contact more than one time with another passenger

Shirley is dealing with a bout of tranxiety, worried that she might have creeped out the handsome man who is sitting in her immediate view.

Passive honk: When driving and a car in front of you does something to annoy you, but you're too non-confrontational and passive aggressive to do anything about it, so when they're finally turning before a light turns red, you let out a honk before they continue driving

Worried about any potential harm he or his car may incur through direct communication, Bill let out his frustration at the red Toyota Prius that cut him off with a passive honk before they jumped on the freeway.

The long walk home: The awkward moment when working at an office and having to walk down a long hallway with another person walking directly from the opposite side, not knowing the proper time to wave, say Hi, or even just to ignore them entirely

After the closer conference room had already been booked by the data team, Kelly reluctantly took the long walk home to the other one down the hall, not knowing if she should say anything to the new guy in I.T. who was walking from the other side.

Misnamer: When you are introduced to someone but forget their name and too much time passes that you can't ask them again what their name is without looking like an asshole

Justin purposely took the longer route to his house so he didn't have to get into a misnamer situation with his friendly neighbor who is maybe named Sara or Rachel.

Acabarassment: When another driver catches you singing along loudly to your car radio, causing you to feel embarrassed

Even though Whitney Houston is one of the most popular singers of all time, Tina still felt a bit of acabarassment when she was caught belting the lyrics to "How Will I Know" when driving on the highway.

Seal the deal: After feeling on the fence about a potential romantic prospect, the act they do that causes you to immediately lose all interest in them

Bethany is wondering if she should stick it out with Brandon. But when she saw him tip less than 10 percent on dinner, he sealed the deal.

The stain that shall not be named: When you spill food on a couch cushion and you flip it over to hide the stain, desperately hoping that you don't stain the other side

It had been a year since he spilled guacamole on the hand-me-down white sofa his older brother gave him, with the stain that shall not be named still lurking in his memory.

Stream-scluded: When you feel left out when a group of friends or co-workers is talking about a popular new television show and you haven't yet seen it

Even if she watched the first three seasons over the weekend, Emily still would not be able to catch up on enough Game of Thrones without her feeling stream-scluded from the rest of the finance department.

Growing pains: When you become a fan of a children's television show but are afraid to let your adult friends know about it without being judged

Victor is enamored with the rich storylines and developed characters on Yo Gabba Gabba, *but is afraid to reveal his passion to the show to those around him.*

Fauxdience: The group one joins when they lie about seeing a movie or TV show, just to be part of the conversation or not have to deal with questions on why they haven't seen it

Not wanting to answer questions why she hadn't seen it yet, Helen joined the fauxidence when she says she loved La La Land, even though she is waiting to watch it online for cheap.

Instagraminclined: Performing some sort of tedious activity just to share on social media

Even though Chester had no appetite and little time to eat teriyaki chicken

tacos, his desire to receive 30+ likes on social media Instagraminclined him to complete the chore.

Timeline cleaning: When you share something on Facebook but don't receive any likes or comments, prompting you to quickly delete it

Although Gerald thought his friends would love the video of a dog twerking, he promptly deleted it after only his Mom liked the video after an hour.

Like of shame: When you're perusing through an old flame's Facebook pictures and accidentally like a photo they posted years ago

Francis hid underneath his blankets after discovering he like of shamed Tarah's picture from Puerto Vallarta three years ago.

Salmonellottery: When you eat meat or food from your refrigerator that possibly is expired because you don't want to go to the store

Not wanting to sit in his car for 15 minutes, Tony took a salmonellottery when cooked the week-old leftover chicken from Chili's.

Quick cycle: Spraying down a pair of old jeans with cologne or perfume because you haven't been able to do laundry that week

Ralph Lauren Polo Blue served as a great quick cycle to Mike's dungarees.

Lunch plus one: When you go with a group of friends or co-workers to lunch, and another acquaintance invites themselves

Despite their best efforts to not be seen leaving the office, Rachel still spotted the group as they got into their car, becoming their lunch plus one.

Zero fun game: When two friends know that they lied to each other about their weekend plans

Bert says he had to wash his hair, and Lance says he needed to do homework. But when they later saw pictures of each other on Facebook at different parties, their friendship quickly became a zero fun game.

Street lurker: When you're walking behind someone at night and purposely turn down a street off your path because you don't want to make them feel like you're following them

John street lurked a quarter mile down La Cienaga before returning back to Wilshire so the person in front of him wouldn't feel uncomfortable.

Minor deposit: When you deposit less than $5 of cash to your checking account so you can be at the proper balance to withdraw $20

With pay day three days away, Gordon had to make a minor deposit to hold him over.

Testy taster: A person who samples too much at a fast food restaurant without realizing there's a long line behind them

15 people were now waiting in line at Panda Express while the testy taster sampled the Szechuan beef.

High Schaudenfriend: The joy one receives when Facebook stalking an enemy or bully from high school and seeing how their life turned out

Even though Kathy had been the bane of her existence during senior year, Teresa felt high schaudenfriend when she saw Kathy had been arrested for drunk and disorderly conduct.

P.T.A-hole: A parent on the P.T.A. who makes all other Mom's and Dad's lives a living hell

Organizing the second grade bake sale should have been a relatively simple task, but the P.T.A-hole turned it into a three-hour-long ordeal.

Grocery glare: The judgment a grocery store clerk gives at the items you're checking out

He didn't plan to do his full grocery shopping until Sunday, but Alex still incited a few grocery glares over his purchase of a big tub of Goldfish crackers and a $5 bottle of wine.

Sweater rental: Purchasing a high end piece of clothing but keeping the tag intact so one can return it later and get their money back

Fiona loved her cardigan from Nordstrom, but it is only a sweater rental, and she had to keep it clean for two more weeks if she wanted her money back.

Virtual solo: When at a concert and one spends more time on their phone recording themselves at the concert than actually watching the band perform

Even though tickets were $100 at the cheapest, every audience member at the Taylor Swift concert is taking their own virtual solo.

Not-so-silent snacking: When a person is in a quiet area but can't help themselves from snacking on something loud and obnoxious

Just as Justin was trying to concentrate on writing this example, the not-so-silent snacking of Funyuns by another library peer continue to throw him off.

En-car: When one arrives at their destination but spends an additional amount of time in their car so they can finish listening to their song

Even though it is crucial they get inside the movie theater to get a good seat, Mike and Miranda took an en-car so they could listen to the guitar solo on "Go Your Own Way."

Gift of laziness: When it's abundantly clear that a gift for a holiday or birthday is purchased immediately before the event took place

Even though he had an entire month to prepare for Christmas, that didn't top Jim from doing a gift of laziness and buying a $20 gas station gift card.

Social media isolation: The lengths one goes to avoid conversation about any pop culture item that they haven't been able to catch up on yet

Jennifer went to great social media isolation lengths when she refused to leave her home or go on her computer until she got a chance to watch the new Star Wars movie.

Death-like: The event when stalking somebody's photos on Facebook or Instagram and you accidentally click like on an image from years ago.

Mark couldn't even make eye contact with Elouise after death-liking a 2007 photo of her in a bikini by the beach.

TECHNOLOGY

How many programmers does it take to screw in a light bulb?

None, that's a hardware problem.

A 12-year-old child named Dan is at home playing video games in the afternoon while his Dad is on the family computer, finishing some last minute business before leaving for work. Usually when the child uses the computer, there are strict parental controls stopping him from looking at anything lewd. But his Dad is in a hurry and left his profile open before rushing out the door.

Without either of his parents returning home for the next couple of hours, Dan has the opportunity to look at whatever he wants. He hops on the computer, goes to Google and types in naked ladies. Suddenly, dozens of pictures appear in the search results area. Dan then types in every possible thing that comes to his young imagination. As he is searching, the garage door unexpectedly opens and Dan hears the unpleasant sound of his Mom's Toyota Camry pulling into the garage. Dan panics and tries to close all the images, but he has too many windows open on the desktop, causing the computer to freeze. His Mom walks inside and Dan turns off the monitor and runs to his room.

Dan is terrified. He listened to his Mom's footsteps as she walks to the computer and turns on the monitor. Suddenly there is silence, he knows he had been caught. "Dan, come down here right now!"

Dan trudges downstairs, ready for the yelling of a lifetime. He approaches his Mom with his head down low, trying to calculate how many weeks he will be grounded. He figures that if he lies, he might get away with it and get only two weeks. If the lie backfires, he might get six. Telling the truth, though, would land him a solid four weeks, so Dan settles for honesty.

"Dan, can you explain the meaning of this?" his Mom says, pointing at the computer with all of the images open.

"Dad went to work and I just wanted to see."

"Well I'm going to have a talk with your Dad about this when he gets home. You can stay in your room until then."

It is two hours until Dan's Dad returns but it feels like two years. When he arrives, he walks upstairs to Dan's room, and sees that his son is clearly disgruntled.

"Hey champ, what's the matter?"

"I got in trouble," Dan says meekly.

"Oh boy, did a bad report card come in the mail? Well we can talk about it later, it isn't the end of the world."

Dan's Mom then yells, saying she needs to speak to his Dad immediately. Dan is left alone again in his room, but can hear through his door muffled yells coming from the kitchen. They are really going at it, arguing harder than he has ever heard them before. Dan opens his door and quietly walks down the stairs to hear what they might be saying. He catches his Mom in the middle of a statement...

"I just, I don't even know what to say to you right now Mark. He's 12 years old."

"I know, I know, it was a mistake" his Dad says.

"I mean, what kind of father leaves his computer open and doesn't even show his son where to find the good stuff?"

My techie husband and I are walking in the desert when he stops to photograph one stunning vista after another. Overcome by the sheer beauty, he pays it his ultimate compliment: "Everywhere I look is a screen saver!"

An artist, a lawyer, and a computer scientist are discussing the merits of a mistress. The artist tells of the passion, the thrill that comes with the risk of being discovered. The lawyer warns of the difficulties: it can lead to guilt, divorce, bankruptcy. Not worth it. Too many problems. The computer scientist says, "It's the best thing that's ever happened to me. My wife thinks I'm with my mistress. My mistress thinks I'm home with my wife, and I can spend all night on the computer!"

A wife asks her husband, a software engineer, "Could you please go shopping for me and buy one carton of milk, and if they have eggs, get six!" A short time later, the husband comes back with six cartons of milk. The wife asks him, "Why the hell did you buy six cartons of milk?" He replied, "They had eggs."

Bill Gates is hanging out with the chairman of General Motors. "If automotive technology had kept pace with computer technology over the past few decades," boasts Gates, "you would now be driving a V-32 instead of a V-8, and it would have a top speed of 10,000 miles per hour. Or, you could have an economy car that weighs 30 pounds and gets a thousand miles to a gallon of gas. In either case, the sticker price of a new car would be less than $50."

"Sure," says the GM chairman. "But would you really want to drive a car that crashes four times a day?"

A man is crossing a road one day when a frog calls out to him and says, "If you kiss me, I'll turn into a beautiful princess." He bends over, picks up the frog, and puts it in his pocket. The frog speaks up again and says, "If you kiss me and turn me back into a beautiful princess, I will tell everyone how smart and brave you are and how you are my hero!" The man takes the frog out of his pocket, smiles at it, and returns it to his pocket. The frog speaks up again and says, "If you kiss me and turn me back into a beautiful princess, I will be your loving companion for an entire week." The man takes the frog out of his pocket, smiles at it, and returns it to his pocket. The frog then cries out, "If you kiss me and turn me back into a princess, I'll stay with you for a year and do ANYTHING you want." Again the man takes the frog out, smiles at it, and puts it back into his pocket. Finally, the frog asks, "What is the matter? I've told you I'm a beautiful princess, that I'll stay with you for a year and do anything you want. Why won't you kiss me?" The man says, "Look, I'm a computer programmer. I don't have time for a girlfriend, but a talking frog is cool."

A wife sends her husband a text message on a cold winter evening: "Windows frozen." The husband sends answer back: "Pour some warm water over them". Some time later husband receives an answer from his wife: "The computer is completely fucked now."

A dying Grandma tells her grandchild, "I want to leave you my farm. That includes the barn, livestock, the harvest, the tractor, and other equipment, the farmhouse and $25 million in cash." The grandchild, absolutely floored and about to become rich says, "Oh Grandma, you are SO generous! I didn't even know you had a farm. Where is it?" With her last breath, Grandma whispers, "Facebook..."

A woman goes into Bass Pro Shop to buy a rod and reel for her grandson's birthday. She doesn't know which one to get, so she just grabs one and goes over to the counter. A Bass Pro Shop associate is standing there wearing dark shades. She says, "Excuse me, sir. Can you tell me anything about this rod and reel?" He says, "Ma'am, I'm completely blind; but if you'll drop it on the counter, I can tell you everything from the sound it makes."

She doesn't believe him but drops it on the counter anyway. He says, "That's a six-foot Shakespeare graphite rod with a Zebco 404 reel and 10-pound test line. It's a good all around combination and it's on sale this week for only $20." She says, "It's amazing that you can tell all that just by the sound of it dropping on the counter. I'll take it!" As she opens her purse, her credit card drops on the floor. "Oh, that sounds like a Master Card," he says.

She bends down to pick it up and accidentally farts. At first she is really embarrassed, but then realizes there is no way the blind clerk could tell it is she who tooted. Being blind, he wouldn't know that she is the only person around. The man rings up the sale and says, "That'll be $34.50, please." The woman is totally confused by this and asks, "Didn't you tell me the rod and reel were on sale for $20? How did you get $34.50?"

He replies, "Yes, ma'am. The rod and reel is $20, but the Duck Call is $11 and the Bear Repellent is $3.50."

A man observes a woman in the grocery store with a three-year-old girl in her basket. As they pass the cookie section, the child asks for cookies and her mother tells her No. The little girl immediately begins to whine and fuss, and the mother says quietly, "Now Ellen, we just have half of the aisles left to go through; don't be upset. It won't be long."

He passes the mother again in the candy aisle. Of course, the little girl begins to shout for candy. When she is told she can't have any, she begins to cry. The mother says, "There, there, Ellen, don't cry. Only two more aisles to go, and then we'll be checking out." The man again happens to be behind the pair at the check-out, where the little girl immediately begins to clamor for gum and bursts into a terrible tantrum upon discovering there would be no gum purchased today.

The mother patiently says, "Ellen, we'll be through this check out stand in five minutes, and then you can go home and have a nice nap." The man follows them out to the parking lot and stops the woman to compliment her. "I couldn't help noticing how patient you were with little Ellen." The mother breaks in, "My little girl's name is Tammy. I'm Ellen."

Dogs

A man and his wife are going for a stroll one night when they spot what is obviously a blind man taking a walk on the other side of the street with his seeing eye dog. "Wow! Isn't that something!" remarks the wife. "Look at that man taking a stroll just like us."

They continue strolling for a few minutes longer when they hear the man let out a loud yelp. The dog has walked him right into a parked car and he has clearly banged his shin pretty hard. Rushing over to help, they are surprised to see the man reach into his pocket and pull out a treat for the dog. "Isn't that weird?" whispers the wife, "giving him a treat even when he's mad?"

"Why are you giving him a treat?" questions the husband.

"I ain't giving him a treat!" says the enraged man, "I'm just trying to find out where his head is, so I can give him a sharp kick in the ass!

Two goldfish are in their tank. One turns to the other and says, "You man the guns; I'll drive."

Joe is a steward for Fly High airlines. He watches as an older lady boards the plane holding a dog in a cage. "Excuse me," says Joe, "dogs are not allowed on board, you have to check it in with the baggage." The lady isn't happy, but Joe is an experienced steward and succeeds in convincing the lady without much of a scene.

Upon arrival, Joe takes a peek in the cage, and to his great surprise, sees that the dog is dead! Frantic that they may get sued, Joe quickly sends one of his underlings out to town to buy a dog that looks exactly the same. Just in the nick of time, the underling arrives with the dog.

They quickly switch dogs and breathes a sigh of relief. "This isn't my dog!" says the lady as soon as she sees it. "I'm sure it is," insists Joe. "I was very careful about where I put it." "It's not my dog," argues the lady. "You see, I was bringing my dog to my hometown to have him buried, and this dog is alive!"

Two blondes suddenly get into bird hunting and are eager to try it out for themselves. They read that a bird dog is a great and useful accessory in bird hunting, so they decide to go to the pet shop and buy one.

They ask for a well trained bird dog and get one. The two blondes immediately go to the woods to try it out. The dog doesn't work. No matter how hard they try, it just doesn't follow their commands.

They become really frustrated and one of the blondes says to her companion, "OK, we'll give him one more try. We'll throw him in the air one more time and if he doesn't fly, we're taking him back to the store!"

Dan opens up the front door at 5:45 p.m. right on the dot, where his dog Sampson will usually greet him. But Sampson is sitting upright when Dan walks in, chew toy on the floor.

"Dan, it's time that you and I had a serious talk."

"Did you just speak?"

"Yes, and frankly, I don't think I've been speaking up enough over the past few years. Please have a seat."

Dan sits down, still a bit unaware of what is going on. Sampson then speaks.

"When you first adopted me, I was a down-on-my-luck dog without a single friend or milk bone in the world. Then you adopted me, and that all changed. I must admit, it is difficult getting used to regular meals and a well-heated home, and I'm not a fan of the talk radio you play in your absence. But Dan, I feel that for every dog, there comes a point where they must decide what mutt they were of the past, and what pooch they wish to be in the future."

"OK...," Dan says.

"I believe it was the Brazilian lyricist and novelist Paulo Coelho who said, 'If you think adventure is dangerous, try routine, it is lethal.' Coelho touches upon an ironic theme here: While routine often brings comfort, that comfort can lead to one not taking risks in life. Do you see what I'm trying to get at here?"

"You want to buy your own kibbles from the pet store from now on?"

"What I want to buy is change. What I want to buy is passion. And Dan, I simply can't have that with you anymore. I don't want to see the one dog park we go to near the Costco off Pine Street: I want to see all the dog parks, those that are by Costco's and those that may be near Sam's Clubs. Do they exist? I don't know, but I want to find out!"

"There actually is one by the Sam's Club near downtown, it's just a bit out of the way, that's why we haven't gone there."

"That's not the point, Dan. I want to see the world and try new things. I don't want my life to just be solely focused on you coming home every day from work and wondering if you're going to take me for a walk and if I want to smell that bush or pee on it, or if I want to sleep on the bed but just after get cozy suddenly decide I want to sleep on the couch and leave you feeling restless. I want passion, I…I want love, Dan! I want love!"

The dog takes a breath, then continues.

"I am ready to leave, so here's how it's going to work. I'll be moving out, and finding a new home at that one beautiful place. I think I remember with lots of bright lights and citizens wearing orange-tattered clothing."

"Wait…are you talking about when we went to Home Depot? That's a store, it isn't a place you live."

"Not by your standards Dan, but I guess that's just another reason why this simply won't work anymore."

"I mean you were a great dog, but hey, you gotta do what you gotta do. I'll probably just go down to the shelter and find another older dog that needs a home. You're always welcome to crash here whenever you want."

"Thank you Dan, I appreciate that."

Sampson gets up from the chair and walks to the bedroom and kicks the door shut with his paw.

"Man," Dan says, "I've gotta get my dogs to stop breaking up with me, this is the third one this year!"

A dog walks into a bar and hops up on a stool. He looks the bartender straight in the eye and says, "Hey, guess what? I can talk. Have you ever seen a talking dog before? Amazing, right? How about a drink?"

The bartender thinks for a moment and says, "Sure, the toilet's right around the corner."

A police officer is sitting his car with his K9 partner in the back seat. A man walks over and asks, "Is that a dog in the back seat?" The officer says, "It sure is." The man responds, "Wow, what did he do?"

A dog walks into a telegraph office and picks up a blank form. He then writes on it, "Woof. Woof. Woof. Woof. Woof. Woof. Woof. Woof. Woof," and hands the form to the clerk.

The clerk takes it off him, looks it over and then says, "You know, there are only nine words here. You could add another 'Woof' for the same price."

The dog shakes his head at the clerk in disbelief and says, "But that would make no sense at all."

A burglar is sneaking through this house one night, when out of the darkness comes a voice, "I can see you, and Jesus can, too."

The burglar freezes in his tracks and is too frightened to move. He waits a few moments and nothing has happened so he moves forward. Again from the darkness comes the voice, "I can see you, and Jesus can, too." The burglar is petrified and too frightened to move a muscle.

After 30 minutes, he decides to do something. He backs very slowly and tentatively to the wall and feels around for a light switch. He switches on the light and there in front of him, sits a cockatoo in a cage, who says, "I can see you, and Jesus can, too."

Greatly relieved, the burglar sighs, "It's just a cockatoo." The cockatoo looks at the burglar and says, "I might be just a cockatoo, but Jesus is a big Rottweiler."

O ne morning Farmer Johnson is riding his kicking mule to market when he meets Jim Boggs, against whom he has an old and concealed grudge. The farmer knows Boggs' weakness lay in bragging and betting: Therefore, he salutes him accordingly.

"How are you, Jim? Fine morning."

"Hearty, Sir," replies Jim. "Fine weather. Nice mule that you are riding. Will he do to bet on?"

"Bet on? Guess he will. I tell you, Jim Boggs, he's the best mule in the county."

"Great thunder! Is that so?" Jim asks excitedly.

"Solid truth, every word of it. Tell you confidentially, I am taking him down for betting purposes. I bet he can kick a fly off any man without its hurting him."

"Now look here, Mr. Johnson," says Jim, "I am not a betting character, but I'll bet you something on that myself."

"Jim, there's no use—don't bet," says the farmer. "I don't want to win your money."

"Don't be alarmed, Mister. I'll take such bets as them every time."

"Well, if you are determined to bet, Jim, I will risk a small stake—say, five dollars."

"All right, Mr. Johnson, you're my man. But who'll he kick the fly off? There's no one here but you and I. You try it."

"No," says Johnson, "I have to be at the mule's head to order him."

Oh, yes," says Jim. "Then probably I'm the man. Well, I'll do it, but you are to bet 10 against my five if I risk it."

"All right," says Farmer Johnson. "Now, there's a fly on your shoulder. Stand still." And the farmer adjusts the mule.

"Whist, Jervey!" says the farmer.

The mule raises his heels with such velocity and force that Boggs rises in the air like a bird and alights on all fours in a muddy ditch, bang up against a rail fence.

Rising in a towering passion, he exclaims: "Yaas, that is smart! I knew your darned mule couldn't do it. You had all that put up. I wouldn't be kicked like that for 50 dollars. Now you can just fork them stakes right over."

"No, sir," says the farmer. "Jervey did just what I says he would. I says he would kick a fly off a man without hurting him, and he did. You see the mule is not hurt by the operation. However, if you are not satisfied, we will try again as often as you wish."

Jim brushes the mud off, looks solemnly at the mule, and then, putting his hand thoughtfully to his brow, remarks: "No, Mr. Johnson. I don't think the mule is hurt, but I didn't understand the bet. You can keep the money."

A woman comes up behind her husband while he is enjoying his morning coffee and slaps him on the back of the head.

"I found a piece of paper in your pants pocket with the name 'Marylou' written on it," she says, furious. "You had better have an explanation."

"Calm down, honey," the man replies. "Remember last week when I was at the dog track? That is the name of the dog I bet on."

The next morning, his wife sneaks up on him and smacks him again.

"What is that for?" he complains.

"Your dog called last night."

A lady rushes into the veterinarian and screams, "I found my dog unconscious and I can't wake him! Do something!"

The vet puts the dog on the examination table and after a few simple tests, he says, "I'm sorry, I don't feel a pulse, I'm afraid your dog is dead."

The lady can't accept this and says, "No, no, he can't be dead! Do something else!"

The vet goes into the other room and comes back with a little cat. The cat jumps up on the table and starts sniffing the dog from head to toe. It sniffs and sniffs up and down the dog, then all of a sudden just stops and jumps off the table and leaves. "Well, that confirms it," the vet says, "your dog is dead."

The lady is very upset but finally settles down. "OK, I guess you're right. How much do I owe you?" The vet says, "That will be $540."

The lady has a fit and asks, "Why is it so much? After all the vet didn't do anything for the dog."

"Well", the vet replies, "it's $40 for the office visit and $500 for the CAT SCAN!"

Upon entering the little country store, a stranger notices a sign saying "DANGER! BEWARE OF DOG!" posted on the glass door.

Inside he notices a harmless old hound dog asleep on the floor beside the cash register.

He asks the store manager, "Is that the dog folks are supposed to beware of?"

"Yep, that's him," he replies. The stranger can't help but be amused. "That certainly doesn't look like a dangerous dog to me. Why in the world would you post that sign?"

"Because", the owner replies, "before I posted that sign, people kept tripping over him."

....

A nursery school teacher is delivering a station wagon full of kids home one day when a fire truck zooms past them. Sitting in the front seat of the fire truck is a Dalmatian. The children fall to discussing the dog's duties.

"They use him to keep crowds back," says one youngster.

"No, he's just for good luck," says another.

A third child begins the argument to a close.

"They use the dogs," she says firmly, "to find the fire hydrant."

....

A man and his dog walk into a bar. The man proclaims, "I'll bet you a round of drinks that my dog can talk."

Bartender: "Yeah! Sure, go ahead."

Man: "What covers a house?"

Dog: "Roof!"

Man: "How does sandpaper feel?"

Dog: "Rough!"

Man: "Who is the greatest baseball player of all time?"

Dog: "Ruth!"

Man: "Pay up. I told you he could talk."

The bartender, annoyed at this point, throws both of them out the door. Sitting on the sidewalk, the dog looks at the guy and says, "Or is the greatest player Mickey Mantle?"

....

An elderly couple is just settling down for bed when the old man realizes he left the lights on in the greenhouse in the back yard.

Then they hear voices.

Three men have broken into the greenhouse.

Scared, they call the police.

The dispatcher replies that he will send an officer as soon as one becomes available as they are all out on calls.

The old man waits for a few minutes and calls Dispatch again.

He tells Dispatch, "Don't worry about sending an officer, I shot the robbers, and now the dogs are eating their bodies!"

In no time at all, police are all over the place and capture the robbers red-handed!

One of the cops asks the old man, "I thought you said you shot the robber and your dogs were eating them!"

"The old man replies, "I thought you said there weren't any officers available!"

L ittle Harold is practicing the violin in the living room while his father is trying to read in the den. The family dog is lying in the den, and as the screeching sounds of little Harold's violin reach his ears, he begins to howl loudly.

The father listens to the dog and the violin as long as he can. Then he jumps up, slams his paper to the floor and yells above the noise, "For Pete's sake, can't you play something the dog doesn't know?!"

F or months he has been her secret admirer. Now, at long last, he has mustered up the courage to ask her the most serious of all questions:

"There are quite a lot of advantages to being a bachelor," he begins, "but there comes a time when a man longs for the companionship of another being: One who will regard him as perfect, as an idol; whom he can treat as his absolute own; who will be kind and faithful when times are hard, and who will share all his joys and sorrows."

To his delight he sees a sympathetic gleam in her eyes. Then she nods in agreement.

Finally, she responds, "I think that's a great idea! Can I help you choose which puppy to buy?"

Paul gets off the elevator on the 40th floor and nervously knocks on his blind date's door. She opens it and is as beautiful and charming as everyone has said.

"I'll be ready in a few minutes," she says. "Why don't you play with Rollo while you're waiting? He does wonderful tricks. He rolls over, shakes hands, sits up, and if you make a hoop with your arms, he'll jump through."

The dog follows Paul onto the balcony and starts rolling over. Paul makes a hoop with his arms and Rollo jumps through—and over the balcony railing! Just then Paul's date walks out.

"Isn't Rollo the cutest, happiest dog you've ever seen?"

"To tell the truth, "he replies, "Rollo seemed a little depressed to me!"

An old man takes his dog to the vet after getting several complaints from the mailman. After examining the dog, the vet says, "Sir, I don't see anything wrong with your dog other than the fact that he is old, and through my years of practice, I have found that if you castrate an old dog, they will get fat and lazy and mellow out quite a bit."

After giving this much thought, the old man says, "OK doc, go ahead, because if I don't do something, my ass is going to end up in jail." Three days later, the old man goes to the vet's office, picks the dog up and takes him home.

That evening, the old man is sitting on his porch reading his paper, and the bulldog is laying by his side. Along comes the mailman, who turns into the old man's front gate to give the old man his mail. Off of the porch jumps the dog, knocks the mailman down, and proceeds to tear his ass up.

The old man comes off of the porch, picks the dog up, places him under his arm and says, "Damn, Mr. Mailman, I'm sorry as hell, but I just don't know what to do with this damn dog! As a matter of fact, I just took him to the vet three days ago and had him castrated."

The mailman gets up, brushes himself off and says, "Well you dumb son-of-a-bitch, you should have had his teeth pulled! Hell, I could tell that he didn't want to screw me when he came off of the porch!"

Two buddies are out for a Saturday stroll. One has a Doberman and the other has a Chihuahua. As they saunter down the street, the guy with Doberman says to his friend, "Let's go over to that bar and get something to drink." The guy with the Chihuahua says, "We can't go in there. We've got dogs with us." The one with the Doberman says, "Just follow my lead." They walk over to the bar and the guy with the Doberman puts on a pair of dark glasses and starts to walk in. The bouncer at the door says, "Sorry, Mac, no pets allowed." The man with the Doberman says, "You don't understand. This is my seeing eye dog." The bouncer says, "A Doberman pinscher?" The man says, "Yes, they're using them now. They're very good." The bouncer says, "Come on in." The buddy with the Chihuahua figured what the heck, so he put on a pair of dark glasses and started to walk in. He knew his would be more unbelievable. Once again the bouncer says, "Sorry, pal, no pets allowed." The man with the Chihuahua says, "You don't understand. This is my seeing eye dog." The bouncer says, "A Chihuahua?" The man with the Chihuahua says, "A Chihuahua? They gave me a freaking Chihuahua?"

CATS

For a man to truly understand rejection, he first must be ignored by a cat.

A man in a movie theater notices what looks like a cat sitting next to him.

"Are you a cat?" asks the man, surprised.

"Yes," the cat replies.

"What are you doing at the movies?" the man asks.

"Well," says the cat. "I liked the book."

A man drives deep into the forest to get rid of his cat. He lets her out at an abandoned place. After one hour he gets a phone call from his wife:

"The cat is back."

The man growls: "OK, can you put her on. I got lost and need directions."

I n front of the local butcher's, an art connoisseur notices a mangy little kitten lapping up milk from a saucer. The saucer, he realizes with a start, is a rare and precious piece of pottery. It is, in fact, a collector's item.

He strolls into the store and offers two pounds for the cat. "He's not for sale," says the butcher.

"Look," says the collector, "that cat is dirty and scabby, but I'm an eccentric. I prefer cats that way. I'll raise my offer to 10 pounds."

"It's a deal," says the proprietor, and pockets the 10 immediately.

"For that amount of money, I'm sure you won't mind throwing in the saucer," says the connoisseur. "The kitten seems so happy drinking from it."

"I can't do that," says the butcher firmly, "That's my lucky saucer. From that saucer, so far this week, I've sold 18 cats."

A woman walks into my aunt's animal shelter wanting to have her cat and six kittens spayed and neutered.

"Is the mother friendly?" my aunt asks.

"Very," says the woman, casting an eye on all the pet carriers. "That's how we got into this mess in the first place."

M y father's secretary is visibly distraught one morning when she arrives at the office and explains that her children's parrot has escaped from his cage and has flown out an open window.

Of all the dangers the tame bird would face outdoors alone, she seems most concerned about what would happen if the bird starts talking.

Confused, my father asks what the parrot could say.

"Well," she explains, "he mostly says, 'Here, kitty, kitty.'"

A n old lady sits on her front porch, rocking away the last days of her long life, when all of a sudden, a fairy godmother appears and informs her that she will be granted three wishes.

"Well, now," says the old lady, "I guess I would like to be really rich."

POOF! Her rocking chair turns to solid gold.

"And, gee, I guess I wouldn't mind being a young, beautiful princess."

POOF! She turns into a beautiful young woman.

"Your third wish?" asks the fairy godmother. Just then the old woman's cat wanders across the porch in front of them. "Ooh—can you change him into a handsome prince?" she asks.

POOF!

There before her stands a young man more handsome than anyone could possibly imagine. She stares at him, smitten. With a smile that makes her knees weak, he saunters across the porch and whispers in her ear, "Bet you're sorry you had me neutered."

Little Tim is in the garden filling in a hole when his neighbor peers over the fence. Interested in what the cheeky-faced youngster is up to, he politely asks, "Whatcha doing, Tim?" "My goldfish died," replies the boy tearfully, without looking up. "And I've just buried him." The neighbor is concerned. "That's an awfully big hole for a goldfish, isn't it?" Tim pats down the last heap of earth then replies, "That's because he's inside your cat."

A man who lives at home with his mother and pet cat goes on a trip to Europe. Before he leaves, he tells his best friend to inform him of any emergencies.

A few days after his departure, his cat climbs up on the roof, falls off and is killed. His friend immediately wires him with the message: "Your cat died!"

In a few hours he is back home, having cut short his trip in grief and anger at his friend whom he says, "Why didn't you break the news to me gradually? You know how close I was to my cat! You could have sent a message 'Your cat climbed up on the roof today' and the next day you could've written, 'Your cat fell off the roof' and let me down slowly that he died."

After a quick memorial service, the bachelor leaves again to continue his trip. A few days later, he returns to his hotel and there is a message waiting for him from his friend.

It reads, "Your mother climbed up on the roof today."

One day, a cat dies of natural causes and goes to Heaven. There he meets the Lord himself.

The Lord says to the cat, "You lived a good life, and if there is any way I can make your stay in Heaven more comfortable, please let me know."

The cat thinks for a moment and says, "Lord, all my life I have lived with a poor family and had to sleep on a hard wooden floor."

The Lord stops the cat and says, "Say no more," and a wonderful fluffy pillow appears.

A few days later, six mice are killed in a tragic farming accident and go to Heaven. Again the Lord is there to greet them with the same offer.

The mice answer, "All of our lives we have been chased. We have had to run from cats, dogs, and even women with brooms. Running, running, running! We're tired of running. Do you think we could have roller skates so we don't have to run anymore?"

The Lord says, "Say no more," and fits each mouse with beautiful new roller skates.

About a week later the Lord stops by to see the cat and finds him in a deep sleep on the pillow.

The Lord gently wakes the cat and asks him, "How are things since you arrived?"

The cat stretches and yawns and replies, "It is wonderful here. Better than I could have ever expected. And those six meals on wheels you sent the other day were the best!"

WILD ANIMALS

A lion walks into a bar, sits down, and orders a beer. The bartender, amazed that the lion can actually talk, gives him a beer.

The lion says, "What do I owe you?"

The bartender stops and thinks for a moment.

"Even though this lion is smart," thinks the bartender, "he probably hasn't been in many bars." So the bartender says, "That'll be 10 dollars." The lion forks over the money and starts drinking his beer.

After a few minutes, the bartender can't restrain his curiosity, so he walks back over to the lion and tries to strike up a conversation.

"You know, we don't get many lions in this bar." The lion looks up from his beer and says, "Well, at 10 bucks a beer, I'm not surprised."

Two guys are walking through a game park and they come across a lion that has not eaten for days. The lion starts chasing the two men. They run as fast as they can and the one guy starts getting tired and decides to say a prayer: "Please turn this lion into a Christian, Lord." He looks to see if the lion is still chasing him, and he sees the lion on its knees. Happy to see his prayer answered, he turns around and heads toward the lion. As he comes closer to the lion, he hears it saying a prayer: "Thank you Lord for the food I am about to receive…"

One day a baby polar bear approaches his mother with a confused expression on his face and says, "Mom? Am I a polar bear?"

"Well of course, son!"

The cub replies, "You're sure I'm not a panda bear or a black bear?"

"No, of course not. Now run outside and play."

But the baby polar bear is still confused, so he approaches his father.

The cub asks, "Dad, am I a polar bear?"

"Why of course son!" the papa polar bear gruffly replies.

The cub continues, "I don't have any grizzly bear or Koala bear in my bloodlines?"

"No son. I'm a polar bear, your mother is a polar bear, and by god, you too are 100 percent purebred polar bear! Why in the world do you ask?"

"Because I'm freezing my BUTT off!!"

There are two cows in a field. The first cow says "moo" and the second cow says "baaaa." The first cow asks the second cow, "Why did you say baaaa?" The second cow says, "I'm learning a foreign language."

You are on a horse, galloping at a constant speed. On your right side is a sharp drop off, and on your left side is an elephant traveling at the same speed as you.

Directly in front of you is another galloping horse but your horse is unable to overtake it.

Behind you is a lion running at the same speed as you and the horse in front of you.

What must you do to safely get out of this highly dangerous situation?

Get your drunk ass off the merry-go-round!

A panda walks into a bar and gobbles some beer nuts. Then he pulls out a gun, fires it in the air, and heads for the door. "Hey!" shouts the bartender, but the panda yells back, "I'm a panda. Google me!" Sure enough, panda: "A tree-climbing mammal with distinct black-and-white coloring. Eats shoots and leaves."

A duck, a skunk, and a deer go out for dinner at a restaurant one night. When it comes time to pay, the skunk doesn't have a scent and the deer doesn't have a buck, so they put the meal on the duck's bill.

A team of little animals and a team of big animals decide to play football. During the first half of the game, the big animals are winning. But during the second half, a centipede scores so many touchdowns that the little animals win the game. When the game is over, the chipmunk asks the centipede, "Where were you during the first half?" He replies, "Putting on my shoes!"

A chicken walks into a library, goes up to a librarian and says, "Book book book." The librarian decides that the chicken wants a book so he gives the chicken a book and the chicken walks away. About 10 minutes later, the chicken comes back with the book, looking a bit agitated, saying, "Book book book." The librarian decides the chicken wants another book so he takes the old book back and gives the chicken another book. The chicken walks out the door. Ten minutes later the chicken comes back again, very agitated, saying, "Book book book!" so quickly it almost sounds like one word. The chicken puts the book on the librarian's desk and looks up, waiting for another book. This time the librarian gives the chicken another book and decides that something weird is happening. He follows the chicken out the door and into the park, all the way to the pond. In the pond is a frog sitting on a lily pad. The chicken gives the book to the frog, who then says, "Reddit, reddit."

A cowboy passes by a ranch and strikes up a conversation with the rancher sitting by the gate.

The cowboy asks the rancher, "Mind if I talk to your dog over there?"

"Damn fool, don't you know dogs can't talk?"

The cowboy replies, "So what's the harm?"

The rancher shrugs, "Go right ahead."

The cowboy ambles up to the dog and says, "Howdy!" The dog replies, "Hello."

The rancher's eyes pop wide open.

The cowboy continues, "Does your master here treat you alright?"

"Sure does. He feeds me, lets me sleep inside, and every day he takes me to the lake."

The cowboy asks the shocked rancher, "Mind if I talk to your horse over there?"

The rancher replies, "Now, I don't know what you're up to, but I know for a fact that horses can't talk."

"Well then, what's the harm?"

"Go right ahead," says the rancher.

The cowboy says to the horse, "Hello." The horse replies, "Hello."

The rancher's jaw drops.

The cowboy asks, "Your owner here treat you OK?"

"Sure," replies the horse, tossing his mane. "He rides me every day, brushes me down, feeds me good, and he keeps me in the barn out of the bad weather."

The cowboy looks satisfied and turns to the rancher, "Are those your sheep over there?"

The rancher looks alarmed and stammers, "Listen, them sheep out there? They're —they're nothing but a bunch of liars!"

A farmer is helping one of his cows give birth when he notices his four-year-old son standing at the fence with wide eyes, taking in the whole event.

The man thinks to himself, "Great, he's four years old and I'm gonna have to start explaining the birds and bees now. No need to jump the gun. I guess I'll let him ask and then I'll answer."

After everything is over, the man walks over to his son and says, "Well son, do you have any questions?"

"Just one," gasps the wide-eyed lad. "How fast was that calf going when he hit that cow?"

Two turkey vultures are preparing to migrate north for the summer but, after talking about it, they decide they were too old to fly all that way, so they decide to take a plane. When they are about to board the aircraft, the flight attendant, noticing that both buzzards are carrying a dead armadillo, asks, "Would you like to check those armadillos through as luggage?" "No thanks," the buzzards reply, "they're carrion."

An eagle swoops down from the sky and eats a mouse. Three hours later, while the eagle is flying, the mouse sticks its head out of the eagle's butt and asks, "How high up are we?"

"About 2,000 feet," the eagle replies.

The mouse replies, "You ain't shittin' me, are you?"

A man staggers into an emergency room with two black eyes and a five iron wrapped tightly around his throat.

"I was having a quiet round of golf with my wife," he tells the doctor, "when she sliced her ball into a pasture of cows. We went to look for it, and I noticed one of the cows had something white in its rear end. I walked over and lifted up the tail, and sure enough, there was my wife's golf ball stuck right in the cow's butt. That's when I made my mistake."

"What did you do?" asks the doctor.

"Well, as I was standing there holding up the tail, I yelled to my wife, 'Hey, this looks like yours!'"

A robin applies for the receptionist's job at the new Best Buy headquarters. The interviewer, a bit nonplussed, tells the robin that the candidate has to be able to type at least 80 words per minute. The robin demonstrates a 100 wpm talent! Not wanting to hire a bird for the job, the interviewer tells the robin that the candidate has to be able to take dictation. The robin surpasses all other candidates. Finally the interviewer thinks he'd be able to get rid of the robin with "The candidate must be bilingual!" The robin replies, "Meow!!"

A lion wakes up one morning with the urge to inflict his superiority on his fellow beasts. So he strides over to a monkey and roars: "Who is the mightiest animal in the jungle?"

"You are, Master," says the monkey, quivering.

Then the lion comes across a warthog.

"Who is the mightiest animal in the jungle?" roars the lion.

"You are, Master," says the warthog, shaking with fear.

Next the lion meets an elephant.

"Who is the mightiest animal in the jungle?" roars the lion.

The elephant grabs the lion with his trunk, slams him against a tree half a dozen times, drops him like a stone and ambles off.

"All right," shouts the lion. "There's no need to turn nasty, just because you don't know the answer."

A little girl is talking to her teacher about whales. The teacher says that it is physically impossible for a whale to swallow a human being because even though whales are very large mammals, their throats are far too small for a human to go down. The little girl says that Jonah was swallowed by a whale. Irritated, the teacher says again that a whale cannot swallow a person and that it is physically impossible. The little girl says, "When I get to Heaven, I will ask Jonah." The teacher says, "What if Jonah went to the other place?" The little girl replies, "Then you can ask him!"

For five years, two sharks and a dolphin have worked side by side every day as window washers, and every night after work they stop for a drink. One day, disaster strikes, and the dolphin falls to his death. The police come to the site and begin asking questions. "Where does he live?" The sharks shrug their shoulders. "Is he married?" The sharks don't know. "What is his name?" The sharks shrug again. "You worked with this guy for five years and you don't know anything about him?" the cop asks. "I know something about him," one shark volunteers. "He has two assholes." "What are you talking about?" says the cop. "Well," says the shark, "Whenever we go for a drink after work the bartender says, 'Here comes the dolphin with the two assholes.'"

A zebra has lived her entire life in a zoo and is getting on a bit, so the zoo keeper decides as a treat that she can spend her final years in bliss on a farm. The zebra is so excited that she gets to see this huge space with green grass and hills and trees and all these strange animals. She sees a big fat weird-looking brown thing and runs up to it all excited.

"Hi! I'm a zebra, what are you?"

"I'm a cow," says the cow.

"Right, and what do you do?" asks the zebra.

"I make milk for the farmer," says the cow.

"Cool."

The zebra then sees this funny looking little white thing and runs over to it.

"Hi, I'm a zebra, what are you?"

"I'm a chicken," says the chicken.

"Oh, right, what do you do?" asks the zebra.

"I make eggs for the farmer," says the chicken.

"Right, great, see ya round."

Then the zebra sees this very handsome beast that looked almost exactly like her without the stripes. She runs over to it and says, "Hi, I'm a zebra, what are you?"

"I am a stallion," says the stallion.

"Wow," says the zebra. "What do you do?"

"Take off your pajamas darling, and I'll show you."

A father and son go hunting together for the first time. The father says, "Stay here and be very quiet. I'll be across the field."

A few minutes later, the father hears a blood-curdling scream and runs back to his son.

"What's wrong?" the father asks. "I told you to be quiet."

The son answered, "Look, I was quiet when the snake slithered across my feet. I was quiet when the bear breathed down my neck. But when the two squirrels crawled up my pant legs and said, 'Should we eat them here or take them with us?' I guess I just panicked."

MATH PROBLEMS

John is roaming around Costco, trying out free food samples. There are five different samples he wants to try, but John can only go around to each booth once every 10 minutes; otherwise, the staff will get suspicious and ask him to leave. How many samples can John eat in two hours?

- 10
- 15
- 20
- 25

Sally is riding on a plane from Los Angeles to New York. The length of the trip is six hours, and every 100 minutes on the trip, Sally will remember that she left something behind at the airport. If Sally had a carry-on bag, an MP3 player, and a novelty Oscar-statuette, how long will it take for her to realize that all the items are missing?

- 3 hours
- 4 hours
- 5 hours
- When she lands at JFK and has to pay $100 in overnight shipping to get her items returned to her

Robert, Veronica, and Francine are all eating dinner at a popular chain restaurant downtown. They plan to split the check evenly between the three of them, except for appetizers, which Robert argues he shouldn't have to pay since he only had a small taste, even though he suggested to the table that they order them. If the total of the entrées is $180 and the total of the Bloomin' Onion, Fried Pickles, and Cheese Poppers is $25, how much will Robert, Veronica, and Francine pay?

- Veronica and Francine will each pay $72.50, while Robert only pays $60
- Veronica and Francine will each pay $60, while Robert pays $40
- Veronica and Francine will each pay $55, while Robert pays $30
- No matter what Veronica and Francine pay, they're still getting screwed over by Robert

Kevin posted a Facebook status saying, "Screw long lines at the post office" at 8:10 p.m. His Mom is asleep when Kevin posts this, but checks Facebook when she wakes up at 7 a.m. How many whole hours will pass before Kevin gets an angry text from his Mom, yelling at him for not being professional on social media?

- 6 hours

- 8 hours

- 10 hours

- 12 hours

Sheila has been on the phone with the cable company trying to cancel her service for three hours. Every 25 minutes, Sheila takes a break from the phone call to scream her lungs out. If the police received two complaints for every time Sheila has screamed on her call, how many complaints will Sheila have against her on her criminal record?

- 6 complaints

- 7 complaints

- 8 complaints

- 9 complaints

Cassie is behind a woman at Baskin Robbins who is insisting on sampling every one of their 31 flavors before she will ultimately decide that she wants just plain old vanilla at the end. It takes the woman 30 seconds to receive a sample, taste it, and say "Hmm, too sweet/too sour/ugh, too many chocolate chips!" before moving onto the next one. If Cassie can only be at Baskin Robbins for 15 minutes, will she ever receive her ice cream?

A. No

B. Yes, but by that point she will have lost her appetite and won't want the ice cream anymore anyway

Max is at a blackjack table at a casino in Las Vegas. For every five hands that Max plays on his own, he wins three of them. But for every five hands where a group of drunken, obnoxious, bachelor party participants join in and don't follow the basic, common sense rules of blackjack, Max wins only one out of five. If Max is at the table for 25 hands, and the bachelor party is there with him for 10 hands before deciding to leave to vomit in a trash can, how many hands will Max win?

- 11
- 13
- 9
- 15

Melanie and Brandon are having their wedding, and cousin Randy is one of the guests. Every 30 minutes, cousin Randy will make two lewd comments to three bridesmaids each, drink one beer, and swipe an entrée from a different table when they aren't looking. If the reception lasts three hours, how many lewd comments, beers and stolen entrées can Randy rack up before he is politely asked to leave?

- 12 lewd comments, 6 beers, 6 entrées
- 10 lewd comments, 4 beers, 4 entrées
- 15 lewd comments, 4 beers, 4 entrées
- 15 lewd comments, 6 beers, 6 entrées

The interior angles of a living room each measure at 108 degrees. Pauline can hang up one of his vintage Dave Matthews Band concert posters for every one side, or wall, of the living room. How many Dave Matthews Band posters will the living room be able to hold?

- 3
- 4
- 5
- 6

Xavier is dumped by his girlfriend Dana. Two times a week, Xavier will look at Dana's Facebook profile and cry after revisiting photos of their relationship. One month after breaking up, Xavier will see photos on Facebook of Dana with her new boyfriend Greg and will cry once more a week than usual. If a month is four weeks, how many times will Xavier cry in three months before finally figuring out that he needs to move on with his life and stop creepily stalking his ex?

- 30
- 32
- 34
- 36

Cassandra is trying to figure out where to go for dinner. Her husband, Mark, never gives her a clear, definitive answer on where to go and there is a 60 percent chance he is disappointed with whatever Cassandra chooses, despite having the opportunity to voice his opinion earlier. If Cassandra suggests three restaurants the couple already likes, four restaurants the food critic in the local newspaper raved about, three restaurants that Cassandra has a Groupon for, and four that her friend Kate from yoga says were good, how many restaurants in total will Mark be disappointed with? (Round to the lowest whole number.)

- 7
- 8
- 9
- All of the above: Mark is impossible to please

Gilbert is watching episodes of a popular cop drama on Netflix on his mobile phone. Gilbert, though, has forgotten to connect to wifi, and the episode is quickly devouring his data plan. If Gilbert has five gigabytes left in his data plan for the month and it takes 1.25 gigabytes to stream an episode, how many episodes of Netflix will Gilbert be able to watch before realizing his error and having to go to T-Mobile and feign ignorance in hopes of getting more data?

- 2
- 3
- 4

- 5

- There is not sufficient enough data to answer the question. We don't know if Gilbert will actually get bored of the cop drama once it's revealed the lead detective is the one behind the gruesome serial murders.

Maurice, Janet, and Morgan are co-workers who all like to get lunch together once a week. Once a month, Rachel, a co-worker from down the hall, will hear about their plans for lunch and invite herself. If there are four weeks in a month, how many lunches will Rachel ruin in the course of two years?

- 12

- 24

- 36

- There is not sufficient data to answer, as the question does not include scenarios where Maurice, Janet, and Morgan purposely give Rachel incorrect directions to wherever they're going, making it impossible for Rachel to attend even though she's already heard about the lunch.

Randy and Roberta are driving with their daughter on an 18-hour-long road trip. To keep their daughter entertained, they provided her with an iPad and a few Disney movies to stream. Their daughter, however, has chosen to watch the same Disney movie over and over. If the movie is two hours long and it takes Randy and Roberta five viewings to memorize all of the songs and dialogue, what percentage of Randy and Roberta's journey will be complete before they're able to memorize the entire film by heart?

- 20 percent

- 30 percent

- 55 percent

- There is not sufficient data to answer, as the question does not consider battery life of the iPad, or how many viewings it will take before Randy and Roberta "accidentally" leave it behind at a rest stop.

Billy is a lazy, 45-year-old man living with his Mom at home. Once a week, his Mom asks him to get a job and move out, and Billy lies and tells her he filled out three applications to local businesses that are hiring. If there are 30 local businesses in the area hiring, how many weeks will it take for Billy's Mom to realize her son is lying and kick him out of the house over being lazy?

- 8

- 10

- 12

- 14

- There is not sufficient data to answer, as Billy could start lying about filling out applications online, or may purposely be blowing his job interviews so he doesn't have to pay rent.

A group of Americans are traveling by tour bus through Holland. As they stop at a cheese farm, a young guide leads them through the process of cheese making, explaining that goat's milk is used. She shows the group a lively hillside where many goats are grazing. "These," she explains, "are the older goats put out to pasture when they no longer produce." She then asks, "What do you do in America with your old goats?" A spry old gentleman answers, "They send us on bus tours!"

A plane is taking off from JFK Airport. After it reaches a comfortable cruising altitude, the captain makes an announcement over the intercom: "Ladies and gentlemen, this is your captain speaking. Welcome to Flight number 293, non-stop from New York to Los Angeles. The weather head is good and, therefore, we should have a smooth and uneventful flight. Now sit back and—OH MY GOD!" Silence follows, and after a few minutes, the captain comes back on the intercom and says, "Ladies and Gentlemen, I am so sorry if I scared you earlier. While I was talking to you, the flight attendant accidentally spilled a cup of hot coffee in my lap. You should see the front of my pants!" A passenger in business class yells, "That's nothing. You should see the back of mine!"

A tourist in Spain goes to a fancy restaurant for dinner. As he looks around, he notices a diner being served a beautifully garnished dish with two gigantic meatballs in the middle. When the waiter asks him for his order, the man asks him about the meatball dish. The waiter explains that the meatballs are bull's testicles, and when the bull loses the bullfight, the bull is brought to the restaurant, and this beautiful dish is made. The diner tells the waiter that he wants the bull's testicles for dinner, but the waiter tells him that only one bull a day is brought to the restaurant, but he can have it tomorrow. The diner agrees. The next day, the diner goes to the restaurant and orders the testicle dish. When his food is brought out, he notices that the meatballs are extremely small. He mentions this to the waiter, and the waiter replies: "Well sir, you have to understand, sometimes the bull wins."

Stuart and Susan are touring Paris on their first year anniversary. Susan has studied French and has even lived in Paris for a year during a study abroad program in college. While she has always encouraged Stuart to learn the language, he finally decided this past year was the perfect time, and that on their one year anniversary, he will surprise her by speaking fluent French. Susan invites Stuart to a small restaurant near the Eiffel Tower, a place she always loved frequenting when she was a student. Some of the staff from Susan's time still work there and will stop by to say Hi as the two are dining.

"Ahh, hello Susan! And this must be your lovely husband Stuart!"

"Yes it is! Stuart, meet Pierre, he's been a waiter here since I was in college!"

"Et de son côté, votre mari n'est jamais allé à l'université!" Pierre says in French to Susan as the two break out in laughter. Pierre wishes the two well as he takes their order walks away from the table.

Stuart is quietly fuming. He doesn't want to ruin the surprise that he has learned French, but also doesn't want to lose his dignity by being called an uneducated idiot by the waiter.

"What did he say when you both started laughing?" Stuart inquires.

"Oh he just says something about my outfit," Susan replies.

Stuart is upset his wife didn't tell the truth, but he forgives her. The two are eating their entrées as Pierre returns to the table.

"Pierre, this is divine. Of all the restaurants I've been to in Paris, none has been able to prepare a Duck Confit with such precision and delicacy as your restaurant."

"It's, um, it's good. It's quite good," Stuart says.

"Votre mari ne connaîtrait pas le bon confit de canard s'il vous mordait sur le cul!" Pierre says to Susan, the two erupting in laughter once again. Pierre walks away, and Stuart is even disgruntled this time.

Stuart knows full well the waiter had said, "Your husband wouldn't know good duck confit if it bit him on the ass," but doesn't want to call Susan out on it yet. The two order a tasty dessert, and once they finish, Pierre quickly arrives with the check.

"Ah, I hope everything tonight was to your satisfaction."

"It was Pierre, everything was just as delicious as it was years ago."

"And Stuart, I hope you enjoyed your first tasting of true French cuisine."

"I did, I can't wait to explore what other scrumptious treats your country has to offer."

Pierre turned to his wife and not-so-quietly says, "Dieu sait qu'il va passer le reste du voyage à la recherche d'un McDonald's!" as the two quietly giggle at the thought of the seemingly uncultured Stuart spending the next few days in a fervent search for a McDonald's.

"Nah, I'm much more of a Burger King guy."

A couple drive down a country road for several miles, not saying a word. An earlier discussion has led to an argument and neither of them wants to concede their position. As they pass a barnyard of mules, goats, and pigs, the husband asks sarcastically, "Relatives of yours?" "Yep," the wife replies, "in-laws."

A very distinguished lady is on a plane arriving from Switzerland. She finds herself seated next to a nice priest whom she asks: "Excuse me Father, could I ask a favor?" "Of course my child, what can I do for you?" "Here is the problem. I bought myself a new sophisticated hair remover gadget for which I paid an enormous sum of money. I have really gone over the declaration limits and I am worried that they will confiscate it at customs. Do you think you could hide it under your cassock?" "Of course I could, my child, but you must realize that I cannot lie." "You have such an honest face Father, I am sure they will not ask you any questions," and she gives him the "hair remover." The aircraft arrives at its destination. When the priest presents himself to customs he is asks, "Father, do you have anything to declare?" "From the top of my head to my sash, I have nothing to declare, my son," he replies. Finding this reply strange, the customs officer asks, "And from the sash down, what do you have?" The priest replies, "I have there a marvelous little instrument designed for use by women, but which has never been used." Breaking out in laughter, the customs officer says, "Go ahead, Father. Next!"

LISTS

6 TYPES OF UBER AND LYFT DRIVERS YOU WILL HAVE

Since the company's founding in 2010, Uber (and subsequently Lyft) have shaped the way humans transport themselves to the airport and after drunken barrages on the town. No longer are we in the days where one needs to sprint upstream on a busy avenue past other desperate people trying to hail a taxi. The ease of pushing a button to hail a ride has revolutionized our lives and has put millions of miles in countless Toyota Priuses. Even though the rideshare economy is relatively young, and the pool of Uber and Lyft contractors incredibly diverse, there are 10 bona fide driver "types" who stand out amongst their peers.

1: THE OVERLY-TALKATIVE DRIVER WHO WANTS TO BE YOUR BEST FRIEND

Sitting down in the back seat of an Uber is usually the unspoken sign for "I have a headache, please do not speak to me." But this driver seems to be lost in Uber-etiquette translation as they speak endlessly, trying to gauge anything from how your day went, to what your thoughts on Tom Brady or the New England Patriots are, to if you believe in an afterlife, and whether you think La La Land is overrated. This driver, while well meaning, ultimately becomes a nuisance, often resulting in you jumping out two miles two soon and walking the rest of the way.

Closest driving relative: The driver who has a Bluetooth or periodically answers phone calls from friends on your ride

Can learn a lesson or two from: The driver who keeps the radio at a reasonable volume.

2: THE UNDERLY TALKATIVE DRIVER WHO JUST WANTS TO BE LEFT ALONE

Just as common as the over-talkative driver is his bizarro-ridesharing counterpart, the underly talkative driver. Your ride is a long 40 minutes, and you try to break bread with this driver through some small, friendly conversation. But every Hi or "How is your day going?" is quickly rebuffed by one or two-word responses, often with a displeasing or disinterested tone. "Good. Sure. It's OK. I like the Patriots." To be fair, Uber drivers have to have the same conversation over and over again throughout the course of their day, so it's understandable they get tired of extended pleasantries. But these drivers make it seem like you have committed a grave injustice against them and their families before even stepping in the car.

Closest driving relative: The driver who ignores you when you suggest a quicker route

Can learn a lesson or two from: The driver who gives out free water in their car

3: THE DRIVER WHO PLAYS LOUD MUSIC AND DOESN'T GET YOUR HINTS TO TURN IT DOWN

It's pretty common to encounter drivers who will offer to hook up your iPod to their stereo and play whatever music you want. And it's also common to have drivers who play no music or radio at all. This driver, however, is trying to turn his Nissan Sentra into a portable EDM or thrash metal show, complete with bass drops and weird techno-screeches. "Excuse me, could you turn it down?" you despairingly scream at this driver. "System of a Down? No close, this is Slayer!" They respond back. They definitely heard what you actually said.

Closest driving relative: The driver who tries to invite you to one of their band's gigs after your ride

Can learn a lesson or two from: Driver who plays quiet NPR or classical music

4: THE DRIVER WHO MYSTERIOUSLY HAS A 3.4 STAR RATING BUT SEEMS LIKE A GREAT PERSON

It's five in the morning. You have a red-eye flight in two hours to catch at the airport, and no drivers are in the nearby vicinity to get you there on time. You start to worry and think about calling a cab or even just shelling out 100 bucks in parking. But suddenly, a tiny car blip appears on your phone's screen. The driver has a 3.4 rating, lower that what you're usually comfortable with, but you're desperate and you accept.

The driver is the single nicest person you've ever met in your entire life. The conversation is friendly and engaging, and they offer you water and gum as they take you to your destination. Five minutes before you arrive, they give you the contact info of their mechanic friend who can help you with car repairs, or their bud in graduate school who can lend you their old GRE study books. You look back with warmth at the ride you shared, but suddenly become paranoid as to what this person may have done to earn a 3.4 rating, and start questioning your sanity if your ride was as great as you think.

Closest driving relative: The driver who brings your mobile phone back to your apartment after you accidentally left in their car two hours after your ride finished

Could learn a lesson or two from: Any driver with a 4.5 or 5 star rating

5: THE DRIVER WHO ONE-UPS EVERY STATEMENT YOU MAKE

You're stoked: It's your first time in New York in several years, and you have a full itinerary of plans and places to visit in four days. This driver is a local: They've spent their whole life in the city and know every building and hot dog vendor inside and out. Their helpfulness quickly turns to annoyance, though, as every time you mention a place you want to go, they immediately insult your selection and provide unsolicited advice.

"Nah, you don't want to go to the Empire State Building observation deck, that's dumb. Check out the Top of the Rock instead."

"Pshh, Shake Shack? You don't want that tourist garbage. Five Napkin Burger is the best in the city."

"Hamilton? Ov-er-rated! Stick with Cabaret or Wicked."

Closest driving relative: The driver who says they can hook you up with free concerts or bottle service at their friends club

Could learn a lesson or two from: The driver who gives you a free coupon to Shake Shack

6: THE DRIVER WHO TRIES TO BUT IN ON YOUR CONVERSATIONS

There you are with your boyfriend or girlfriend, talking about how much fun Hamilton was as you go to get some last-minute custard from Shake Shack. Suddenly, your driver barges in:

"Yeah, I saw the show when Lin-Manuel was starring. Incredible, right?" Yeah, you say, trying to keep this conversation to a two-person maximum. The topic shifts to seeing if you can get your coach seats back home shifted up to first class.

"Oh, you don't want to do that. Keep your miles for another trip, you won't remember the comfort of the ride as much as going to another place entirely." The driver clearly isn't getting it, and you don't even respond to their latest statement. Finally, you have one last talk about what movie you want to watch in your hotel room before going to bed.

"Listen, *Home Alone* is great, but *Home Alone 2* is the masterpiece of the franchise. Five-star movie," they say, as you give them a one-star review.

Closest driving relative: Driver who desperately wants to be your friend after your ride is over

Could learn a lesson or two from: Driver who appreciates original *Home Alone* over *Home Alone 2*

7 EXCUSES TO USE TO GET OUT OF ADULT SOCIAL SITUATIONS IF YOU DON'T HAVE KIDS

While stressful, child rearing can reap immense personal benefits for one's life. Outside of endless love and purpose that a baby can bring, parents also have the ability to say no to any invite or social gathering should they find unappealing just by playing the "we have to get home, our baby is sick" card. For any non-parent adults who wish they could just walk out of boring company barbeques, bizarre art gala openings of old high school friend's, or just want to spend a night at home without speaking to another human, here are some excuses just as strong as the kid card and won't raise any eyebrows that could lower your social clout.

1: I CAN'T GO, I LEFT MY SPACE HEATER ON!

This immediately generates the urgency to leave than leaving one's stove on, and for those who aren't well versed in cooking abilities, is significantly more believable. At the same time, friends who hear this excuse might call you out on it: If you live in a home or apartment that has central air, there really isn't that much need for a space heater. But if you leave enough in a hurry, they won't really think twice.

2: My neighbor broke up with their spouse/got fired/is sad the Patriots won the Super Bowl and I need to comfort them

Using a spouse, friend, or co-worker as an excuse can generate suspicion, and cause your peers to ask that person if they're feeling better at a later occasion, increasing the chance of your lie being revealed. Neighbors, though, are anonymous and interchangeable: Even for people who have been to your home countless of times in the past, they still haven't met all of the people who live near you, and would have to trust you when you say you struck up a friendship with the nice 80-year-old woman down the street. Be cautious with details given, as new visitors may want to meet you best bud Agnes the next time they come visit.

3: I have to study for (any graduate or professional exam)

This one causes initial early suspicion when used, since you would have likely told your friends about your plans to head back to law school or realize your lifelong dream of getting a master's in sports sociology. But you just need to provide a phony exam date in the near future. That way when people ask how you did, you can just nod off, giving the impression that you bombed, and that will stop all line of questioning.

4: I'm dog-sitting for my aunt

This is an especially useful excuse that can be applied on numerous occasions. Dog-sitting for your parents means that your parents have to have a dog and live in the same area for this to fly. But few people outside of your immediate family actually know how many aunts you have and what types of canines they may or may not own. If you're still feeling cautious, suggest your aunt owns a more aggressive dog breed: "Jack Russell Terriers are great, but Aunt Margaret's can be one vicious mutt."

5: I have to pick up relative/friend/co-worker for the airport

Do NOT use your spouse or romantic partner in this excuse: They have too many close ties to you and can easily generate a web of lies. Friends and co-workers won't question you picking up a relative. Relatives and friends won't think twice about you having to leave to get a co-worker. And co-workers may be surprised to learn you actually have friends outside the office but won't question your absence.

6: I HAVE TICKETS TO [FILL-IN-THE-BLANK] MOVIE

This one is tricky, because whomever you tell this excuse to will want to hear about your opinions about the movie after you see it. This can quickly be remedied though by reading a Wikipedia article about said movie before watching it and becoming familiar with any talking points your friends may bring up, or even just seeing the movie itself. For science fiction films, be prepared to answer any questions about universe building, and how prequel/reboot films weren't nearly as good. For romance movies, talk about how the couple was unrealistic and would never work in real life. For action films, talk about how awesome the car chase was, and how cool the explosion was and the fight with the bad guy at the end.

7: MY STOMACH HURTS

Arguably the weakest excuse, because of its commonplace usage and its awareness of being an excuse. But just because so many people have resorted to feigned stomach pains as ways of getting out of social obligations doesn't necessarily mean that your pains aren't true and honest in this particular moment. Maybe just throw in a fart or two to make it more believable.

THE 5 TYPES OF ANNOYING PLANE PASSENGERS YOU WILL SIT NEXT TO, AND HOW TO DEFEAT THEIR OBNOXIOUSNESS

Despite the level of complaints levied at the airline industry, traveling by plane is usually a pretty seamless procedure. Only once every blue moon does a bag get lost, turbulence rocks your plane, or inclement weather impedes your travel plans (which frankly, should be somewhat expected in winter months). The biggest nuisance that actually comes from flying originates in those who occupy the much-too-cramped seats next to us on the multi-hour long journey across the U.S. in this hurtling torpedo of steel.

1: THE PARENT WHO ENCOURAGES THEIR CHILD'S BAD BEHAVIOR OR COMPLETELY IGNORES IT

Traveling with babies can be obnoxious, but really there's little parents can do to soften the cries of young ones on a flight. Parents with children at toddler age or above don't seem to get the hint that their cherished young one isn't such a "special, little guy or girl" in the eyes of other passengers on the plane. Their kid wails and kicks and screams, but the parent just lets them do it, out of ignorance or even just so their kid can express themselves. Ask this parent nicely to see if they can keep their child under control, and if they rebuke your request, pass a note to the child later on that says, "Santa Claus and the Easter Bunny aren't real" for some delicious, cabin-pressured petty revenge.

2: THE PASSENGER WITH THEIR HEADPHONES UP TOO LOUD

To be fair, it's hard to gauge just how high your headphones are when wearing them in public. This passenger, usually found in the window seat with their head resting on their fist, just may not actually know that the entire front cabin can hear his playing of Daft Punk's "Robot Rock" on repeat. The catch-22, though, is that this passenger does not have the immediate sensory awareness to notice if you're trying to get them to lower their volume. The best revenge is to blast music on your headphones equally as loud, while gently tapping your foot on theirs. (Bonus points if you can do it off-beat to whatever track they're listening to.) This way if they try to request you stop, they'll be faced with the same dilemma you had while sitting next to them.

3: THE PASSENGER WHO USES THE RESTROOM TOO FREQUENTLY

People have to go when they have to go, and for some with health afflictions, they may have to go more than others. But then there are people who sit in the window seat (even after you offer to switch your aisle seat) and use the facilities at least once every hour on your six-hour trip. Even worse than that, they take time to stretch and convene with the flight attendants. To get your revenge, pretend to be asleep any time they try to make their way to the aisle, and when you get "woken up," decide to use the restroom at that very same minute.

4: THE PASSENGER WHO LEAVES A MESS WITH THEIR FOOD ON THE AIRPLANE

It seems impossible for someone to make such a mess with a small bag of peanuts, an eight-ounce cup of Diet Coke, and a Slim Jim bought back at the terminal. Yet this passenger has done it, claiming your row as his or her own personal trash can, with no regard for anyone in the nearby vicinity. Wait until this passenger gets up to use the restroom or falls asleep, and then leave a mess of your own in their chair.

5: THE PASSENGER WHO TRIES TO REMOVE A SUITCASE FROM THE OVERHEAD COMPARTMENT MULTIPLE TIMES MID-FLIGHT.

What could possibly be up there that you need to access your bag so often? You already have your laptop, a magazine and a neck pillow sitting at your chair. What else could you possibly need from overhead, you wonder, as their ass crack dangles in front of your face. What's even more frustrating isn't so much that this passenger needs to get something from their overhead bag, but when they finally access it, they realize the item they needed was with them all along, or that they don't even want what they were looking for anymore. Next time this happens, do the same at their seat, but spend at least 10-15 minutes shuffling through your items. If they're sitting in window, do the same but at your actual seat.

UNOFFICIAL STATE TOURISM MOTTOS

- Alabama: Roll Tide Roll! Over our crippling-low educational and health standards.
- Alaska: Let's be honest, you're never going to visit here.
- Arizona: The heat might make you think it's hell, but the golf courses will convince you it's heaven.
- Arkansas: Home of Wal-Mart and not much else.
- California: Listen, you can't afford to live anywhere here, no matter how much you make.

- Colorado: We've got weed and John Denver really liked us.

- Connecticut: We're like the Boss mode of pretentious New Yorkers

- Delaware: We're the first state to ever exist and the first people forget about.

- Florida: Cash out your 401(k) here in oranges.

- Georgia: Just like peaches aren't as tasty as oranges, we're a second resort compared to Florida.

- Hawaii: We look forward to you spending thousands of dollars on your honeymoon here.

- Idaho: Hey, we've got potatoes, at least that's something.

- Iowa- We've got corn, a good writing school and Captain Kirk from Star Trek was born here.

- Kansas: We hope you enjoy your drive through our state until you eventually get to where you really wanted to go: Colorado or Missouri.

- # Kentucky: We spend the whole year waiting for a horse race. But it's a great one!

- Louisiana: New Orleans smooth jazz and tasty treats will make you forget about the rest of the state's poor quality of life.

- Maine: We're home to the second-most famous Portland in the U.S., but if you want to just go to Canada, that's fine too.

- Maryland: We've got the Orioles, the Naval Academy, and are home to The Wire.

- Massachusetts: When we're not shoveling snow, we're being bandwagon Boston sports fans.

- Michigan: Historic college football will help you forget you're living in Michigan.

- Minnesota: The closest glimpse you can get of Canada without having to use your passport.

- Mississippi: We don't know if you'll ever visit our state, but we're damn sure you know how to spell it correctly.

- Missouri: Our second-most famous city has the bordering state's name in it. And our most famous city has a giant arch. That counts for something.

- Montana: The skies are just as big as our boredom.

- Nebraska: Admit it, you don't know anyone who's ever been to or lived in Nebraska.

- Nevada: Do the shit here that's illegal to do wherever you're from.

- New Hampshire: A great place to fill up on gas during your drive from Massachusetts to Vermont.

- New Jersey: Home of Frank Sinatra, Bruce Springsteen, and the people who like to tell you it's the home of Frank Sinatra and Bruce Springsteen.

- New Mexico: Previously a myth until *Breaking Bad* confirmed this is in fact a real place.

- New York: Come for the pizza, stay because the crippling snowstorm cancelled your flight.

- North Carolina: Home to Michael Jordan and an almost Super Bowl-winning team.

- North Dakota: Only remembered as the state that doesn't have Mount Rushmore.

• Ohio: Even LeBron James tried to escape for a little bit.

- Oklahoma: There's a musical named after us! Also known as Texas' Hat.

- Oregon: Every resident gets a free Subaru Outback after 15 years of living here.

- Pennsylvania: Our cities are diverse, and we love to screw up presidential elections.

- Rhode Island: Home to a top-notch arts school and the setting of Family Guy.

- South Carolina: One of our cities has great food and history. The others, not so much.

- South Dakota: The destination of countless family road trips that no one really ever wanted to go on anyways.

- Tennessee: Home to some of the best music you can't stand to listen to.

- Texas: We're still unsure if there's anyone actually living anywhere between El Paso and Dallas.

- Utah: You can experience some of the best outdoors in the world, but we'll be damned if you ever try to drink a beer above 2.0 alcohol level here.

- Vermont: Just like Bernie Sanders, only relevant for a few months of the year.

- Virginia: Chances are Dave Matthews has played a concert on the very sidewalk you're walking on.

- Washington: Almost as expensive as California but with better Starbucks.

- West Virginia: You know us from that one Country Roads song

- Wisconsin: If you can name another city here besides Green Bay, Madison, or Milwaukee, you get to become mayor of it.

- Wyoming: The best fireworks destination for Coloradans.

WHAT YOUR DOG BREED SAYS ABOUT YOU

- Labrador retriever: Even though you have a family of five, you're still the only one who takes care of your dog.

- German shepherd: Chances are you haven't properly trained this dog and are too lazy to do so in the future.

- Golden retriever: You couldn't build a white picket fence on your property, so this is the next best thing.

- Bulldog: The perfect addition to your La-Z-Boy chair. You've also used countless towels to clean up its drool.

- Beagles: You have fun playing with them, but they have fun annoying your neighbors with high-pitched barks while you're at work.

- French Bulldogs: You have a natural affinity for vampires and love playing with ears.

- Yorkshire Terriers: The perfect dog to carry in your purse and to take on the airplane for a one-day trip, even though you could have easily found a sitter for the pet at home.

- Poodle: Chances are, you have enough money to pay someone else to take care of this dog.

- Rottweiler: People judge you for having one, even though their poodles and Pomeranians are significantly more misbehaved.

- Boxers: No matter how much coffee you drink, you don't have enough energy to keep up with these guys.

- Pointers: You live on a giant farm

Random thoughts and musings while sitting in traffic on the 405

- Los Angeles' 405 is one of the largest freeways in the country and is home to some of the worst gridlock, turning what should be a quick and simple five-minute jaunt into a screw-up of imaginable proportions. Here are random thoughts, and musings while spending an extended hour on the 405.

- "I could probably watch the entire new season of Game of Thrones right now."

- "I wonder if that Hummer driver has ever actually been off-road in their life. Also, when was the last time I actually ever saw a Hummer?"

- "This Prius just merged into my lane from the left-hand lane that was going at the same speed. They don't even need to go right, what's the point of coming over here?"

- "This driver literally got on and off for one mile. ONE MILE. WHAT WAS THE POINT OF GETTING ON THE HIGHWAY?"

- "Prius driver is back in my line, they clearly grew old or existentially depressed from being in the left hand side."

- "You know what, I'm going to start playing an episode of Game of Thrones right now, I don't care how much cell phone data I use. I'll just listen to it through the radio like an audio book. (Loud, graphic violence occurs.) OK, never mind."

- "Do countries in Europe and across the world have this problem with traffic? Do they just really get everywhere they need to go on time? Is the fact that their cars are smaller contribute to their lack of traffic? Would the American automobile industry be faring better overseas if we made smaller cars? That's it, just have Ford, Dodge, etc., focus on making less wide cars that are still cool. We'd make a killing!"

- "What's the proper balance between public transportation and driving? When riding the subway, you have to deal with overcrowded trains and train traffic, but with cars you have this. Perhaps the best case scenario is some sort of public transportation cars that you can drive."

- "That man is eating Kung Pao Chicken as he's driving. Not a sandwich, not an apple, actual Kung Pao Chicken with a fork and everything. He's pouring soy sauce on his rice at every stop. And he's not even eating it from a to-go box, it's from an actual plate! This guy has an actual plate in his car! Who does that? How dirty is the bottom area of his vehicle?"

- "You know, Kung Pao chicken sounds really good right now. I could get off here and go to that one place that has really good Yelp reviews, it'd just be another 30 minutes."

- "That Honda Civic is literally so low to the ground that it is causing sparks as it drives. It's maybe a 1993, 1994 car, why put in thousands of dollars worth of body work into it? Why not just buy a newer used civic and fix that up? It's like buying a pair of $5 sneakers from Wal-Mart, and then spending $55 over the course of two years to repair them, when you could just spend $55 on a new pair of sneakers that would last you for years from the get go."

- "My Nikes are getting kind of old though. Eh, I'll wait 'til the holidays to get new ones."

- "Why don't they teach how to use a manual shift in Driver's Ed? Literally half of the population doesn't know how to use one, it's something that could be easily done in one session and bam, everyone would be that much more skilled."

- "I wonder who is the first ever mechanic who thought to themselves, 'I could make up any fake problem about this car and their driver will pay for it.' At what point since the early 1900s to today did the technology become so advanced that the average driver is unfamiliar with issues plaguing the car? How many millions and even billions of dollars have been funneled to unnecessary car repairs? Was there just one guy who started doing this and every lying mechanic descendent from him? Steve from Philly, that's the guy who first thought to tell a customer they needed to have their tires horizontally shifted so their car could drive fast, and now he's like the Messiah of mechanics."

- "How well do billboards actually work on the American public? Yeah, there's the whole subliminal part of it, where if you saw a billboard for McDonald's and were thinking about where to get dinner later, you might end up going there. But for something like 'Dj Chow and the Mutt on KYSS 104.6,' how much of their audience has been generated from billboards? Is there a group of the driving public who actually bases each decision they make off of what they see on billboards on the highway? That they actually contact those personal injury lawyers and buy that expensive athlete-sponsored cologne and actually relaxed for the very first time when they saw a billboard that said 'Take some time to relax'?"

- "That person's license plate says "EAT SH8" Eat shate? What's shate? Do they mean shit? Why not just EAT SH1T or EAT 5H1T? Why even have a vulgarity like that for a license plate? What's the point? Did any of these other drivers to anything to upset you? What do you have against us? Was that really the best use of your 50 dollars? How many tickets has that vulgarity caused you? Are you even employed?"

- "This person is honking at me. Why? What's the point? I am not the sole cause for this traffic. I do not hold the keys to relieving you of this situation, it is not my ill intent to you to put you through this, why take out your frustration on me?"

- # "Oh shit, I had my turn signal on, that's probably why they were honking. My bad!"

- "I wonder when was the point where Google Maps became popular enough that it could accurately tell how much traffic was in front of you. It seems like it was only speculation for a few good years, that if multiple cars with

Google Maps were driving slow, that must have meant everyone was driving slow, even though those few slow drivers could have easily been the exception. I wonder if there's some random area in the world that they haven't quite figured out yet. Like the roads in Allentown, Pennsylvania, are just too confusing or the patterns of drivers are just too difficult to map, so when it says there's no traffic there's a bunch of traffic and when there's supposedly gridlock it's smooth sailing. I wonder if someone who is actually manning the Google Maps app has the ability to just screw anyone over they want, like pick a road that they know their ex-girlfriend or boss is driving on and say there's going to be no traffic but BAM! they find themselves in 1-2 hours and miss whatever they were going to go to. Seems like an awful lot of power for one person to have, but it is possible! I wonder if that's what's happening now..."

- "Oh no wait, looks like it was just a fender bender. OK, then!"

SPORTS

BASKETBALL

What do you call 12 millionaires around a TV watching the NBA Finals?

The Brooklyn Nets

The psychology instructor finishes a lecture on mental health and proceeds to give an oral quiz to the freshman class.

Speaking specifically about manic depression, the instructor asks, "How would you diagnose a patient who walks back and forth screaming at the top of his lungs one minute, then sits in a chair weeping uncontrollably the next?"

A young man in the rear of the room raises his hand and answers, "A basketball coach?"

Bobby Knight, having led a full life, dies. When he gets to heaven, God is showing him around. They come to a modest little house with a faded Hoosiers flag in the window. "This house is yours for eternity, Bobby," says God. "This is very special; not everyone gets a house up here."

Bobby feels special indeed and walks up to his house. On his way up the porch, he notices another house just around the corner. It is a three-story mansion with a black and gold sidewalk, 50-foot tall flagpole with an enormous Purdue flag and, in every window, a Boilermaker logo.

Bobby looked looks at God and says, "God, I'm not trying to be ungrateful, but I have a question. I was a good coach, I won three NCAA titles, more than 600 games and I even went to the Hall of Fame. So why does Gene Keady get a better house than me?"

God chuckles, and says, "Bobby, that's not Gene Keady's house, it's mine!"

BASEBALL

A first grade teacher explains to her class that she is a Boston Red Sox fan. She asks her students to raise their hands if they are Red Sox fans, too. Not really knowing what a Red Sox fan is, but wanting to be like their teacher, hands explode into the air. There is, however, one exception. A girl named Mary has not gone along with the crowd. The teacher asks her why she has decided to be different. "Because I'm not a Red Sox fan." "Then," asks the teacher, "what are you?" "Why I'm proud to be a New York Yankees fan," boasts the little girl. The teacher is a little perturbed now, her face slightly red. She asks Mary why she is a Yankees fan. "Well, My Dad and Mom are Yankees fans, and I'm a Yankees fan, too!" The teacher is now angry. "That's no reason," she says loudly. "What if your Mom is a moron, and your Dad is a moron, what would you be then?" A pause, and a smile. "Then," says Mary, "I'd be a Red Sox fan."

It's career day in elementary school where each student talks about what his or her Dad does. Little Johnny is last, and finally the teacher calls on him to talk about his Dad. Johnny comes to the front of the class. My Daddy is a dancer at a gay bar. He takes off his clothes for other men, and if they pay him enough money, he goes into the alley and performs sex acts on them." The teacher is shocked, and she calls for an early recess for the rest of the class. She sits down with Johnny and asks him if this is really true about his Dad. Johnny says; "No, but I was too embarrassed to say he played for the Rockies."

A father and son are outside Wrigley Field, and the young son is asking his father to buy him a "Cardinals Suck" T-shirt. The father hesitates, but finally tells his son, "You can have the shirt if you promise never to say that word." "That's right," says the T-shirt vendor, wanting to make the sale. "'Suck' isn't a very nice word." "No," replies the father. "I meant the word 'Cardinals.'"

A doctor at an insane asylum decides to take his patients to a baseball game.

For weeks in advance, he coaches his patients to respond to his commands.

When the day of the game arrives, everything seems to be going well. As the National Anthem starts, the doctor yells, "Up, Nuts!" And the patients comply by standing up.

After the anthem, he yells, "Down, Nuts!" And they all sit back down in their seats.

After a home run is hit, the doctor yells, "Cheer, Nuts!" They all break out into applause and cheer.

When the umpire makes a particularly bad call against the star of the home team, the Doctor yells, "Booooo Nuts!!!" and they all started booing and cat calling.

Thinking things are going very well, the doctor decides to go get a beer and a hot dog, leaving his assistant in charge.

When he returns, there is a riot in progress. Finding his assistant, the doctor asks, "What in the world happened? "

The assistant replies, "Well, everything was going just fine till a vendor passed by and yelled PEANUTS!"

A recent Scottish immigrant attends his first baseball game in his new country and after a base hit he hears the fans roaring RUN, RUN! The next batter connects heavily with the ball and the Scotsman stands up and roars with the crowd in his thick accent: "R-r-run ya bahstard, r-run will ya!" A third batter slams a hit and again the Scotsman, obviously pleased with his knowledge of the game, screams, "R-r-run ya bahstard, r-r-run will ya!" The next batter held his swing at three and two and as the ump calls a walk the Scotsman stands up yelling, "R-r-run ya bahstard, r-r-run!" All the surrounding fans giggle quietly and he sits down, confused.

A friendly fan, sensing his embarrassment whisper, "He doesn't have to run, he's got four balls." After this explanation the Scotsman stands up in disbelief and screams, "Walk with pr-r-ride, man! Walk with pr-r-ride!!"

T wo old men have been best friends for years, and they both live to their early 90s, when one of them suddenly falls deathly ill. His friend comes to visit him on his deathbed, and they're reminiscing about their long friendship, when the dying man's friend asks, "Listen, when you die, do me a favor. I want to know if there's baseball in heaven."

The dying man says, "We've been friends for years, this I'll do for you." And then he dies.

A couple days later, his surviving friend is sleeping when he hears his friend's voice. The voice says, "I've got some good news and some bad news. The good news is that there's baseball in heaven."

"What's the bad news?"

"You're pitching on Wednesday."

This couple just recently got a divorce and they decided to move away from each other and go their separate ways. So, the father sits down and talks with his son and he says, "Son, I think that it is best that you go and live with your mother." The kid says, "No, I won't because she beats me." Then, the mother comes in and talks to the son, "I think it is best that you go and live with your father" "NO NO," he replies, "he beats me!" So then both the parents sit down and say to their son, "Well, if we both beat you, then who do you want to live with?" The son says, "The Diamondbacks. They can't beat anyone."

What are O.J. Simpson's favorite baseball teams?

The Red Sox and the Dodgers.

A conceited new rookie is pitching his first game. He walks the first five men he faces and the manager takes him out of the game. The rookie slams his glove on the ground as he yells, "Damn it, the jerk took me out when I had a no-hitter going."

FOOTBALL

A New York high schooler named Tommy is hanging out with a group of teenagers in the park after midnight. They're a rambunctious bunch, getting into trouble, smoking cigarettes and drinking under age, a few of them with criminal records. One of teens gets the idea to break into Old Man Marley's house and steal his beloved football signed by Tom Brady. Old Man Marley is a grump, always yelling at neighbors and a complete shut-in, but is a big football fan, and that football is his prized possession.

The teens then head over to Old Man Marley's house and sneak in through the back window of the living room where the football is held. They can hear Old Man Marley's snoring from the top of the steps, and figure they're in the clear since he's sound asleep. They take the football that's stacked on top of a mantle and start kicking it around, rubbing ketchup and mustard over it, and even poking it with forks and knives. Tommy is a bit reluctant to participate, but then jumps in with the rest of the crowd. As they're having fun, they hear: "Freeze! Put your hands up!" A cop has entered through Old Man Marley's basement, and he tells the teens that they have triggered the silent alarm. They each go to the police station and are questioned by police before each of their parents picks them up.

Tommy rides next to his Mom in the car in the 30-minute ride from the station. She is clearly furious but isn't saying a word to him. Tommy then decides to speak up. "Mom, I'm sorry, it's such a stupid mistake. We were just having fun but it got out of hand. And yeah, Old Man Marley's a jerk but that doesn't mean that we can just mess with him or his possessions. And now that's on my criminal record forever, God knows how that will impact any job I apply for or if it'll hurt my chances at getting into college. I know how disappointed—"

Tommy's Mom abruptly cuts him off. She speaks with pure furor in her voice. "Disappointed? Oh buddy, don't even tell me about disappointed. You have no idea how pissed off I am right now." Tommy is nearly in tears as his Mom yells like he's never seen her yell before: "You broke into that old man's house, who's what, 90 years old and nearly blind and deaf. You committed a felony, you'll probably get suspended from school, you'll have to do a bunch of community service so now we won't be able to go on our family trip anymore. But really Tommy, what kind of idiot takes a signed football from Tom Brady and doesn't set fire to it? I mean sure, the knives and the forks were clever, and the ketchup is a nice touch, but anytime you get a football signed by Brady, you gotta burn that thing to pure toast!"

GOLF

Four old-timers are playing their weekly game of golf, and one remarks how nice it would be to wake up on Christmas morning, roll out of bed and without an argument, go directly to the golf course, meet his buddies and play a round.

His buddies all chime in and say, "Let's do it! We'll make it a priority, figure out a way and meet here early Christmas morning."

Months later, that special morning arrives, and there they are on the golf course.

The first guy says, "Boy this game cost me a fortune! I bought my wife such a diamond ring that she can't take her eyes off it."

Number 2 guy says, "I spent a ton, too. My wife is at home planning the cruise I gave her. She is up to her eyeballs in brochures."

Number 3 guy says, "Well, my wife is at home admiring her new car, reading the manual."

They all turned to the last guy in the group who is staring at them like they have lost their minds.

"I can't believe you all went to such expense for this golf game. I woke up, slapped my wife on the butt and said, 'Well babe, Merry Christmas! It's a great morning for either sex or golf' and she said, 'Take a sweater.'"

Four retired men have played golf together once a week for many years. One day on 16th hole that runs alongside the highway, a funeral procession drives by. One man says to the others, "Stop and remove your hats, show some respect."

Afterward, one of the other men asks what got into him. "I have never seen you show anybody any respect."

The first man replies: "I was married to her for 65 years."

A man is addressing the ball when an announcement comes over the loud-speaker: "Will the gentleman on hole number one please not hit from the Ladies' tee box."

The man backs away, a little distracted, then approaches his ball again. As he does, the same announcement comes over the loud-speaker: "Will the gentleman on hole number one please not hit from the Ladies' tee box."

The man is getting irritated now, and after backing away from his shot, approaches his ball one more time. This time the announcement came: "We really need the gentleman on hole number one to move off of the Ladies' tee box!"

To which the man turns around and yells: "And I really need the announcer to shut up and let me play my second shot!"

A woman is out golfing one day when she hits the ball into the woods. She goes into the woods to look for it and finds a frog in a trap. The frog says to her, "If you release me from this trap, I will grant you three wishes."

The woman frees the frog, and the frog says, "Thank you, but I failed to mention that there is a condition to your wishes. Whatever you wish for, your husband will get times 10!"

The woman says, "That's OK." For her first wish, she wants to be the most beautiful woman in the world. The frog warns her, "You do realize that this wish will also make your husband the most handsome man in the world, an Adonis to whom women will flock." The woman replies, "That's OK, because I will be the most beautiful woman and he will have eyes only for me."

So, KAZAM! She's the most beautiful woman in the world!

For her second wish, she wants to be the richest woman in the world. The frog says, "That will make your husband the richest man in the world. And he will be 10 times richer than you." The woman says, "That's OK, because what's mine is his and what's his is mine."

So, KAZAM! She's the richest woman in the world!

The frog then inquires about her third wish, and she answers, "I'd like a mild heart attack."

Moral of the story: Women are clever. Don't mess with them.

Attention female readers: This is the end of the joke for you. Stop here and continue feeling good.

Male readers, continue reading....

The man has a heart attack 10 times milder than his wife.

Moral of the story: Women think they're so smart. Let them continue to think that way and just enjoy the show.

P.S.: If you are a woman and are still reading this, it only goes to show that women never listen!

DOCTORS
&
LAWYERS

Doctors

A pipe bursts in a doctor's house. He calls a plumber. The plumber arrives, unpacks his tools, does mysterious plumber-type things for a while, and hands the doctor a bill for $600.

The doctor exclaims, "This is ridiculous! I don't even make that much as a doctor!"

The plumber quietly answers, "Neither did I when I was a doctor."

I got my haircut and had an eye appointment on the same day because I have a fetish for being told where to look.

A man goes to see his doctor because he is suffering from a miserable cold. His doctor prescribes some pills, but they don't help.

On his next visit, the doctor gives him a shot, but that doesn't do any good.

On his third visit, the doctor tells the man, "Go home and take a hot bath. As soon as you finish bathing, throw open all the windows and stand in the draft."

"But doc," protests the patient, "if I do that, I'll get pneumonia."

"I know," says the doctor, "I can cure pneumonia."

A guy goes to the doctor:

"Doc, I can't stop singing 'The Green, Green Grass of Home.'"

"That sounds like Tom Jones Syndrome."

"Is it common?"

"It's not unusual."

A doctor and his wife are having a big argument at breakfast.

"You aren't so good in bed either!" he shouts and storms off to work.

By midmorning, he decides he'd better make amends and phones home. After many rings, his wife picks up the phone.

"What took you so long to answer?"

"I was in bed."

"What were you doing in bed this late?"

"Getting a second opinion."

Why do doctors slap babies' butts right after they are born?

To knock the manhood off the smart ones

One night a man and a woman are both at a bar knocking back a few beers. They start talking and come to realize that they're both doctors. After about an hour, the man says to the woman, "Hey. How about if we sleep together tonight? No strings attached. It'll just be one night of fun." The woman doctor agrees to it.

So they go back to her place and he goes in the bedroom. She goes in the bathroom and starts scrubbing up like she's about to go into the operating room. She scrubs for a good 10 minutes. Finally she goes in the bedroom and they have sex for an hour or so.

Afterward, the man says to the woman, "You're a surgeon, aren't you?" "Yeah, how did you know?" The man says, "I could tell by the way you scrubbed up before we started." "Oh, that makes sense," says the woman." You're an anesthesiologist aren't you?" "Yeah," says the man, a bit surprised. "How did you know?" The woman answers, "Because I didn't feel a thing."

"Doctor," the embarrassed man says, "I have a sexual problem. I can't get aroused for my wife anymore."

"Mr. Thomas, bring her back with you tomorrow and let me see what I can do."

The next day, the worried fellow returns with his wife. "Take off your clothes, Mrs. Thomas," the medic says. "Now turn all the way around. Lie down please. Uh-huh, I see. OK, you may put your clothes back on."

The doctor takes the husband aside. "You're in perfect health," he says. "Your wife didn't make me aroused at all either."

A woman, calling Mount Sinai Hospital, says, "Hello, I want to know if a patient is getting better."

The voice on the other end of the line says, "What is the patient's name and room number?"

She says, "She's Sarah Finkel, in Room 302."

He says, "Oh, yes. Mrs. Finkel is doing very well. In fact, she's had two full meals, her blood pressure is fine, she's going to be taken off the heart monitor in a couple of hours and if she continues this improvement, Dr. Cohen is going to send her home Tuesday."

The woman says, "Thank God! That's wonderful! Oh! That's fantastic! That's wonderful news!"

The man on the phone says, "From your enthusiasm, I take it you must be a close family member or a very close friend!"

She says, "I'm Sarah Finkel in 302! Cohen, my doctor, doesn't tell me a thing."

An elderly couple is going to their doctor for a checkup. The man goes in first. "How're you doing?" asks the doctor. "Pretty good," answers the old man. "I'm eating well, and I'm still in control of my bowels and bladder. In fact, when I get up at night to pee, the good Lord turns the light on for me."

The doctor decides not to comment on that last statement and goes into the next room to check on the man's wife. "How're you feeling?" he asks. "I'm doing well," answers the old woman. "I still have lots of energy and I'm not feeling any pain." The doctor says, "That's nice. It sounds like you and your husband are both doing well.

"One thing, though: Your husband says that when he gets up to pee at night, the good Lord turns the light on for him. Do you have any idea what he means?"

"Oh no," says the woman, "he's peeing in the refrigerator again."

A young woman goes to her doctor complaining of pain. "Where are you hurting?" asks the doctor.

"You have to help me, I hurt all over," says the woman.

"What do you mean, all over?" asks the doctor. "Be a little more specific."

The woman touches her right knee with her index finger and yells, "Ow, that hurts!" Then she touches her left cheek and again yells, "Ouch! That hurts, too!" Then she touches her right earlobe, "Ow, even THAT hurts!" she cries.

The doctor checks her thoughtfully for a moment and tells her his diagnosis: "You have a broken finger."

LAWYER

What's the difference between a lawyer and a vulture?

Lawyers accumulate frequent flyer points.

The attorney tells the accused, "I have some good news and some bad news."

"What's the bad news?" asks the accused.

"The bad news is, your blood is all over the crime scene, and the DNA tests prove you did it."

"What's the good news?"

"Your cholesterol is 130."

An investment banker decides she needs in-house counsel, so she interviews a young lawyer. "Mr. Peterson," she says. "Would you say you're honest?"

"Honest?" replies Peterson. "Let me tell you something about honesty. My father lent me $85,000 for my education, and I paid back every penny the minute I tried my first case."

"Impressive. And what sort of case was that?"

"Dad sued me for the money."

A judge is sentencing criminal defendants when he sees a vaguely familiar face. He reviews his record and finds that the man is a career criminal, except for a five-year period in which there were no convictions.

"Milton," the judge asks, puzzled, "how is it you were able to stay out of trouble for those five years?"

"I was in prison," he answers. "You should know that—you were the one who sent me there."

"That's not possible," the judge says. "I wasn't even a judge then."

"No, you weren't the judge," the defendant counters, smiling mischievously. "You were my lawyer."

A man phones a lawyer and asks, "How much would you charge for just answering three simple questions?"

The lawyer replies, "A thousand dollars."

"A thousand dollars!" exclaims the man. "That's very expensive isn't it?"

"It certainly is," says the lawyer. "Now, what's your third question?"

A truck driver used to amuse himself by running over lawyers he saw them walking down the side of the road. Every time he saw a lawyer walking along the road, he swerved to hit him and there would be a loud THUMP. Then he would swerve back on the road.

One day, as the truck driver is driving along the road, he sees a priest hitch-hiking. He thinks he'll do a good deed and pulls the truck over.

"Where are you going, Father?" The truck driver asks.

"I'm going to the church five miles down the road," replies the priest.

"No problem, Father! I'll give you a lift. Climb in the truck." The happy priest climbs into the passenger seat and the truck driver continues down the road. Suddenly, the truck driver sees a lawyer walking down the road.

Instinctively he swerves to hit him. At the last moment he remembers there is a priest in the truck with him, so he swerves back to the road and narrowly misses the lawyer.

Certain he should've missed the lawyer, the truck driver is very surprised and immediately uneasy when he hears a loud THUMP. He feels really guilty about his actions and so turned to the priest and says, "I'm really sorry Father. I almost hit that lawyer."

"That's OK," replies the priest. "I got him with the door."

How many lawyers does it take to screw in a light bulb?

None, lawyers only screw us.

How do you tell if it is really cold outside?

A lawyer has his hands in his own pockets.

What's the difference between a good lawyer and a great lawyer?

A good lawyer knows the law. A great lawyer knows the judge.

What's the difference between an accident and a calamity?

It's an accident when a bus full of lawyers plunges off the road into a river. It's a calamity if they can swim.

A lawyer is standing in a long line at the box office. Suddenly, he feels a pair of hands kneading his shoulders, back, and neck. The lawyer turns around.

"What the hell do you think you're doing?"

"I'm a chiropractor, and I'm just keeping in practice while I'm waiting in line."

"Well, I'm a lawyer, but you don't see me screwing the guy in front of me, do you?"

A lawyer married a woman who had previously divorced 10 husbands. On their wedding night, she tells her new husband, "Please be gentle, I'm still a virgin."

"What?" says the puzzled groom. "How can that be if you've been married 10 times?"

"Well, Husband #1 was a sales representative; he kept telling me how great it was going to be.

"Husband #2 was in software services; he was never really sure how it was supposed to function, but he said he'd look into it and get back to me.

"Husband #3 was from field services; he said everything checked out diagnostically but he just couldn't get the system up.

"Husband #4 was in telemarketing; even though he knew he had the order, he didn't know when he would be able to deliver.

"Husband #5 was an engineer; he understood the basic process but wanted three years to research, implement, and design a new state-of-the-art method.

"Husband #6 was from finance and administration; he thought he knew how, but he wasn't sure whether it was his job or not.

"Husband #7 was in marketing; although he had a nice product, he was never sure how to position it.

"Husband #8 was a psychologist; all he ever did was talk about it.

"Husband #9 was a gynecologist; all he did was look at it.

"Husband #10 was a stamp collector; all he ever did was—God! I miss him! But now that I've married you, I'm really excited!"

"Good," says the new husband, "but why?"

"You're a lawyer. This time, I know I'm going to get screwed!"

A doctor notices a sidewalk stand that says Brains for Sale. He goes over to investigate and sees a sign that says Doctor brains $8 a pound and another sign that says Paramedic brains $12 a pound, Nurse brains $30 a pound, Truck driver brains $40 a pound and Lawyer brains $90 a pound.

So he asks the man behind the cash register, "How come a doctor's brains are only worth $8 and a lawyer's are worth $90?"

The man replies, "Do you know how many lawyers it takes to make a pound of brains?"

A man sits down at a bar, looks into his shirt pocket and orders a double scotch.

A few minutes later, the man again peeks into his pocket and orders another double. This routine is followed for some time, until after looking into his pocket, the man tells the bartender he'd had enough.

The bartender says, "I've gotta ask you. What's with the pocket business?"

"Oh," says the man, "I have my lawyer's picture in here, and when he starts to look honest, I know I've had enough."

A physician, an engineer, and an attorney are discussing who among them belonged to the oldest of the three professions represented. The physician says, "Remember, on the sixth day, God took a rib from Adam and fashioned Eve, making him the first surgeon. Therefore, medicine is the oldest profession."

The engineer replies, "But, before that, God created the heavens and earth from chaos and confusion, and thus he is the first engineer. Therefore, engineering is an older profession than medicine."

Then, the lawyer speaks up. "Yes," he says, "but who do you think created all of the chaos and confusion?"

A prominent lawyer's son dreams of following in his father's footsteps. After graduating from college and law school with honors, he returns home to join his father's firm, intent on proving himself to be a skilled and worthy attorney.

At the end of his first day at work, he rushes into his father's office, and says, "Father, father! The Smith case, that you always said would go on forever—the one you have been toiling on for 10 years—in one single day, I settled that case and saved the client a fortune!"

His father frowns and scolds his son, "I did not say that it would go on forever, son. I said that it could go on forever. When you saw me toiling on that case for days and weeks at a time, didn't it ever occur to you that I was billing by the hour?"

At the height of a political corruption trial, the prosecuting attorney attacks a witness. "Isn't it true," he bellows, "that you accepted $5,000 to compromise this case?" The witness stares out the window, as though he hasn't heard the question. "Isn't it true that you accepted $5,000 to compromise this case?" the lawyer repeats. The witness still does not respond. Finally, the judge leans over and says, "Sir, please answer the question." "Oh," the startled witness says to the judge, "I thought the attorney was talking to you."

N ASA is interviewing professionals to be sent to Mars. Only one can go and cannot return to Earth. The first applicant, an engineer, is asked how much he wants to be paid for going. "A million dollars," he answers, "because I want to donate it to M.I.T." The next applicant, a doctor, is asked the same question. He asks for $2 million. "I want to give a million to my family," he explains, "and leave the other million for the advancement of medical research." The last applicant is a lawyer. When asked how much money he wants, he whispers in the interviewer's ear, "Three million dollars." "Why so much more than the others?" asks the interviewer. The lawyer replies, "If you give me $3 million, I'll give you $1 million, I'll keep $1 million, and we'll send the engineer to Mars."

THE DOG AND THE CAT

The dog and the cat meet up for dinner once a month to catch up. They share stories about each other's lives, how things were going at work, and how their children were doing. The two used to split the check evenly, even if one of them has gotten a soda or an appetizer the other didn't share. But after four or five dinners, the cat will get up to use the restroom right when the check comes, and won't return to the table until the dog has paid for it. The cat says he will get the dog back next time, but next time is always delayed, and the cat always has an excuse up its paw on why it can't pay then. The dog gets fed up and hatches a plan. The dog invites the cat out on his birthday and the two go to a great restaurant in a crappier part of town. The dog never explicitly says that he will pay for the food, although it is implied. The dog orders appetizers, side dishes, plenty of martinis and desserts, which the cat is happy to partake in, thinking that his meal is complimentary. When the check comes, the cat still gets up to use the restroom, thinking that the dog will take care of it. But the cat sees an "Out of Order" sign on the restroom door, and that there isn't another one in the nearby vicinity. The cat then is forced to sit back down, where the dog replies, "Oh, I left my wallet at home! Well, you owe me for next time anyways." The cat reluctantly pays and suddenly is busy the next month for dinner.

Never dine with a feline who will dodge the bill over nine lifetimes.

THE GOAT AND THE FROG

The goat and the frog are best friends from college who decide to share an apartment after moving to the same city. At first things are great: They both pay their bills on time, keep the apartment nice and clean, and when they have guests over, they are respectful and follow all necessary house rules. But after a few weeks, the goat stops picking up after himself at the apartment. He will bring home guests who yell and bellow into the early morning hours. When the frog asks the goat for rent, the goat replies that he's low on cash, even though he will spend money on weekend trips, new cars, and rounds for everybody at the bar. The frog gets fed up and starts to mimic the goat's behavior to give him a taste of his own medicine. He smokes cigarettes inside, invites rambunctious guests over, and leaves half-eaten flies and sticky lily pad residue all over the apartment. The goat is annoyed but can't say a thing since he has done the same thing to the frog. After a few days of living in filth, the goat starts to pick up around the apartment again and pays his rent on time.

Before you swallow any shit-covered insects, give the flies a taste of their own medicine.

THE BEAR AND THE MOOSE

The bear and the moose arrive at the front door of the office at the same time every day. The moose drives directly from home without making any stops, but the bear gets to the area a little bit earlier and uses his extra 15 minutes to buy coffee and donuts for his fellow co-workers. Naturally, the bear has a lot to carry in his hands and has trouble opening the front doors. The moose, though, never once bothers to help him, always nudging the door open with his antler and scurrying inside before he can help out the bear. The bear offers to buy coffee for the moose, and even invites him out to Trivia Night with co-workers as a friendly gesture, but the moose still doesn't budge to open the door. On a Friday, the bear gets to the door a few seconds earlier than the moose, coffee in hand, and "accidentally" drops the coffee on him. The moose shrieks and runs around to the nearest stream to cool himself down as the bear laughs.

If you're going to be cold to people, be ready to expect a hot surprise in return.

THE ROBINS AND THE PARROT

The three robins like to have fun at the office but still do their jobs well. They share jokes they find on the Internet and harmless funny pictures with one another, but only when they have finished all of their respective duties. The robins started noticing, though, that upper management has an intimate knowledge of the jokes and good humor they share, almost as if their cubicle nest is being spied on. The robins then discover that a parrot who works in administration had been telling upper management all of their jokes, listening closely but never interjecting themselves. The robins are dismayed by this but craft a clever idea. One of the robins approaches the parrot and casually mentions how they all got offers to work in a competing tree, even though those offers aren't real. They will make 10% more on their current salary and even get a nice holiday bonus at the end of the year. Just as they plan, the parrot tells the higher-up birds, and the robins end up getting a big raise.

If a bird is telling secrets about you, feed them false information to help yourself out.

THE WOLF AND THE SHEEP

The sheep is out with her flock for a night on the town. They go to a few different bars and have a couple of drinks, enjoying each other's company. But at one bar there is a wolf lurking in the corner, gazing with creepy intent at the sheep. The wolf approaches the sheep's table and offers to buy them drinks. The sheep politely decline. The wolf insists that the sheep take him up on his kind gesture. They once again politely say no and ask to be left alone. The wolf doesn't get the message. The sheep get a brilliant idea. The sheep start talking to the wolf and getting a bit more friendly. When the wolf goes in for a kiss, the sheep feigns illness, vomiting all over his sweater.

If you're going to be an obnoxious wolf going after sheep, remember to bring some extra clothing.

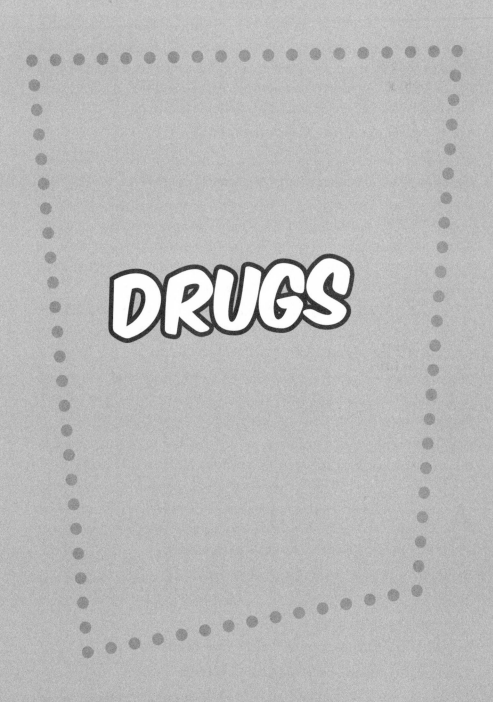

Why did the junkie freak out?

There was an unexpected narc at the door.

....

A married couple can't find a babysitter so they are forced to take Timmy, their five-year-old son to a rock concert. The concert is pretty rowdy, but the five-year-old seems fine and is enjoying himself. Suddenly, a big plume of marijuana smoke lingers towards where the family is sitting.

"Mommy, Daddy, what's that smell?" The child asks.

"Oh that? Err, umm, that's what we call adult flowers. At concerts and other events like this, people like to burn those flowers because they like the smell."

The kid seemed to buy it. A week later, the kid is at home with a new babysitter while his parents are away. The babysitter rummages through the parent's dresser and goes outside on the family's patio to smoke a joint, and the kid instantly recognizes the smell. When the parents come home and the babysitter leaves, they ask him how his night was with the new sitter.

"It was awful! He made me do my homework and didn't let me watch any cartoons!" The parents laugh at this, and ask him what else. "Then he went outside and lit some adult flowers."

The parents are upset that the new sitter had smoked with their son around. They press him for more info. "How long did he smoke? Did he give you any? Was he acting weird?"

"No," Timmy says, "but he told me to tell you that your guy's stuff is terrible, and he'll sell you a dime bag of some real good shit for only 15 bucks."

....

A speed freak is out walking one fine evening. He finds a poor person on the street and helps him up. The poor person says, "Son, I'm a genie. And since you helped me, I'll give you three wishes."

The speed freak says, "I want a big bag of meth!"

OK, the genie says. POOF, the bag appears! They prepare some thick long white lines and share it between the two of them.

The next morning the genie asks, "What's the second wish?"

"I want two big bags of meth," says the speed freak.

OK, says the genie. POOF! And they prepare it and snort it between the two of them.

The next morning the genie asks, "And the third wish?"

"I want four big bags of meth!"

POOF! So, they prepare lots of big lines and share it between the two of them.

Much later the genie gets up and says, "OK, it's time for me to go."

The genie takes a couple of steps, pauses, turns around and says, "OK, just one more wish."

Three guys die in a car wreck, and they all go to Hell. When they arrive, the Devil asks each of the men what their sin was.

The first guy says, "It's gotta be the booze, I'm always drunk." The Devil decides to lock him in this room for 100 years with nothing but shelves of every kind of alcohol you could dream of. The guy's thinking, "Yeah! Look at all this alcohol!" and runs into the room.

The second guy says, "It's the women! I could never stay faithful to my wife." The devil opens the second door and nothing but the finest-looking naked women that you have ever seen. And, he would be the only guy in there for 100 years. He can't believe it. He goes in and the Devil shuts the door.

The third man says, "It's gotta be the weed, I'm always tokin' up!" The Devil opens the third door to reveal nothing but fields of 10-foot tall, icky, sticky, take-a-toke, make-ya-choke, chronic, green, death weed. The stoner can't believe it. He goes in and takes a seat Indian style with his back to the door and the Devil shuts the door behind him.

One hundred years go by and the Devil comes back to check on the three men. He opens the first door and the man comes crawling out. He's got an empty bottle in one hand, he's completely naked, hasn't shaved or showered in years, and is covered in his own puke.

"I'll never drink again!" he says.

The devil tells him that at least he learned something and decides to give him a second shot at life.

The devil then opens the second door and the man comes running out even faster than when he went in.

"I'm gay!" he screams.

The devil decides that at least he learned not to cheat on his wife and gives him another chance as well.

The devil then comes to the third door. He opens it and nothing has changed.

The stoner is still sitting in the same position that he was 100 years ago.

The devil asks him if he learned anything.

The stoner turns around as a tear rolls down his cheek: "You got a light, man?"

A little rabbit is happily running through the forest when he stumbles upon a giraffe rolling a joint. The rabbit looks at her and says, "Giraffe, my friend, think about what you're doing to yourself! Come with me running through the forest, you'll see, you'll feel so much better!"

The giraffe looks at him, looks at the joint, tosses it and goes off running with the

rabbit.

Then they come across an elephant doing coke. So the rabbit again says, "Elephant my friend, why do you do this? Think about what you're doing to yourself! Come running with us through the pretty forest, you'll see, you'll feel so good!"

The elephant looks at them, looks at his razor, mirror and all, then tosses them and starts running with the rabbit and giraffe.

The three animals then come across a lion about to shoot up some smack. "Lion my friend, why do you do this? Think about what you're doing to yourself! Come running with us through the sunny forest, you will feel so good!"

The lion looks at him, puts down his needle, and starts to beat the shit out of the little rabbit.

The giraffe and elephant watch in horror, then finally obtain the presence of mind to pull the lion off the rabbit. "Lion," they reprimand, "why did you do this? He is merely trying to help us all!"

The lion answers, "That little jerk has me running around the forest like an idiot for hours every time he's on Ecstasy!"

Jesus is worried about the drug epidemic plaguing the world. In an effort to solve this dilemma, he decides that a few apostles would return to earth and fetch a sample of each drug, so they can understand what these substances do.

Two days after the operation is implemented, the disciples return. Jesus, waiting at the door, lets in each disciple:

"Who is it?"

"It's Mark." Jesus opens the door.

"What did you bring, Mark?"

"Marijuana from Colombia."

"Very well son, come in."

Another soft knock is heard.

"Who is it?"

"It's Matthew." Jesus opens the door.

"What did you bring, Matthew?"

"Cocaine from Bolivia."

"Very well son, come in."

At the next knock Jesus asks, "Who is it?"

"It's John." Jesus opens the door.

"What did you bring, John?"

"Crack from New York."

"Very well son, come in."

Someone starts pounding on the door.

"Who is it?"

"It's Judas." Jesus opens the door.

"What did you bring, Judas?"

"FREEZE! THIS IS THE POLICE!"

A stoner stumbles out of a party and starts to walk home. On the way, he bumps into a guy who is all bloody and mangled. The guy limps up to the stoner and screams, "Call me an ambulance!" The stoner looks at him for a second, smiles and says, "You're an ambulance!"

A stoner wants to learn about ice fishing. So he gathers all the necessary equipment and goes to the nearest frozen ice. About 20 feet out, he cuts a hole in the ice. "There's no fish there!" booms a voice. The stoner shrugs and moves out another 50 feet and starts to cut another hole. "There's no fish there, either!" booms the voice. The stoner shouts, "Is that you God?" "No," says the voice, "I own the damn ice rink!"

A stoner walks into an appliance store and asks the owner, "How much for that TV set in the window?" The owner looks at the set, then looks at the stoner, and says, "I don't sell stuff to potheads." So the stoner tells the owner that he'll quit smoking pot and will come back the next week to buy the TV. A week later, the stoner comes back and says, "I quit smoking pot. Now, how much for that TV set in the window?" And the store owner says, "I told you I don't sell to potheads!" So the stoner leaves again. He comes back a week later and says, "How much for that TV?" The owner says, "I'm not going to tell you again, I don't sell to potheads!" The giggling stoner looks back at the owner and says, "How can you tell I'm a pothead?" The owner looks back and says, "Because that's a microwave!"

Join the marijuana movement: It's a joint effort.

"Hello there, is this the DEA?"

"Yes, how can we help you, sir?"

"I'm calling to report my neighbor Bob Smith! He is hiding marijuana inside his firewood."

"Thank you very much for the call, sir."

The next day, the DEA agents descend on Bob's house.

They search the shed where the firewood is kept.

Using axes, they bust open every piece of wood, but can't find any marijuana.

They curse at Bob and leave.

The phone rings at Bob's house.

"Hey, Bob! Did the DEA come?" says his best friend.

"Yeah!"

"Did they chop your firewood?" his best friend asks.

"Yep."

"Happy Birthday, buddy!" his best friend replies.

Two guys are picked up by the cops for smoking crack and appear in court before the judge. The judge says, "You seem like nice young men, and I'd like to give you a second chance rather than jail time. I want you to go out this weekend and try to show others the evils of drug use and persuade them to give up drugs forever. I'll see you back in court Monday."

Monday, the two guys are in court, and the judge says to the first one, "How did you do over the weekend?" "Well, your honor, I persuaded 17 people to give up drugs forever." "17 people? That's wonderful. What did you tell them?" "I used a diagram, your honor. I drew two circles like this: I told them this (the big circle) is your brain before drugs and this (small circle) is your brain after drugs." "That's admirable," says the judge.

To the second man, the judge asks: "And how did you do?"

"Well, your honor, I persuaded 156 people to give up drugs forever." "156 people! That's amazing! How did you manage to do that!" "Well, I used the same two circles. I pointed to the small circle and told them, 'This is your butt before prison…'"

TEACHERS & EDUCATION

What is a math teacher's favorite sum?

Summer!

Teachers who take class attendance are absent-minded.

Teacher: Billy, you know you can't sleep in my class.

Billy: I know. But maybe if you were just a little quieter, I could.

Stressing the importance of a good vocabulary, the teacher tells her young charges, "Use a word 10 times, and it shall be yours for life."

From somewhere in the back of the room comes a small male voice chanting, "Amanda, Amanda, Amanda, Amanda, Amanda, Amanda, Amanda, Amanda, Amanda, Amanda."

Does it count as differentiated instruction if I print their worksheets in different colors?

Pupil: I don't think I deserved zero on this test!

Teacher: I agree, but that's the lowest mark I could give you!

What do you call a teacher without students?

Happy

Teachers deserve a lot of credit. Of course, if we paid them more, they wouldn't need it.

Teacher: I want you to tell me the longest sentence you can think of.

Pupil: Life imprisonment!

Where do door-makers get their education?

The school of hard knocks

What do you call a teacher without students?

Broke...oh wait, that's a regular teacher.

Teacher: Why have you got cotton wool in your ears, do you have an infection?

Pupil: Well, you keep saying that things go in one ear and out the other, so I am trying to keep them it all in!

A kid comes home from his first day at school. Mum asks, "What did you learn today?" The kid replies, "Not enough. I have to go back tomorrow."

Pupil: Teacher, would you punish me for something I didn't do?

Teacher: Of course not.

Pupil: Good, because I didn't do my homework.

There is one person in our district who is all about "No Child Left Behind":

The bus driver.

What kinds of tests do they give witches?

Hex-aminations

Teacher: You copied from Fred's exam paper, didn't you?

Pupil: How did you know?

Teacher: Fred's paper says "I don't know" and yours says "Me, neither"!

A little boy isn't getting good marks in school. One day he makes the teacher quite surprised. He taps her on the shoulder and says, "I don't want to scare you, but my Daddy says if I don't get better grades, somebody is going to get a spanking."

The admissions board at Harvard University is about to sit down to begin looking at applications for new undergraduate students. This is going to be the most competitive year in the school's history.

"I have Kevin Sanders here from Provo, Utah," the admissions counselor says. "He's at the top of his class, president of student council, stellar SAT scores, and his essay of how he defeated cancer is truly inspirational. He is Harvard material if I've ever seen it."

The head of the admissions committee agrees. "Kevin sounds like a great fit. Send him his acceptance letter right away. OK, who's next?"

"Ruth here is a student from Sacramento. She has a perfect 4.0 GPA and volunteers at a homeless shelter after school. Her SAT scores are good, but nothing jaw-dropping. I say let's send a rejection letter and maybe let her in if we have more room."

"Sounds like a plan. Who's next?"

"Dylan here is a 17-year-old from Corpus Christi, Texas, but now lives in California. He currently has a 2.6 weighted GPA, 1.9 unweighted, is on probation and has to complete 100 hours of mandatory community service before he graduates, otherwise he's going to jail for a petty larceny offense. For his extra-curriculars, he wrote down kicking ass and taking names, and for volunteer work, he says volunteering is for losers. He hasn't submitted any SAT scores yet, and when I inquired why he didn't take the SATs, he says he is too busy hanging out at Hot Topic but to call me back when I can get some Adderall. I have to tell you, Dylan here is bona fide Harvard material."

The head of the admissions committee is stunned. "You can't be serious. This kid sounds like a complete nuisance. I'd honestly be uncomfortable letting him walk around on the campus as a visitor, let alone study here."

"But see, that's just the thing! He's the complete opposite of conventional Harvard material. And we're always talking about reshaping the image of the university. Some of our more uppity students could take a lesson or two from Dylan in the art of doing kick flips on his skateboard! And asking for a water cup from Chipotle but then filling it up with soda anyway."

Conflicted, the admissions head finally says, "What the hell, let the kid in. Harvard will be good for him."

A week later, Ruth comes home to find two letters from Harvard in her mailbox. The first is a boilerplate rejection letter from the university. She is sad but not overly disappointed, it is more a pipe dream than anything. The second letter, though, is addressed to Dylan, who apparently lives at the same address. Ruth is utterly baffled and walks inside with the letters, and explains the situation to her Mom.

"Well honey, I can see why you're so conflicted, it'd be difficult to pretend to be someone else for four years, you'd be living a lie."

"Oh, I'm not conflicted about that, Mom, but how on earth am I going to learn how to do a kickflip on a skateboard before school starts in three months? You need at least a year to learn that!"

Tom has just started a job at a financial consulting firm in Manhattan. It is his first high-paying job, something that he has been working for his entire life, and he is absolutely stoked to start his first day.

Tom greets all his new co-workers, sat down in his office, overlooking Fifth Avenue, when his boss walks in and wishes him good luck. As the door is closed, Tom looks out the window with excitement and then wonders to himself, "Wait, what am I actually supposed to do?"

Tom's official title is Account Manager, and from the job description, he is supposed to manage communication between five of the firm's biggest accounts. It seems like a big responsibility, but he quickly notices that all of the communication goes directly to his assistant and lower-level account executives. Tom's excitement quickly fades into disdain, as his job is essentially pointless.

All he has to do every day is show up, sit in his office and do nothing. Tom first tries to see if he could do nothing but watch movies on Netflix all day and get away with it. He does with no problem. Tom then shows up at work, takes a cab to a country club in Long Island, plays 18 holes of Golf, drinks three beers and comes back to work without a peep or question on where he was. One time, Tom even decides to fly to London for a quick two-day trip, just so he could see a highly acclaimed play in the West End. No one says a thing, but asks why he is humming so many show tunes, and mentions he has seen the show on Broadway a few blocks down the street. He decides to take an entire month off, since he knows the office will never notice. It seems the more time he spends away, the more praise he receives from his superiors.

But one day Tom is ravaged by guilt. His career that he had worked so hard for throughout this whole life has become a joke, he just can't do it anymore. So he approaches the VPs and comes clean: "I haven't been working at the office as much as you think I have. In fact, I haven't been working at all, I've been taking trips by the barrelful, dodging out on work, and always coming up with excuses for my subordinates to do my work. I am so sorry."

The VPs are stunned: "Wait a minute, so you haven't been doing your actual job, have been slacking off, throwing your actual work to your underlings, and taking all the credit?"

"Yes," Tom says meekly.

"Well then," the VP says, "how'd you like a promotion? Your executive material if I've ever met it."

The vice-president of a local company has quite a problem. He is told by his boss to lay off one of his employees, either Mary or Jack. His choice is a tough one because Mary has been a devoted employee for 10 years and Jack is a fine worker who has a family to support. At night, the VP tosses and turns in his sleep trying to decide which of his employees he will lay off. Finally he decides that the first one to come to work tomorrow will be the one. Morning finally comes and the VP waits at the office for one of the two employees to arrive. At 8:55 Mary walks into the office. "I've got a difficult decision," the VP says, "I either have to lay you or Jack off."

"Oh? Jack off," Mary says, "I've got a headache."

A man is up for his yearly performance review and is certain that he is going to get fired from work. His sales numbers are down, his clients are leaving to other firms, and it just seems like there is no reason to keep him around. The man decides that if he is going to get fired, he is going to half-ass everything at work the last week before. So the man stops showering, he shows up late, he takes long lunches and wastes every single minute that he is on the clock. The time of his performance review comes around, and the man is mangy and dirty, he has a ketchup stain on his shirt, and when he opens his mouth foul breath pours out. His supervisor announces that he's getting promoted with a 50 percent raise. The main is befuddled: Why is he getting promoted when all of his previous work has gone to shit?

"Honestly," his boss answers, "you've been the best thing for moral around here! All the other employees work harder so they won't have to end up like you."

Reaching the end of a job interview, the Human Resources Officer asks a young engineer fresh out of the Massachusetts Institute of Technology, "And what starting salary are you looking for?" The engineer replies, "In the region of $125,000 a year, depending on the benefits package." The interviewer inquires, "Well, what would you say to a package of five weeks' vacation, 14 paid holidays, full medical and dental, company matching retirement fund to 50 percent of salary, and a company car leased every two years, say, a red Corvette?" The engineer sits up straight and says, "Wow! Are you kidding?" The interviewer replies, "Yeah, but you started it."

Two factory workers are talking. The woman says, "I can make the boss give me the day off." The man replies, "And how would you do that?" The woman says, "Just wait and see." She then hangs upside down from the ceiling. The boss comes in and says, "What are you doing?" The woman replies, "I'm a light bulb." The boss then says, "You've been working so much that you've gone crazy. I think you need to take the day off." The man starts to follow her and the boss says, "Where are you going?" The man says, "I'm going home, too. I can't work in the dark."

A boss says to his secretary, "I want to have sex with you, but I will make it very fast. I'll throw $5,000 on the floor and by the time you bend down to pick it up, I'll be done." She thinks for a moment then calls her boyfriend and tells him the story. Her boyfriend says, "Do it, but ask him for $10,000. Then pick up the money so fast, he won't even have enough time to undress himself." She agrees. After half an hour passes, the boyfriend calls the girlfriend and asks, "So what happened?" She responds, "The bastard is using quarters!"

A guy goes in for a job interview and sits down with the boss.

The boss asks him, "What do you think is your worst quality?"

The man says, "I'm probably too honest."

The boss says, "That's not a bad thing, I think being honest is a good quality."

The man replies, "I don't care about what you think!"

A salesman drops in to see a business customer. Not a soul is in the office except a big dog emptying wastebaskets. The salesman stares at the animal, wondering if his imagination could be playing tricks on him. The dog looks up and says, "Don't be surprised. This is just part of my job."

"Incredible!" exclaims the man. "I can't believe it! Does your boss know what a prize he has in you? An animal that can talk!"

"Please don't!" says the dog. "If he finds out I can talk, he'll make me answer the phone, too!"

A man joins a big multinational company as a trainee. On his first day he dials the pantry and shouts into the phone, "Get me a coffee quickly!"

The voice from the other side responds, "You fool! You've dialed the wrong extension! Do you know who you're talking to, dumbo?"

"No", replies the trainee.

"It's the Managing Director of the company, you fool!"

The man shouts back, "And do you know who YOU are talking to, you fool?"

"No," replies the Managing Director.

"Good!" replies the trainee and puts down the phone.

A company, feeling it is time for a shake-up, hires a new CEO. This new boss is determined to rid the company of all slackers. On a tour of the facilities, the CEO notices a guy leaning on a wall. The room is full of workers and he thinks this is his chance to show everyone he means business!

The CEO walks up the guy and asks, "And how much money do you make a week?"

Unconcerned, the young fellow looks at him and replies, "I make $150 a week. Why?"

The CEO then hands the guy $150 in cash and screams, "Here's a week's pay, now get out and don't ever show your face here again!" Feeling pretty good about his first firing, the CEO looks around the room and asks, "Does anyone want to tell me what that lazy scumbag did here?"

With a sheepish grin, one of the other workers mutters, "He's the pizza delivery guy."

One day, a mime is visiting the zoo and attempts to earn some money as a street performer. As soon as he starts to draw a crowd, the zookeeper grabs him and drags him into his office.

The zookeeper explains to the mime that the zoo's most popular attraction, a gorilla, died suddenly and the keeper fears that attendance at the zoo will fall off.

He offers the mime a job to dress up as the gorilla until they can get another one. The mime accepts the offer. So, the next morning, before the crowd arrives, the mime puts on the gorilla suit and enters the cage.

He discovers that it's a great job. He can sleep all he wants, play and make fun of people, and he draws larger crowds than he ever did as a mime on the street. However, eventually the crowd tires of him, and he tires of just swinging on auto tires.

He notices that the people are paying more attention to the lion in the next cage. Not wanting to lose the attention of his audience, he climbs to the top of his cage, crawls across a partition, and dangles from the top of the lion's cage. Of course, this makes the lion furious, but the crowd loves it.

At the end of the day the zookeeper comes and gives the mime a raise for being such a good attraction. Well, this goes on for some time, the mime keeps taunting the lion, the crowd grows larger, and his salary keeps going up.

Then, one day, when he is dangling over the top of the lion's cage, he slips and falls. The mime is terrified.

The lion raises himself up and prepares to pounce. The mime is so scared that he begins to run around the cage with the lion in hot pursuit.

Finally, the mime starts screaming, "Help! Help me!" The lion is quick and pounces. The mime soon finds him flat on his back looking up at the angry lion.

The lion says, "Shut up, you idiot, or we'll both lose our jobs!"

Knock Knock!

Who's there?

To.

To who?

To whom.

Knock Knock!

Who's there?

Tara.

Tara Who?

Tara McClosoff.

Knock Knock!

Who's there?

Dewey.

Dewey who?

Dewey have to do these jokes all night?

Knock Knock!

Who's there?

Ivanna Seymour.

Ivanna Seymour who?

Ivanna Seymour Butts.

Knock Knock!

Who's there?

Idaho!

Idaho who?

I da ho! Where da John?

Knock Knock!
Who's there?
Interrupting cow
Interrupting cow wh—
MOOO!

Knock Knock!

Who's there?

Aardvark.

Aardvark who?

Aardvark a hundred miles and aardvark one hundred more just to be the man who aardvarked one hundred miles to end up at your door.

Knock Knock!

Who's there?

Nicholas!

Nicholas who?

Knicker less girls shouldn't climb trees.

Knock Knock!

Who's there?

Madam.

Madam who?

Ma dam foot got caught in the door!

Knock Knock!

Who's there?

Ho-ho.

Ho-ho who?

You know, your Santa impression could use a little work.

Knock Knock!

Who's there?

Nana.

Nana who?

Nana your business who's there.

Knock Knock!
Who's there?
Control Freak.
Con—
OK, now you say, "Control Freak who?"

Knock Knock!

Who's there?

Noah.

Noah who?

Noah good place we can get something to eat?

Knock Knock!

Who's there?

Butch, Jimmy, and Joe.

Butch, Jimmy, and Joe who?

Butch your arms around me, Jimmy a little kiss, and never let me Joe.

Knock Knock!

Who's there?

Yah.

Yah who?

No thanks, I prefer Google.

SHOPPING

I think PetSmart is probably the only place you're allowed to cat call.

An older man approaches an attractive younger woman at a shopping mall.

"Excuse me, I can't seem to find my wife. Can you talk to me for a couple of minutes?"

The woman, feeling a bit of compassion for the old fellow, says, "Of course, sir. Do you know where your wife might be?"

"I have no idea, but every time I talk to a beautiful woman with breasts as lovely as yours, she seems to appear out of nowhere."

One day a man goes to a pet shop to buy a parrot. The assistant takes the man to the parrot section and asks the man to choose one. The man asks, "How much is the yellow one?" The assistant says, "$2,000." The man is shocked and asks the assistant why it's so expensive. The assistant explains, "This parrot is a very special one. He knows typewriting and can type really fast." "What about the green one?" the man asks. The assistant says, "He costs $5,000 because he knows typewriting and can answer incoming telephone calls and takes notes." "What about the red one?" the man asks. The assistant says, "That one's $10,000." The man says, "What does HE do?" The assistant says, "I don't know, but the other two call him boss."

I live above a noisy tennis shop and recently a friend came over and asked what the commotion was downstairs. I said it's all the ratchet.

"IKEA customer support, how may I help you?" a cheerful agent says on the phone.

"Hel…hello," Hubert says nervously, "I need help. It's…it's something with my furniture."

"Alright sir, what type of furniture is it?"

"A dres…a dresser."

"OK, and what seems to be the problem, sir? Are you missing any of the materials? Are some materials broken? Are you having trouble trying to build the item?"

"No, none of that. It's just, I assembled the furniture, and I encountered no problems doing so."

The other side of the phone is silent for a few agonizing seconds.

"Say again, sir?"

"This cabinet I bought from IKEA, I took it out of the box, assembled it with the provided tools, and now it works great. Something must be terribly wrong."

The customer service agent takes a few moments to compose herself. She can't believe what she is hearing.

"Sir, I don't mean to call you a liar, but what you say makes absolutely no sense. It's just impossible."

Hubert understands the agent's apprehension to believe his story. But he submits photos of the cabinet to IKEA and even invites some of the company's senior officials to tour his home and look at the cabinet. They too can't believe their eyes and quickly apologize to Hubert for any emotional hardship he's endured during the cabinet's construction and they encourage him to share his story until they can come to a decision as to what to do.

In the late of the night, the senior officials write a one-page letter and submit it to The New York Times, with just seconds to spare before their print deadline hits. A few hours later, people across the world are stunned as they read the unbelievable news:

"To our faithful customers,

"IKEA has always been a company that has valued transparency. You have made us a part of your homes by including our bed frames and futons as part of your possessions. For that, it is only just that IKEA informs you of any possible news or items that are necessary for you to hear.

"On February 16, Hubert, a man from Allentown, PA, was able to build one of our most popular dressers without conflict. He had the necessary amount of supplies to build the item, was able to follow instructions, and finished the dresser in less time than expected. As of writing this, Hu-

bert's dresser is still working perfectly. It hasn't gotten stuck in anyway or fallen apart randomly in the middle of the night.

"Clearly, this is not what IKEA stands for as a company. We are issuing an immediate recall to anyone who has purchased the same dresser as Hubert within the past two years. Even if your dresser is functioning as expected, by teetering lopsided or with a stuck drawer, we cannot say with confidence that your item would unexpectedly start working perfectly. We greatly regret this error and apologize to anyone who is harmed."

The company's stock takes a small tumble, but consumers ultimately have faith in Ikea and praise them for being transparent and dealing with the situation with such class. Hubert is left wondering if maybe he is at fault in any way by building his dresser without error.

He goes to his basement, where he has stuck the perfectly functioning dresser in the midst of the brouhaha. Next to it is the empty box the dresser had arrived in, and inside are the instructions. When Hubert looks at them, his heart is struck with fear. It isn't IKEA's fault, after all, but his own. It turns out that as Hubert was building the dresser, he was looking at the instructions upside down.

"I'd like to buy some gloves for my wife," the young man says, eyeing the attractive sales girl, "but I don't know her size."

"Will this help?" she asks sweetly, placing her hand in his.

"Oh, yes," he answers. "Her hands are just slightly smaller than yours."

"Will there be anything else?" the salesgirl queries as she wraps the gloves.

"Now that you mention it," he replies, "she also needs a bra and panties."

A husband and wife are shopping in their local Wal-Mart. The husband picks up a case of Budweiser and puts it in their cart.

"What do you think you're doing?" asks the wife.

"They're on sale, only $10 for 24 cans," he replies.

"Put them back, we can't afford them," demands the wife, and so they carry on shopping.

A few aisles further on, the woman picks up a $20 jar of face cream and puts it in the basket.

"What do you think you're doing?" asks the husband.

"It's my face cream. It makes me look sexy and beautiful for you when we're making love," replies the wife.

Her husband retorts: "So does 24 cans of Budweiser at half the price!"

HOLIDAY

Why is Santa's little helper depressed?

Because he has low elf esteem

The Santa Claus at the shopping mall is very surprised when Emily, young lady aged about 20 years old, walks up and sits on his lap. Now, we all know that Santa doesn't usually take requests from adults, but she smiles very nicely at him, so he asks her, "What do you want for Christmas?"

"Something for my mother, please," replies Emily sweetly.

"Something for your mother? Well, that's very loving and thoughtful of you," smiles Santa. "What do would you like me to bring her?"

Without turning a hair, Emily answers quickly, "A son-in-law."

I got the worst Christmas gift last year! Someone got me the new set of Christian Candles. Which, if someone gets you that, do not use the Judas Candle: It'll burn you every time.

Jennifer is a pretty 18-year-old girl. In the week before Christmas, she saunters up to the curtain counter, and is trying to decide which of the many types of tinsel she will buy. Finally, she makes her choice and asks the spotty youth who is manning the fabric section: "How much is this gold tinsel garland?"

The spotty youth points to the Christmas mistletoe above the counter and says: "This week we have a special offer, just one kiss per meter."

"Wow, that's great," says Jennifer, "I'll take 12 meters."

With expectation and anticipation written all over his face, the boy measures out the tinsel, wraps up the garland, and gives it to Jennifer.

She then calls to an old man who has been browsing through the Christmas trees and says: "My Grandpa will settle the bill."

On the first Christmas, the first of three Wise Men step carefully into the stable but sinks his golden slipper into a big pile of manure. "Jesus Christ!" he yells. The woman beside the manger turns to her husband and says, "Now, Joseph, isn't that a better name for the kid than Irving?"

Why is Christmas just like a day at the office?

You do all the work and the fat guy with the suit gets all the credit.

A week before Christmas, Peter writes a letter to Santa Claus and throws it in

the mailbox. The mail carrier gets the letter and does not know where to send it. So he opens it and reads:

"Dear Santa Claus, this Christmas I'd love to get a teddy bear, a construction set, and water-based paints."

The mail carrier is unhappy, because there is no Santa Claus and Peter will receive no gift. So the mail carrier and the other mailmen decide to gather some money, and buy and send Peter the gifts he asked for in his letter. But they have only enough money for the teddy bear and constructor set. They decide to send Peter an incomplete package with only two gifts.

The day after Christmas, Peter again writes a letter to Santa and the mail carrier opens it and reads: "Dear Santa Claus, thank you for the wonderful teddy bear and constructor set! Unfortunately, I did not get water-based paints. Probably the postmen have stolen it."

A boy begs his father to get him a Christmas tree this year.

Every year, the boy asks and the father tells him, "I don't want to pay for it."

But the son kept begging. Unable to bear his son's whining, he picks up his axe one day and heads out of the house.

Thirty minutes later, he returns with a great big Christmas tree. "How did you cut it down so fast?" his son asks.

"I didn't cut it down," the father replies. "I got it at a tree lot."

"Then why did you bring an axe?"

"Because I didn't want to pay."

After the annual office Christmas party blowout, John wakes up with a pounding headache, cotton-mouthed, and utterly unable to recall the events of the preceding evening. After a trip to the bathroom he is able to make his way downstairs, where his wife puts some coffee in front of him.

"Louise," he moans, "tell me what went on last night. Is it as bad as I think?"
"Even worse," she assures him in her most scornful one. "You made a complete ass of yourself, succeeded in antagonizing the entire board of directors, and insulted the chairman of the company to his face."

"He's an arrogant, self-important jerk, piss on him!"

"You did. All over his suit," Louise informs him. "And he fired you."

"Well, screw him," says John.

"I did. You're back at work on Monday."

The Sunday before Christmas, a pastor tells his congregation that the church needs some extra money. He asks the people to consider donating a little more than usual into the offering plate. He says that whoever gives the most will be able to pick out three hymns. After the offering plates are passed, the pastor glances down and notices that someone has placed a $1,000 bill in offering.

He is so excited that he immediately shares his joy with his congregation and says he'd like to personally thank the person who placed the money in the plate. A very quiet, elderly, saintly looking lady all the way in the back shyly raises her hand. The pastor asks her to come to the front.

Slowly she makes her way to the pastor. He tells her how wonderful it is that she gave so much and, in thanks, asks her to pick out three hymns. Her eyes brighten as she looks over the congregation, points to the three most handsome men in the building and says, "I'll take him and him and him."

Three men die on Christmas Eve and go to heaven, where they're met by Saint Peter. "In order to get in," he tells them, "you must each produce something representative of the holidays."

The first man digs into his pockets and pulls out a match and lights it. "This represents a candle of hope." Impressed, Peter lets him in.

The second man pulls out a tangle of keys and shakes them. "These are bells." He's allowed in too.

"So," Peter says to the third man, "what do you have?"

The third man proudly shows him a pair of red panties.

"What do these have to do with Christmas?" asks Peter.

"They're Carol's."

Just before Hanukkah, Miriam, a grandmother, is giving directions to her grown up grandson who is coming to visit with his wife. "You come to the front door of the condominium complex. I am in apartment 2B."

Miriam continues, "There is a big panel at the door. With your elbow, push button 2B. I will buzz you in. Come inside, the elevator is on the right. Get in, and with your elbow, hit 2. When you get out, I am on the left. With your elbow, hit my doorbell."

"Grandma, that sounds easy," replies Jonathan, the grandson, "but why am I hitting all these buttons with my elbow?"

To which she answers, "You're coming to visit empty handed?"

Admiring the Christmas trees displayed in his neighbor's windows, Nathan asks his father, "Daddy, can we have a Hanukkah Tree?"

"What? No, of course not," says his father.

"Why not?" asks Nathan.

Bewildered, his father replies, "Well, Nathan, because the last time we had dealings with a lighted bush, we spent 40 years in the wilderness."

A woman goes to the post office to buy stamps for her Hanukkah cards. She says to the clerk, "May I have 50 Hanukkah stamps?" The clerk says, "What denomination?" The woman says, "Oh my God. Has it come to this? Give me 6 Orthodox, 12 Conservative, and 32 Reform."

My mother once gave me two sweaters for Hanukkah. The next time we visited, I made sure to wear one. As we entered her home, instead of the expected smile, she said, "What's the matter? You didn't like the other one?"

It is Hanukkah and the tiny village is in fear of not having any latkes because they have run out of flour. Rudi, the rabbi, is called upon to help solve the problem.

He says, "Don't worry, you can substitute matzo meal for the flour and the latkes will be just as delicious!"

Shela looks to her husband and says, "Morty, you think it'll work?" and Morty says, "Of course! Everybody knows Rudolph the Rab knows grain, dear!"

On New Year's Eve, Marilyn stands up in the local pub and says that it is time to get ready. At the stroke of midnight, she wants every husband to be standing next to the one person who has made his life worth living. Well, it is kind of embarrassing. As the clock strikes, the bartender is almost crushed to death.

On New Year's Eve, Daniel is in no shape to drive, so he sensibly leaves his van in the car park and walks home. As he is wobbling along, he is stopped by a policeman. "What are you doing out here at four o'clock in the morning?" asks the police officer.

"I'm on my way to a lecture, answers Roger.

"And who on earth, in their right mind, is going to give a lecture at this time on New Year's Eve?" inquires the constable sarcastically.

"My wife."

Roxanne is taking an afternoon nap on New Year's Eve before the festivities. After she wakes up, she confides to Todd, her husband, "I just dreamed that you gave me a diamond ring for a New Year's present. What do you think it all means?"

"Aha, you'll know tonight," answers Todd, smiling broadly.

At midnight, as the New Year is chiming, Todd approaches Roxanne and hands her a small package. Delighted and excited, she opens it quickly.

There in her hand is a book called *The Meaning of Dreams*.

John, at a New Year's party, turns to his friend, Dave, and asks for a smoke. "I thought you made a New Year's resolution and that you don't smoke," Dave says.

"I'm in the process of quitting," replies John with a grin. "I am in the middle of phase one."

"Phase one?" asks David.

"Yeah," laughs John, "I've quit buying."

Martha has a parrot called Brutus. The only problem is that Brutus cusses something awful. Now Martha is having her in-laws over for Thanksgiving, and so she needs to train Brutus quickly not to swear.

Just before her mother-in-law is due, Brutus cusses terribly, so Martha puts him in the freezer for two minutes to literally cool off. Then she opens the door and takes out the parrot along with the turkey.

"And have you learned your lesson about cussing?" Martha asks the parrot.

Brutus the parrot takes one look at the dead turkey and says, "I sure have. But I have one I have a question: What did the turkey do?"

A grandma is showing the children a painting of the Pilgrim Family on a Thanksgiving Day card that they have received, and she comments, "The Pilgrim children enjoyed going to church with their mothers and fathers and praying to God."

One of the grandsons looks at her doubtfully and asks, "Then why is their father carrying that rifle?"

E ddie in Dallas calls his son in New York just before Thanksgiving and tells him, "I am sorry to tell you but your mother and I are divorcing. I just cannot take any more of her moaning. We can't stand the sight of each other anymore. I am telling you first, Eddie, because you are the eldest. Please tell your sister."

When Eddie calls his sister Julie, she says, "No way are they getting divorced! I will go over and see them for Thanksgiving!"

Julie phones her parents and tells them both, "You must NOT get divorced. Promise you won't do anything until I get over there. I'm calling Eddie, and we'll both be there with you tomorrow. Until then, don't take any action, please listen to me," and hangs up.

The father puts down the phone and turns to his wife and says, "Good news," he says. "Eddie and Julie are coming for Thanksgiving and they are both paying their own way."

One Halloween, a trick-or-treater comes to my door dressed as Rocky in boxing gloves and satin shorts. Soon after I give him some goodies, he returns for more. "Aren't you the same 'Rocky' who left my doorstep several minutes ago?" I ask. "Yes," he replies, "but now I'm the sequel. I'll be back three more times tonight too."

T wo men are walking home after a Halloween party and decide to take a shortcut through the cemetery just for laughs. Right in the middle of the cemetery, they are startled by a tap-tap-tapping noise coming from the misty shadows. Trembling with fear, they find an old man with a hammer and chisel, chipping away at one of the headstones. "Holy cow, Mister," one of them says after catching his breath, "You scared us half to death. We thought you were a ghost! What are you doing working here so late at night?" "Those fools!" the old man grumbles. "They misspelled my name!"

A cabbie picks up a nun. She gets into the cab, and the cab driver won't stop staring at her. She asks him why is he staring and he replies, "I have a question to ask you but I don't want to offend you." She answers, "My dear son, you cannot offend me. When you're as old as I am and have been a nun a long as I have, you get a chance to see and hear just about everything. I'm sure that there's nothing you could say or ask that I would find offensive."

"Well, I've always had a fantasy to have a nun kiss me." She responds, "Well, let's see what we can do about that: #1, you have to be single and #2, you must be Catholic."

The cab driver is very excited and says, "Yes, I am single and I'm Catholic too!" The nun says, "OK, pull into the next alley." He does and the nun fulfills his fantasy. But when they get back on the road, the cab driver starts crying.

"My dear child, says the nun, why are you crying?" "Forgive me sister, but I have sinned. I lied, I must confess, I'm married and I'm Jewish." The nun says, "That's OK, my name is Kevin and I'm on my way to a Halloween party."

MONEY

I met a man the other day named Flanagan and he tells me he's a happy man. I ask him why.

"Well," he says, "the IRS has been after me for 20 years, driving me mad, to get money out of me, driving me crazy with worry. But this morning I got a letter from them and it says FINAL NOTICE.

"Thank God," he says, "I won't be hearing from them again."

A man has three girlfriends, but he does not know which one to marry. So he decides to give each one $5,000 and see how each of them spends it.

The first one goes out and gets a total makeover with the money. She gets new clothes, a new hairdo, manicure, pedicure, the works, and tells the man, "I spent the money so I could look pretty for you because I love you so much."

The second one goes out and buys new golf clubs, an iPad, a television, and a stereo and gives them to the man. She says, "I bought these gifts for you with the money because I love you so much."

The third one takes the $5,000 and invests it in the stock market, doubles her investment, returns the $5,000 to the man and reinvests the rest. She says, "I am investing the rest of the money for our future because I love you so much."

The man thinks long and hard about how each of the women spent the money and decides to marry the one with the biggest breasts.

Abe and Esther are flying to Australia for a two-week vacation to celebrate their 40th anniversary. Suddenly, over the public address system, the Captain announces, "Ladies and gentlemen, I am afraid I have some very bad news. Our engines have ceased functioning and we will attempt an emergency landing. Luckily, I see an uncharted island below us and we should be able to land on the beach. However, the odds are that we may never be rescued and will have to live on the island for the rest of our lives!" Thanks to the skill of the flight crew, the plane lands safely on the island. An hour later Abe turns to his wife and asks, "Esther, did we pay our $5,000 PBS pledge check yet?" "No, sweetheart," she responds. Abe, still shaken from the crash landing, then asks, "Esther, did we pay our American Express card yet?" "Oh, no! I'm sorry. I forgot to send the check," she says. "One last thing, Esther. Did you remember to send checks for the Visa and MasterCard this month?" he asks. "Oh, forgive me, Abie," begs Esther. "I didn't send that one, either." Abe grabs her and gives her the biggest kiss in 40 years. Esther pulls away and asks him, "What is that for?" Abe answers, "They'll find us!"

John asks his wife, Mary, what she wants to celebrate their 40th wedding anniversary. "Would you like a new mink coat?" he asks. "Not really," says Mary. "Well how about a new Mercedes sports car?" says John. "No," she responds. "What about a new vacation home in the country?" he suggests. She again rejects his offer with, "No thanks." Frustrated he finally asks, "Well what would you like for your anniversary?" "John, I'd like a divorce," answers Mary. John thinks for a moment and replies, "Sorry dear, I wasn't planning to spend that much."

One Sunday, while counting the money in the weekly offering, the pastor of a small Florida church finds a pink envelope containing $1,000. It happens again the next week. The following Sunday, he watches as the offering is collected and sees a little old lady put the distinctive pink envelope in the plate. This goes on for weeks until the pastor, overcome by curiosity, approaches her. "Ma'am, I couldn't help but notice that you put $1,000 a week in the collection plate," he states. "Why yes," she replies, "every week my son sends me money, and I give some of it to the church." The pastor replies, "That's wonderful, how much does he send you?" The old lady says, "$10,000 a week." The pastor is amazed. "Your son is very successful; what does he do for a living?" "He is a veterinarian," she answered. "That is an honorable profession," the pastor says. "Where does he practice?" The old lady says proudly, "In Nevada. He has two cat houses in Las Vegas and one in Reno."

One day a man goes to an auction. While there, he bids on an exotic parrot. He really wants this bird, so he gets caught up in the bidding. He keeps on bidding, but he keeps getting outbid, so he bids higher and higher and higher. Finally, after he bids way more than he intended, he wins the bid. The price is high but the fine bird is finally his!

As he is paying for the parrot, he says to the auctioneer, "I sure hope this parrot can talk. I would hate to have paid this much for it, only to find out that he can't talk!"

"Don't worry," says the auctioneer, "He can talk. Who do you think kept bidding against you?"

A lady walks into a fancy jewelry store. She browses around, spots a beautiful diamond bracelet, and walks over to inspect it. As she bends over to look more closely, she inadvertently breaks wind. Very embarrassed, she looks around nervously to see if anyone has noticed her little accident and prays that a salesperson doesn't pop up right now. As she turns around, her worst nightmare materializes in the form of a salesman standing right behind her. Cool as a cucumber and displaying complete professionalism, the salesman greets the lady with, "Good day, Madam. How may we help you today?" Very uncomfortably, but hoping that the salesman may not have been there at the time of her little accident, she asks, "Sir, what is the price of this lovely bracelet?" He answers, "Madam, if you farted just looking at it, you're going to shit when I tell you the price."

For his birthday, Little Patrick asks for a 10-speed bicycle. His father says, "Son, we'd give you one, but the mortgage on this house is $80,000 and your mother just lost her job. There's no way we can afford it." The next day the father sees Little Patrick heading out the front door with a suitcase. So he asks, "Son, where are you going?" Little Patrick tells him, "I was walking past your room last night and I heard you tell Mom you were pulling out. I heard her tell you to wait because she is coming too. And I'll be damned if I'm sticking around here by myself with an $80,000 mortgage and no transportation."

Before going to Europe on business, a man drives his Rolls-Royce to a Manhattan bank and goes in to ask for an immediate loan of $5,000. The loan officer is quite taken aback and requests collateral. "Well, then, here are the keys to my Rolls-Royce," the man says. The loan officer promptly has the car driven into the bank's underground parking for safekeeping, and gives him $5,000. Two weeks later, the man walks through the bank's doors, and asks to settle up his loan and get his car back. The loan officer checks the records and tells him, "That will be $5,000 in principal, and $15.40 in interest." The man writes out a check, thanks the loan officer, and starts to walk away. "Wait sir," the loan officer says, "while you were gone, I found out you are a millionaire. Why in the world would you need to borrow?" The man smiles.

"Where else could I securely park my Rolls-Royce in Manhattan for two weeks and pay only $15.40?"

The United Way realizes that it has never received a donation from the city's most successful lawyer. So a United Way volunteer pays the lawyer a visit in his lavish office. The volunteer opens the meeting by saying, "Our research shows that even though your annual income is over two million dollars, you don't give a penny to charity. Wouldn't you like to give something back to your community through the United Way?"

The lawyer thinks for a minute and says, "First, did your research also show you that my mother is dying after a long, painful illness and she has huge medical bills that are far beyond her ability to pay?" Embarrassed, the United Way rep mumbles, "Uh... no, I didn't know that."

"Secondly," says the lawyer, "my brother, a disabled veteran, is blind and confined to a wheelchair and is unable to support his wife and six children." The stricken United Way rep begins to stammer an apology, but is cut off again.

"Thirdly, did your research also show you that my sister's husband died in a dreadful car accident, leaving her penniless with a huge mortgage and three children, one of whom is disabled and another has learning disabilities requiring an array of private tutors?"

The humiliated United Way rep, completely beaten, says, "I'm sorry, I had no idea." And the lawyer says, "So...if I didn't give any money to them, what in the hell makes you think I'd ever give any to you?"

At a country club party, a young man is introduced to an attractive girl. Immediately he begins paying her court and flatters her outrageously. The girl likes the young man, but she is taken a bit aback by his fast and ardent pitch. She is amazed when after 30 minutes, he seriously proposes marriage.

"Look," she says. "We only met a half hour ago. How can you be so sure? We know nothing about each other."

"You're wrong," the young man declares. "For the past five years I've been working in the bank where your father has his account."

Einstein dies and goes to heaven only to be informed that his room is not yet ready. "I hope you will not mind waiting in a dormitory. We are very sorry, but it's the best we can do and you will have to share the room with others," he is told by the doorman.

Einstein says that this is no problem at all and that there is no need to make such a great fuss. So the doorman leads him to the dorm. They enter and Albert is introduced to all of the present inhabitants. "See, here is your first roommate. He has an IQ of 180!"

"That's wonderful!" says Albert. "We can discuss mathematics!"

"And here is your second roommate. His IQ is 150!"

"That's wonderful!" says Albert. "We can discuss physics!"

"And here is your third roommate. His IQ is 100!"

"That's wonderful! We can discuss the latest plays at the theater!"

Just then another man moves out to capture Albert's hand and shake it. "I'm your last roommate and I'm sorry, but my IQ is only 80."

Albert smiles back at him and says, "So, where do you think interest rates are headed?"

A guy walks into a bank and says to the teller at the window, "I want to open a goddamn checking account."

To which the lady replies, "I beg your pardon, what did you say?"

"Listen up dammit, I said I want to open a goddamn checking account right now."

"Sir, I'm sorry, but we do not tolerate that kind of language in this bank!"

The teller leaves the window and goes over to the bank manager and tells him about her situation. They both return and the manager asks, "What seems to be the problem here?"

"There's no damn problem," the man says, "I just won $50 million in the lottery and I want to open a goddamn checking account in this damn bank!"

"I see, sir," the manager says, "and this bitch is giving you a hard time?"

BLUE COLLAR OR "REDNECK" COLLAR

Two rednecks go on a fishing trip. They rent all the equipment: The reels, the rods, the wading suits, the rowboat, the car, and even a cabin in the woods. They spend a fortune. The first day they go fishing, they don't catch anything. The same thing happens on the second day, and on the third day. It goes on like this until finally, on the last day of their vacation, one of the men catches a fish.

As they're driving home, they're really depressed. One guy turns to the other and says, "Do you realize that this one lousy fish we caught cost us 1,500 bucks?"

The other guy says, "Wow! Then it's a good thing we didn't catch any more!"

There are some backwoods hillbillies living across the river from each other, who feud constantly. John hates Clarence with a passion and never passes up a chance to throw rocks across the river at Clarence.

This goes on for years until one day the Corps of Engineers comes to build a bridge across that river. John is elated; he tells his wife that finally he is going to get the chance to cross over and whip Clarence.

He leaves the house and returns in a matter of minutes. His wife asks what is wrong, didn't he intend to go over the bridge and whip Clarence?

He replies that he never had really seen Clarence up close and didn't realize his size until he started over the bridge and saw the sign: "CLEARANCE 8 FT 3 IN"

A redneck husband, who has six children, begins to call his wife "mother of six" rather than by her first name. The wife, amused at first, chuckles.

A few years down the road, the wife has grown tired of this. "Mother of six," the redneck would say, "what's for dinner tonight? Get me a beer!" She gets very frustrated.

Finally, while attending a party with her husband, he jokingly yells out, "Mother of six, I think it's time to go!" The wife immediately shouts back, "I'll be right with you, father of four!"

A redneck couple gets married and is on their honeymoon. The woman changes into a sexy outfit and lies on the bed. She looks sheepishly up at her new hubby and whispers, "Please be gentle with me. I'm a virgin."

The man gets up screaming, grabs his trousers and runs home to tell his father.

His father comforts him by saying, "Now, now. It'll be OK, son. If she wasn't good enough for her own family, then she isn't good enough for ours."

At the police station, Bubba explains to the police officer why his cousins shot him.

"Well," Bubba begins, "We wuz havin' a good time drinking, when my cousin Ray picked up his shotgun and says, 'Hey, der ya fellows wanna go hunting?'"

"And then what happened?" the officer interrupts.

"From what I remember," Bubba says, "I stood up and says, 'Sure, I'm game.'"

Deep in the back woods of Eastern Kentucky, a hillbilly's wife goes into labor in the middle of the night, and the doctor is called out to assist in the delivery.

Since there is no electricity, the doctor hands the father-to-be a lantern and says, "Here, you hold this high so I can see what I am doing!"

Soon, a baby boy is brought into the world. "Whoa there," says the doctor. "Don't be in such a rush to put that lantern down! I think there's another one coming."

Sure enough, within minutes, he has delivered a baby girl. "Hold that lantern up, don't set it down, there's another one!" says the doctor.

Within a few minutes, he has delivered a third baby. "No, don't be in a hurry to put down that lantern, it seems there's yet another one coming!" cries the doctor.

The redneck scratches his head in bewilderment, and asks the doctor, "You reckon it might be the light that's attractin' 'em?"

A redneck takes his daughter to the gynecologist.

They wait in the doctor's office when finally the doctor comes in and asks the father: "Well, what are we here for today?"

The father answers: "To get my daughter on birth control, Doc."

"Well, is your daughter sexually active?" asks the Doctor.

"No," answers the redneck, "she just lays there like her mother."

MOVIES, TV, & MUSIC

HARRY POTTER AT THE END OF THE SCHOOL YEAR, IF HIS PARENTS DIDN'T DIE:

Mom: Harry, it's so good to see my sweet boy!

Harry: Yeah Mom, I'm always glad to come home to my two loving parents.

Dad: More importantly, we need to talk about your OWL scores.

Mom: He's just walking in the door, can't this wait, James?

Dad: We do not pay top galleons for such poor marks!

Harry: I'm sorry Dad, it is just a tough year with the whole school being attacked by ADULT evil wizards. It's just tough to study when you're fearing for your life!

Mom: Maybe try studying when you're hiding?

Dad: You're a disappointment!

Harry: I never wanted to learn magic tricks anyway!

Dad: They're spells! We don't use the "T-word" in this house!

Mom: Can't we have one summer where we don't yell at each other?!?

Dad: I'm going to apparate to get a butterbeer and wish my son could learn to catch a golden snitch in under five minutes!

Harry: Why can't I just paint?!

The directors of *La La Land* and *Moonlight* meet up for lunch a week after the Oscars, where *La La Land* had been mistakenly announced as the winner of Best Picture, before an official came onstage and announced *Moonlight* had actually one. The two are happy to see each other but are still upset over the events that unfolded.

"It just sucks, because I felt for a moment like my movie won and then that was taken away from me." "Yeah I hear you, even when they announced Moonlight had won, it still didn't feel like we did because of that whole fiasco."

"Maybe we could petition to the Academy to split the award, kind of like a tie, but it'd have both of our names on it" the *La La Land* director says. "Hey yeah, I like that! It'd bring some closure to the situation, and I don't mind sharing the award with you!" They then go to the Academy and pitch their idea.

"I have no problem with that," the president of the Academy says, "but we only have a certain amount of space in the Oscar records for one movie title, and having both won't fit. We'll have to combine them," the president of the Academy says, and the directors agreed.

A few weeks later, a husband and wife are walking on the Hollywood Walk of Fame when they see a golden plaque that read "2017 Best Picture Winner: *Moo La Land*." "Hey hub, did you ever see that movie? It sounds unfamiliar," the wife asks. "Never heard of it, but it couldn't be any worse than *Hacksaw Ridge*."

I was invited to a Hollywood wedding. Traffic was heavy, so I got there late—just in time for the divorce.

On a nice summer day during his show's hiatus, Conan O'Brien meets up with David Letterman for lunch on the Venice Beach boardwalk. As they try to talk, people keep stopping Conan and asking him for pictures and autographs, but no one seems to bother Dave.

"Ever since I grew this really long beard, started wearing sunglasses, wrapped a bandana around my head and wore dirty old beanie wherever I go, nobody recognized me anymore! There might be times when someone thinks they do, but they aren't ever quite sure, so they leave me alone."

"Wow that's a great idea," Conan says. So he buys an elaborate fake beard, a ratty old beanie, cheap sunglasses from the boardwalk and a bandana from Goodwill. He puts it all on and meets up with Dave again for lunch. Except this time, nobody bothers him.

Conan simply thinks it's too good to be true, so he starts asking people nearby if they recognize the pair. "Nope!" one person says. "Can't say that I do!" says another. But they ask one more person.

"Excuse me sir, do you recognize us?"

The gentleman walks over to get a closer look at the scraggly looking men.

"Yeah, I do."

"So you know who we are?"

"Yeah I know who you guys are, and I don't mean to be rude here, but from the looks of it, Jay Leno must've really fucked you guys over."

How much cocaine did Charlie Sheen take?

Enough to kill *Two and a Half Men*.

It had been 30 years since "Piano Man" came out, and Billy Joel is still a global star. But he has always been curious as to what the real-life characters from his song are up these days, so he organizes a reunion for all of them to meet at the same bar they hung out at years ago.

The group gathers and Billy starts going around the room, asking what each of them is up to.

"Well I'm no longer a real estate novelist," says Paul, "but just a regular real estate agent. Gave up on the old Great American Novel thing a few years ago. But I did get married though, met her on eHarmony!"

Davey is next. "Finally got out of the Navy 10 years ago, but really missed being at sea, so now I work on an oil rig."

A suave-looking man in an expensive suit speaks next. "Gave up the bar game 20 years ago, moved to Hollywood with 500 bucks in my pocket, got cast in a hit TV show, and I just won my third Oscar last year."

The gang is having a good time, recounting old memories from the bar, but Billy realizes there is someone missing. "Hey, whatever happened to that old man? You know, the one would tell me to play him a memory?"

The gang looks uneasy. "I know what happened to him," Paul says. "Oh no, did he pass away?" Billy asks. "No, he got put on the sex offender list and is serving 30 years in prison for lewd conduct after making love to that tonic and gin."

Meryl Streep is sitting in her Beverly Hills Mansion surrounded by awards and framed accolades, but she feels empty. Even after winning those Oscars and being the toast of the town for all her life, she feels like she's never had a true, challenging role. But Meryl suddenly has an idea and calls her agent.

"Mel, I got it, the greatest role of all time in the greatest movie of all time. It's a biopic of my own life where I play myself. It's only a role that I could play and it'll be the greatest in history."

Mel is skeptical about the idea but he talks with studio execs and they green-light the picture. A year later, *Streep: The Story of Meryl* premieres in theaters, detailing every moment of Meryl's life, from her first movie role to her pitching the idea for this very own biopic. The movie is a failure commercially and crit-ically. Meryl calls her agent to ask what went wrong.

"I guess some people just thought it was unrealistic. Not even Meryl Streep could do something as overwrought as play herself."

P laying opening night at Carnegie Hall had been Victoria's dream job since she was a little girl. But Victoria's voice is gone, and she can't go on. If she screws this up, she'll be out of a career.

Victoria has twelve hours before she has to go on and she tries every herbal remedy she can find online, but to no avail. But Victoria isn't going to give up this chance. So she thinks of a last-ditch, Hail Mary effort: She will lip-synch to a pre-recorded track. It sounds nothing like her, but she is still small enough in the opera scene for no one to really know exactly what her voice sounds like. The only thing they don't know about her is that she is good.

It seems asinine, but the audience is primarily composed of people in their 70s or 80s with poor hearing and eyesight, and they probably can't even hear or tell the difference. Only the sound technician, and also her co-performer Sebastian, will be able to tell, so she lets them in on the secret.

When it comes time for her big fake solo, a roar of applause sweeps over the theater, with every audience member standing up and applauding as pas-sionately as possible. They are utterly enticed by Victoria and don't suspect a thing.

Rave reviews in the New York newspapers enable the show to go on tour na-tionally. Victoria is initially enthralled by this news: She is finally a global opera sensation, but she realizes she'll have to do the performance lip-synched every night for the rest of the tour, otherwise rumors might percolate on why her voice sounds so drastically different.

The show goes from New York to Chicago to San Francisco to Denver to Los Angeles and every city in between, with Victoria earning rave reviews and more and more notoriety. Sebastian is furious at all the attention she is getting over him. So at the performance in San Francisco, he tells the technician to play a different track, one that has nothing to do with opera, when it is Victoria's time to come onstage. And once she opens her mouth, she'll be humiliated and banished from the opera world.

The first 20 minutes of the performance go off without a hitch. When the time for her solo comes, Victoria walks onstage, just as the sound technician readies the song. She opens her mouth and the technician presses play as Cyndi Lauper's "Girls Just Want to Have Fun" blasts through the speakers. The crowd is frantic and confused, and Victoria has a panic attack, running offstage. The director appears and tries to brush it off as a technical difficulty but everyone in the audience knows the truth as they scurry out of the theater. Victoria's opera career has just crumbled before her eyes and Sebastian is swimming in schadenfreude.

Victoria finds herself in a deep depression the next morning, knowing full well she is the laughing stock of the opera world. But she decides to read a review from the San Francisco Chronicle about the performance. When she gets to the final line, she spits out her coffee:

"She doesn't look quite like she did when she was in her prime, and still needs vocal training, but the opera world is happy Cyndi Lauper is now performing in their ranks."

Thanksgiving break comes along and Dorothy is staying at Aunt Em and Uncle Henry's house. Her relationship with them has soured ever since she got in trouble for teleporting random places with her ruby red slippers. When Dorothy enters the house, she is confused as she follows her aunt, but fury strikes her bones as she sees Uncle Henry with Lion, Scarecrow, Tin Man and even Oz himself. She is getting an intervention.

Everyone in the room is holding a few papers in their hands, except for Aunt Em and Uncle Henry, who are more than just hosting the gathering. The first to speak is Tin Man.

"Dorothy. I remember when I first met you. I didn't even know what it meant to be alive. You were just so radiant and cheery and friendly, it was like you sent a jolt into my cold empty body. You showed me just how much one person could accomplish if they set their heart to something. But seeing you now, it's devastating. I'm not sure if you remember, but over spring break, you teleported yourself into my living room to crash on my couch. You were wearing a sombrero hat and an oversized, ketchup-stained I Love Puerto Vallarta T-shirt. I know you can do better, Dorothy. Don't do it for me, do it for you."

Scarecrow stands up out of his chair to speak. "You don't have to stand up Scarecrow, you can sit," Lion tells him, but Scarecrow demands to stand, thinking it will make his message clearer.

"Dorothy, all I ever wanted ever since I was just a small bundle of hay was to have a brain. I thought it'd never happen, but those doubts were removed and newfound intelligence harvested in its place when I went on my journey with you. You were so young but so smart and insightful. But now you're using your slippers to teleport into the dean's office after dark to cheat on exams. And now it just brings a tear to my eye to see you're not even using your gifted brain. What you're doing is stupid, and you're so smart. Please don't forget that."

Dorothy is starting to feel some remorse, but is still in denial as Lion spoke.

"You know what I thought of when I first saw you? I said Hmm, that little girl is a coward. I did! I said exactly that under my breath when I was getting ready to roar at the three of you. You all jumped in fear, but only you Dorothy had the gall to actually hit me and say Shame on you! I was stunned! Nobody had ever stood up to me like that before. And it made me think if some little girl from Kansas could hold her own against me, then I could summon the courage to hold my own against anyone. But I have to say Dorothy, I was wrong. What you're doing right now is cowardly. Using your ruby red slippers to teleport into the cafeteria and grab food and teleport back to your dorm room without having to make any new friends is cowardly. Zapping to an empty field where you can be alone after you don't get invited to a party is cowardly. I know college is tough. But Dorothy, if you can defeat the goofball Oz, you can conquer this."

Dorothy has already wiped away a few tears from her eyes. Dorothy apologizes to her three dear old friends as they share a hug. Oz, though, sits awkwardly in the corner, everyone having forgotten he is there.

"Umm, excuse me, what the hell?"

The four of them look at Oz. "Oh I'm sorry Oz," Dorothy says, "I guess we forgot you were here."

"Yeah, I guess you did, otherwise you wouldn't have told those awful stories about me! That creepy Oz! That cowardly Oz! What the hell! I came here to help!"

Oz storms out of the house and jumps into his hot air balloon, muttering harsh words about Dorothy and her friends under his breath as he floats through the sunset.

"Don't worry," Dorothy says. "I transported to Oz and spiked his coffee earlier. He's going to learn there's no place like irritable bowel syndrome."

Nickelback & 50 Cent just announced their tour. Tickets will go on sale at noon for a record low price of just 0.45 cents.

For the first time in his life, Bruce Springsteen has writer's block. He calls up his manager Jon Landau to confide his artistic struggle, hoping that Jon can provide some sage words of wisdom to help Springsteen find new inspiration.

"I mean, is there a factory closing down anywhere? Or something wrong with the environment? Or some ruthless politician or global tyrant causing havoc on the world?

"Let's take a look! Nope, nothing, looks like everyone is happy and AOK" Jon says. "But I think I found something. There's this one guy named Steve who lives in Kansas City, and all of his social media posts are just complaining about different things. He's the only unhappy person out there. Maybe you could do something about this guy."

Twelve months later, the "Steve from Kansas City" tour is the best-selling of Springsteen's career, with critics praising Bruce for his tender live performances and the album's soulful, deep cuts. Despite the accolades, the world is dying to meet the mysterious Steve who had inspired Springsteen's album.

And with the last stop of the tour at Kauffman Stadium in Kansas City, the world would finally get their chance when it is announced Steve will be in the show's audience.

Springsteen has made it through his three-hour-long concert and comes out for his customary encore. As Bruce readies to perform the most popular track from the album, "Steve gets into trouble with his in-laws at Christmas after re-gifting the Outback Steakhouse gift card they gave him for his birthday," the moment finally arrives as Steve steps onstage.

"You know, I never met an American whose heart is as wide and whose soul is as strong as Steve here. And I know you, the hard-working folk of Kansas City, are proud to call him one of your own." The crowd erupts in cheers and chants Steve's name in unison as Bruce hands his beloved guest the microphone with the world ready to hear him speak for the first time.

"Umm, I'm actually from St. Louis."

The crowd's deafening yells turn into collective, confused murmuring.

"Say again, son?" Springsteen asks.

"St. Louis, I'm from St. Louis, I was just visiting some college friends in Kansas City when you flew out."

"You must be joking."

"No, I'm from St. Louis, I told you that several times, but you just ignored me and kept playing on your guitar, singing incoherent lyrics to yourself. I'm not going to lie, I feel kind of violated by this whole thing, I'm not some American sob story, I'm not from Kansas City, I'm upper middle class, I drive a Prius. Sorry to disappoint you guys."

Steve drops the mic and walked off stage, the stadium in uncomfortable silence. But Springsteen readies his guitar, approaches the microphone, and chooses to do one more time what he has always done best: Sing.

"Ohhhh you'll never meet a guyyy, like Steve from St. Louisss…"

What's green and smells like bacon?

Kermit's finger

C arl reflects back to when he first flew to Dino Island as a budding young archaeologist tasked with approving or disapproving Burnson's crazy scheme: A theme park featuring dinosaurs who were cloned from DNA found in fossilized crab legs. But the dinosaurs have escaped, and Carl has run out of food. He isn't afraid of dying, but will regret not telling his paleontologist colleague Annie how he really feels about her.

He puts on his trusty cowboy hat and red bandana scarf and books it toward the Visitor's Center, about a half mile away. Carl reaches the front of the Visitor's Center and swings the ornately decorated doors open. He steps inside, picks up a stray tree trunk and jams it through the door handles to block any mischievous dinosaurs from entering. Carl gasps for air: He is in more physical pain and exhaustion than at any other point in his life, but he is ecstatic. He's made it. He is still alive.

"Oh, hey Carl. Where have you been for the last month?"

Carl turns around and is flabbergasted to see Annie, Burnson, and the rest of the crew from his trip, sitting down for dinner in the middle of the Visitor's Center.

"Wait, what? You're alive?"

"Of course we are," Annie says, "what, did you think we died or something?"

Carl is still gasping for air. "I saw…I saw the T-Rex…it was about to bite down... bite down on you."

"Ahh, typical Carl seeing things," says the eccentric Burnson. "While I'm not a believer in the psychological idea that past behavior is the best predictor of future behavior, I must say that I'm not surprised to see Carl overreacting."

"Overreacting? There were dinosaurs! They were about to kill us?"

"Let me explain, Carl," Burnson says. "When the dinosaurs broke free, they weren't trying to eat us, they were trying to build their own society that is not chained in captivity. This island is rightfully theirs, and they just want to reclaim it, but they don't want to hurt us though. I must admit, when I designed this park, I was thinking of Sally and Bobby here as nothing more than overgrown reptilian pets," Burnson says while petting two of the raptors. "But they're so much more than that, and these creatures I helped bring into the world deserve a life of their own that isn't just being a theme park attraction."

Carl is perplexed. He has devoted his entire life to studying dinosaurs and their habits, but now he sees how civilized they are. He then joins the rest of his team, as they laugh and shares stories, as the two veclociraptors Bobby and Sally listen from a distance.

"So I get Annie and Carl, and you get the guy whose wearing all black and the others, OK?"

"Fine," the raptor says, "but we're going to have to hit the elliptical for a week straight after this."

Two blondes living in Oklahoma are sitting on a bench talking, and one blonde says to the other, "Which do you think is farther away, Florida or the moon?"

The other blonde turns and says, "Helloooooooooo, can you see Florida?"

A blonde and a redhead have a ranch. They have just lost their bull. The women need to buy another, but only have $500. The redhead tells the blonde, "I will go to the market and see if I can find one for under that amount. If I can, I will send you a telegram." She goes to the market and finds one for $499. Having only one dollar left, she goes to the telegraph office and finds out that it costs one dollar per word. She is stumped on how to tell the blonde to bring the truck and trailer. Finally, she tells the telegraph operator to send the word "comfortable." Skeptical, the operator asks, "How will she know to come with the trailer from just that word?" The redhead replies, "She's a blonde so she reads slow: 'Come for the bull.'"

A blonde is down on her luck. In order to raise some money, she decides to kidnap a kid and hold him for ransom. She goes to the playground, grabs a kid, takes him behind a tree, and tells him, "I've kidnapped you." She then writes a note saying, I've kidnapped your kid. Tomorrow morning put $10,000 in a paper bag and put it under the pecan tree next to the slide on the north side of the playground. Signed, A Blonde.

The blonde then pins the note to the kid's shirt and sends him home to show it to his parents. The next morning, the Blonde checks, and sure enough, a paper bag is sitting beneath the pecan tree. The Blonde opens up the bag and finds the $10,000 with a note that says, How could you do this to a fellow blonde?

Three blondes are in an elevator when the elevator suddenly stops and the lights go out. They try using their mobile phones to get help, but have no luck. Even the phones are out.

After a few hours of being stuck with no help in sight, one blonde says to the others "I think the best way to call for help is by yelling together."

The others agree with the first, so they all inhale deeply and begin to yell loudly: "Together, together, together."

Three women go down to Mexico one night to celebrate college graduation.

They get drunk and wake up in jail, only to find that they are to be executed in the morning, though none of them can remember what they did the night before.

The first one, a redhead, is strapped in the electric chair and is asked if she has any last words.

She says, "I just graduated from Trinity Bible College and believe in the almighty power of God to intervene on the behalf of the innocent."

They throw the switch and nothing happens.

They all immediately fall to the floor on their knees, beg for forgiveness, and release her.

The second one, a brunette, is strapped in and gives her last words.

"I just graduated from the Harvard School of Law and I believe in the power of justice to intervene on the part of the innocent."

They throw the switch and again, nothing happens.

Again they all immediately fall to their knees, beg for forgiveness and release her.

The last one, a blonde, is strapped in and says, "Well, I'm from the University of Texas and just graduated with a degree in Electrical Engineering, and I'll tell ya right now, ya'll ain't gonna electrocute nobody if you don't plug this thing in."

A blonde, a brunette, and a redhead are trying out for a new NASA experiment on sending women to different planets. First, they call the brunette in and ask her a question. "If you could go to any planet, what planet would you want to go to and why?" After pondering the question she answers, "I would like to go to Mars because it seems so interesting with all the recent news about possible extra-terrestrial life on the planet." They say, "Well OK, thank you." And they tell her that they will get back to her.

Next, the redhead enters the room and the NASA people ask her the same question. In reply, "I would like to go to Saturn to see all of its rings." Again,

"Thank you" and they will get back to her. Finally, the blonde enters the room and they ask her the same question they asked the brunette and the redhead. She thinks for a while and replies, "I would like to go to the sun." The people from NASA reply, "Why, don't you know that if you went to the sun you would burn to death?" The blonde smirks and puts her hands on her hips. "Are you guys dumb? I'd go at night!"

A blonde is on a four-engine plane crossing the Atlantic. All of a sudden there's a loud bang. The pilot announces over the intercom, "I'm sorry, one of our engines has just shut off. We'll be delayed 45 minutes."

Suddenly there's another bang. Once again, the intercom clicks on and the pilot expresses his regret that they'll be delayed two hours.

Shortly thereafter, there is a third bang and the pilot announces that they'll be delayed three hours.

The blonde turns to the guy sitting beside her and says, "Man, if the fourth engine shuts off, we'll be up here all day."

A blonde goes to the doctor with burns on both of her ears and her right hand. "Sit down and tell me how it happened," says the doctor.

"I was ironing my clothes when I received a call. Instead of picking up the phone, I picked up the iron and burned my ear."

"'What about the other ear and your hand?" the doctor asks.

She replies, "I tried to call for an ambulance."

A blind man enters a bar and finds his way to a barstool. After ordering a drink, and sitting there for a while, the blind guy yells to the bartender, "Hey, you wanna hear a blonde joke?" The bar immediately becomes absolutely quiet.

In a husky, deep voice, the woman next to him says, "Before you tell that joke, you should know something. The bartender is blonde, the bouncer is blonde and I'm a six-foot-tall, 200-pound blonde with a black belt in karate. What's more, the fella sitting next to me is blonde and he's a weightlifter. The woman to your right is a blonde, and she's a pro wrestler. Think about it seriously, mister. You still want to tell that blonde joke?"

The blind guy says, "Nah, not if I'm gonna have to explain it five times."

Two blondes decide to split a can of Diet Coke. One blonde opens the can, and pours half the contents into her own glass, and half into her friend's glass. Before tossing the can, she stops to read the nutritional information on the side. "'Only one calorie per can'," she reads aloud. "Hmm," murmurs the other blonde. "I wonder which glass has the calorie?"

A blonde is taking online flying lessons. It is time for her to take her flying test. The instructor tells her to go up 1,000 feet and radio back. Then he instructs her to go up to 2,000 feet and radio back. Again, he instructs her to go up to 3,000 feet and radio back. She takes the helicopter up to 1,000 feet and radioes back. She is doing well, so she goes on up to 2,000 feet and radioes back. Still doing well, she goes on up to 3,000 feet. This time, she crashes in the field. The instructor asks her what happened. The blonde says, "When I got to 3,000 feet, I got cold so I turned off the big fan."

A blonde is standing in front of a soda machine outside of a local store. After putting in 60 cents, a root beer pops out of the machine. She sets it on the ground, puts 60 more cents into the machine, and pushes another button; suddenly, a Coke comes out the machine! She continues to do this until a man waiting to use the machine becomes impatient. "Excuse me, can I get my soda and then you can go back to whatever stupid thing you are doing?" The blonde turns around and says, "Yeah right! I'm not giving up this machine while I'm still winning!"

A blonde, a brunette, and a redhead are stuck on an island. One day, the three of them are walking along the beach and discover a magic lamp. They rub and rub, and sure enough, out pops a genie.

The genie says, "Since I can only grant three wishes, you may each have one."

The brunette says, "I've been stuck here for years. I miss my family, my husband, and my life. I just want to go home." POOF!

The brunette gets her wish and she is returned to her family. Then, the redhead says, "I've been stuck here for years as well. I miss my family, my husband, and my life. I wish I could go home too." POOF! The redhead gets her wish and she is returned to her family.

The blonde starts crying uncontrollably. The genie asks, "My dear, what's the matter?" The blonde whimpers, "I wish my friends were still here."

Three women are about to be executed. One is a brunette, one a redhead, and the other a blonde. The guard brings the first woman, the brunette, forward and the executioner asks if she had any last requests. She says no and the executioner shouts "READY! AIM!" and suddenly the brunette yells, "EARTHQUAKE!"

Everyone is startled and looks around. She escapes. So they bring up the redhead and ask if she has any last requests.

She says no, and the executioner shouts "READY! AIM!" and suddenly the redhead yells "TORNADO!" Everyone is startled and looks around. She escapes.

Well, by now, the blonde has it all figured out. They bring her forward and the executioner asks if she had any last requests. She says no and the executioner shouted "READY! AIM!" and the blonde yells, "FIRE!"

A blonde is playing Trivial Pursuit one night. It is her turn. She rolls the dice and she lands on Science & Nature. Her question is, "If you are in a vacuum and someone calls your name, can you hear it?" She thinks for a time and then asks, "Is it on or off?"

A young blonde woman is distraught because she fears her husband is having an affair, so she goes to a gun shop and buys a handgun.

Then one day she comes home and finds her husband in bed with a beautiful redhead. She grabs the gun and holds it to her own head. The husband jumps out of bed, begging and pleading with her not to shoot herself. Hysterically the blonde responds to the husband, "Shut up: You're next!"

A blonde teacher is going on a school trip with her third graders. After she and the class had been waiting on the station for almost three hours, it becomes too much for her. She walks up to the staff and says: "I don't care what you say anymore, we're getting on the next train even if it only has first and second class written on it!"

A blonde sees a posting on a bulletin board that says, "Cruise, Only $5." She goes to the address on the back and hands the receptionist $5. The receptionist nods to a burly man reading a newspaper. He walks over to the blonde and knocks her unconscious.

The blonde wakes up tied to a log floating down river. To her right, she sees one of her blonde friends. "Do you think they're going to serve food on this trip?" she asks.

The other blonde replies, "They didn't last year."

A brunette is standing on some train tracks, jumping from rail to rail, saying "21, 21, 21…" A blonde walks up, sees her and decides to join her. She also starts jumping from rail to rail, saying "21, 21, 21…"

Suddenly, the brunette hears a train whistle and jumps off the tracks just as the blonde is splattered all over the place. The brunette goes back to jumping from rail to rail, counting "22, 22, 22…"

A blonde is on vacation in the depths of Louisiana. She wants a pair of genuine alligator shoes, but doesn't want to pay the high prices.

After unsuccessfully haggling with of one of the shopkeepers, the blonde says, "Maybe I'll just go out and catch my own alligator, so I can get a pair of shoes at a reasonable price."

Later in the day, the shopkeeper spots the young woman standing waist deep in the water, shotgun in hand.

She takes aim at an alligator, kills it and hauls it onto the swamp bank. Lying nearby are several more of the dead creatures. The shopkeeper watches in amazement as the blonde flips the alligator on its back and shouts in frustration, "Damn, this one isn't wearing any shoes either!"

Two blondes are in a bar watching the television when the news comes on. It shows a guy on a bridge who is about to jump, obviously suicidal. "I'll bet you $10 he'll jump," says Betty.

"Bet you $10 he won't," replies Amber. Then, the guy on the television closes his eyes and throws himself off the bridge. The second blonde hands the first her money.

"I can't take your money," says Betty. "I cheated you. The same story was on the five o'clock news."

"No, no. Take it," says Amber. "I saw the five o'clock news too. I just didn't think the guy is dumb enough to jump again!"

A guy takes his blonde girlfriend to her first football game. They have great seats right behind their team's bench.

After the game, he asks her how she liked the experience. "Oh, I really liked it," she replies, "especially the tight pants and all the big muscles, but I just couldn't understand why they were killing each other over 25 cents." Dumbfounded, her date asks, "What do you mean?"

"Well, they flipped a coin, one team got it, and then for the rest of the game, all they kept screaming was, 'Get the quarterback! Get the quarterback!' I'm like, hello? It's only 25 cents!"

A teenage blonde girl has been talking on the phone for about half an hour, and then she hangs up.

"Wow!," says her father, "That was short. You usually talk for two hours. What happened?"

"Wrong number," replies the girl.

A blonde has been attending Blonde International Training College, a school set up to give blondes a chance to make it in the real world, for 10 years. She keeps failing this one class that she needs to graduate: Basic math. The administrators need to get her out to make room for new students, but can't just give her the grade. So, they instead decide to ask her a simple math question at the graduation ceremony. If she answers correctly, she graduates.

Sure enough, she fails the class again, and shouldn't walk across the stage, but the admins invite her to the ceremony. They stand her before everyone and say, "Although you lack one class for graduation, we have decided to pass you if you can answer this one question: What is two plus two?" The blonde thinks about it for a while and finally says, "Four."

The crowd stands up in objection and demands, "Give her another chance!!"